Tourist information · 1:100 000 maps

- ✠ Abbey or priory
- ♪ Aquarium or dolphinarium
- ⌂ Art gallery
- ⊠ Art collection / museum
- ⌖ Bird sanctuary or aviary
- ⌂ Castle
- † Cathedral
- ⌂ Church of interest
- ⋔ Country park
- ⌇ County show ground
- ⌇ Farm park
- ✿ Garden
- ⌐ Golf course
- ⚓ Historic ship
- ⌂ House
- ⌂ House and garden
- ⌂ Local museum
- ⚓ Marina
- ◇ Maritime museum / Military museum
- ▨ Motor racing circuit
- ⌂ Museum
- Ⓟ Picnic area
- ♞ Racecourse
- ♞ Roman antiquity
- ⌂ Safari park
- ⌂ Preserved railway
- ⌼ Theme park
- Tourist information centre
- 𝑖 – open all year
- 𝑖 – open seasonally
- ◯ Transport collection
- ⁛ Ancient monument
- Earthwork
- Windmill
- Watermill
- Other place of interest

Key to map pages

Aberystwyth · Wolverhampton · Walsall · Dudley · Birmingham · Coventry · Kidderminster · Banbury

Hereford · Bromyard · Worcester · Stratford-upon-Avon · **74** · **75** · **76** · **77** · Great Malvern · Newtown · Bidford-on-Avon · Pershore · Evesham · Upton upon Severn · Broadway · Chipping Campden · Ledbury · Ashchurch

Brecon · Dymock · Winchcombe · Moreton-in-Marsh · King's Thorn · Tewkesbury · Stow-on-the-Wold · Chipping Norton · Ross-on-Wye · **68** · **69** · Gloucester · Cheltenham · **72** · **73** · Symonds Yat · **70** · **71** · Bourton-on-the-Water · Woodstock · Monmouth · Cinderford · Burford · Witney · Oxford · Raglan · Coleford · Blakeney · Painswick

Carmarthen · Lydney · Sharpness · Stroud · Cirencester · Fairford · Lechlade on Thames · Abingdon · Tintern Parva · Berkeley · Dursley · Nailsworth · Kemble · Faringdon · **66** · **67** · Llanelli · Chepstow · **62** · **63** · Tetbury · **64** · **65** · Wantage · Didcot · Swansea · Thornbury · Malmesbury · Wootton Bassett · Wantage

Newport · Almondsbury · Yate · Chipping Sodbury · Swindon · Portishead · Filton · Cardiff · Clevedon · Bristol · **56** · **57** · Corsham · Chippenham · Calne · Marlborough · Thatcham · Penarth · Keynsham · Bath · **58** · **59** · Hungerford · Newbury · Reading · Barry · **54** · **55** · Bradford on Avon · Melksham · Devizes · **60** · **61** · Weston-super-Mare · Congresbury · Radstock · Trowbridge · Pewsey · Burbage · Basingstoke · Axbridge · Blagdon · Ludgershall · Whitchurch

Ilfracombe · Combe Martin · Lynmouth · Burnham-on-Sea · Cheddar · Westbury · Andover · **42** · **43** · Lynton · Porlock · Minehead · Highbridge · Wedmore · Wells · Shepton Mallet · Warminster · Shrewton · **50** · **51** · **52** · **53** · Braunton · Barnstaple · Simonsbath · Dunster · Watchet · **46** · **47** · Frome · Amesbury · Winchester · Westward Ho! · Nether Stowey · Glastonbury · **48** · **49** · Bruton · Mere · Wilton · Salisbury

Clovelly · Bideford · South Molton · Bishop's Nympton · Bampton · Taunton · Henstridge · Shaftesbury · Fordingbridge · Southampton · **31** · **32** · **33** · **34** · **35** · **36** · **37** · Yeovil · Sherborne · **38** · **39** · **40** · **41** · Shebbear · Hatherleigh · Lapford · North Tawton · Tiverton · Kentisbeare · Chard · Crewkerne · Yetminster · Wimborne Minster · Ringwood · Lyndhurst · Holsworthy · Silverton · Honiton · Beaminster · Cerne Abbas · Blandford Forum · Ferndown

Whitstone · Okehampton · Crediton · Whimple · Axminster · Maiden Newton · Tolpuddle · New Milton · Lymington · **18** · **19** · **20** · **21** · **22** · **23** · **24** · **25** · **26** · **27** · Christchurch · Ashwater · Mary Tavy · Exeter · Ottery St Mary · Lyme Regis · Bridport · Dorchester · Bournemouth · Launceston · Moretonhampstead · Sidmouth · Wool · Wareham · **28** · **29** · Tavistock · Widecombe in the Moor · Budleigh Salterton · Weymouth · Corfe Castle · Exmouth · Dawlish · West Lulworth · Swanage

Gunnislake · Callington · Yelverton · Buckfast · **14** · **15** · Torbay · Torquay · Liskeard · **10** · **11** · Totnes · Paignton · Saltash · Plymouth · Ivybridge · Brixham · East Looe · Torpoint · Dartmouth · **12** · **13** · Kingsbridge · Salcombe

G000292708

Outdoors

Animal attractions

Listed here is a wide range of selected activities for both children and adults – and many are suitable for both. Some do not need advance booking, but it is always best to telephone first to check both availability and opening times.

Bournemouth

Oceanarium *Bournemouth* Ocean displays of climates and wildlife from around the world. 01202 311993 www.oceanarium.co.uk **28 B1**

Bristol

Bristol Zoo Aquarium *Bristol* Variety of species, large landscaped displays from around the world. 0117 9747399 www.bristolzoo.org.uk **56 B3**

Bristol Zoo Gardens *Bristol* 0117 9747399 www.bristolzoo.org.uk **56 B3**

Horse World *Whitchurch, Bristol* Equine rescue centre. 01275 540173 www.horseworld.org.uk **56 C4**

Cornwall

Blue Reef Aquarium *Newquay* Undersea safari. 01637 878134 www.bluereefaquarium.co.uk **7 C7**

DairyLand Farm World *Newquay* Winner of four national awards. Real working farm. Adventure playground, milking parlour, horse-rides and nature trails. 01872 510246 www.dairylandfarmworld.com **7 D8**

Mevagissey Aquarium *Mevagissey* Displays of the fish found in local waters. 01726 843305 **5 B8**

Monkey Sanctuary *Looe* 01503 262532 www.ethicalworks.co.uk/monkeysanctuary **9 E8**

National Seal Sanctuary *Gweek* Britain's largest seal rescue facility. 01326 221361 www.sealsanctuary.co.uk **4 E2**

Newquay Zoo *Newquay* Feedings and displays. 01637 873342 www.newquayzoo.co.uk **7 C7**

Paradise Park *Hayle* Collection of rare birds. 01736 753365 www.paradisepark.org.uk **3 C7**

Porfell Animal Land *Nr Lanreath* Wild and domestic animals in natural environments. 01503 220211 www.porfellanimalland.co.uk **9 D6**

Screech Owl Sanctuary *St Columb* Care and rehabilitation for sick and injured owls. 01726 860182 www.owlsanct.freeserve.co.uk **8 C1**

Shire Horse Farm and Carriage Museum *Treskillard* All three breeds of heavy English horses. Over 40 horse-drawn vehicles. 01209 713606 **4 C1**

Springfields Fun Park & Pony Centre *Nr Newquay* Large all weather family fun centre. Pony rides and farm animals. 01637 881224 www.springfieldsponycentre.co.uk **8 C1**

Tamar Otter Sanctuary *Launceston* 01986 893470 www.ottertrust.org.uk **18 C2**

Tamar Valley Donkey Park *Gunnislake* Children's centre; petting area and donkey rides. 01822 834072 www.donkeypark.com **10 A4**

The Cheese Farm *Upton Cross* Milking, calf-rearing and farmyard activities; cheese-making; animal park and nature walk; museum. 01872 870879 www.cornishyarg.co.uk **9 A8**

Devon

Big Sheep *Bideford* Farm-based attraction with indoor play area. 01237 472366 www.thebigsheep.co.uk **42 F3**

Buckfast Butterfly Farm and Dartmoor Otter Sanctuary *Buckfastleigh* Tropical garden housing exotic butterflies and moths. Large landscaped otter enclosures. 01364 642916 www.ottersandbutterflies.co.uk **14 B2**

Canonteign Falls and Farm Park *Nr Chudleigh* England's highest natural waterfall. Wildlife and woodland nature reserve. 01647 252434 www.canonteignfalls.com **21 D6**

Combe Martin Wildlife & Dinosaur Park *Ilfracombe* Safari park. 8-ha (20-acre) home to otters, gibbons etc. Life-size dinosaur models including a 6.7-m (22-ft) Tyrannosaurus Rex. 01271 882486 www.dinosaur-park.com **43 B7**

Exmoor Zoo *Bratton Fleming* 170 species. 01598 763352 www.exmoorzoo.co.uk **43 C8**

Jungleland *Barnstaple* Chipmunks, terrapins, birds and fish in exotic settings under cover. 01271 343884 **43 E6**

Miniature Pony and Animal Farm *Moretonhampstead* Animals and adventure play area. 01647 432400 www.miniatureponycentre.com **20 D4**

National Shire Horse Centre *Dunstone* More than 40 shire horses on 24-ha (60-acre) farm. Butterfly house, pet's area and adventure playground. 01752 880268 **11 E7**

North Devon Farm Park *Barnstaple* 15th-century farm house. Farm park and rare breeds centre. 01271 830255 www.farmpark.co.uk **43 E7**

Pennywell Farm & Wildlife Centre *Buckfastleigh* Shire horses, falconry displays, pets corner and play areas. 01364 642023 www.pennywellfarmcentre.co.uk **14 C2**

Quince Honey Farm *South Molton* Watch honey bees at work through glass booths. 01769 572401 www.quincehoney.co.uk **33 A7**

Shaldon Wildlife Trust *Shaldon* Many rare and endangered species. 01626 872234 www.shaldonwildlifetrust.org.uk **15 A6**

Skinners Ash Farm *Fenny Bridges* Pony rides, rare breeds, pets' area. Wild birds and hatcheries. 01404 850231 www.skinners-ash-farm.co.uk **22 A4**

The World of Country Life *Exmouth* Falconry displays, deer park safari. Farm centre, petting area and nursery. Historical exhibits and play areas. 01395 274533 www.worldofcountrylife.co.uk **22 D2**

Dorset

Abbotsbury Swannery *Abbotsbury* World-famous swan sanctuary. 01305 871858 www.abbotsbury-tourism.co.uk **25 D6**

Farmer Palmer's Farm Park *Organford* Feeding, milking demonstrations. Tractor-trailer ride. Indoor and outdoor play areas. 01202 622022 www.farmerpalmer.co.uk **27 B5**

Kingston Maurward Gardens and Animal Park *Dorchester* Children can feed unusual animals. 01305 215003 www.kmc.ac.uk/gardens **26 B1**

Lyme Regis Marine Aquarium & Cobb History *Lyme Regis* Dorset's waters. 01297 444230 **24 B1**

Monkey World Ape Rescue Centre *Wareham* 01929 462537 www.monkeyworld.org **26 C3**

New House Farm *Mosterton* Llama trekking. 01308 868674 www.ukllamas.co.uk **37 E7**

Putlake Adventure Farm *Langton Matravers* Bottle feed lambs. Picnic and play areas, farm trail, pony rides and trailer rides. Barn owls and ferret racing. 01929 422917 www.putlakefarm.co.uk **27 E7**

The Children's Farm and the Smuggler's Barn *Abbotsbury* Ancient barn and children's farm animal petting area 01305 871817 www.abbotsbury-tourism.co.uk **25 D6**

Weymouth Sea Life Park *Weymouth* Seal sanctuary, tropical shark nursery, blue-whale splash pool, stingrays, and otter centre. 01305 788255 www.sealifeeurope.com/uk/weymouth/home.htm **25 D8**

Worldlife and Lullingstone Silk Farm *Sherborne* Conservation and environmental displays. Tropical jungle with butterflies. Silk farm. 01935 474608 **38 C1**

Gloucestershire

Birdland Park & Gardens *Bourton-on-the-Water* 2.8 ha (7 acres) inhabited by more than 500 birds, including flamingos, pelicans and penguins. Also tropical, temperate and desert houses. 01451 820480 www.birdland.co.uk **72 C2**

Butts Farm Rare Farm Animals *South Cerney* A working farmstead with a wide variety of animals. Petting and feeding. 01285 869414 www.thebuttsfarmshop.com **65 C5**

Cotswold Falconry Centre *Moreton-in-Marsh* Breeding and conservation. Eagles, hawks, owls and falcons. 01386 701043 www.cotswold-falconry.co.uk **72 A2**

Cotswold Farm Park *Cheltenham* Gloucestershire Rare breeds conservation. Adventure playground, pets corner. 01451 850307 www.cotswoldfarmpark.co.uk **71 B8**

Folly Acres *Stroud* Working farm, Rural Conservation area. 01452 766822 **64 A2**

Folly Farm Waterfowl *nr Bourton-on-the-Water* Also farm animals, llamas and rheas. 01451 820940 **71 C8**

National Birds of Prey Centre *Newent* More than 110 aviaries with 85 species. World's leader in captive breeding. 01531 820286 www.nbpc.co.uk **69 C8**

Prinknash Bird and Deer Park *Cranham* Unusual birds from all over the world. Other animals including deer and African pygmy goats. 01452 812727 www.prinknash-bird-and-deer-park com **70 E3**

North Somerset

Court Farm Country Park *Banwell* 2325 sq m (25,000 sq ft) of indoor play areas, animals. 01934 822383 www.courtfarmcountrypark.co.uk **55 E7**

Seaquarium *Weston-super-Mare* 01934 613361 www.seaquariumweston.co.uk **55 D6**

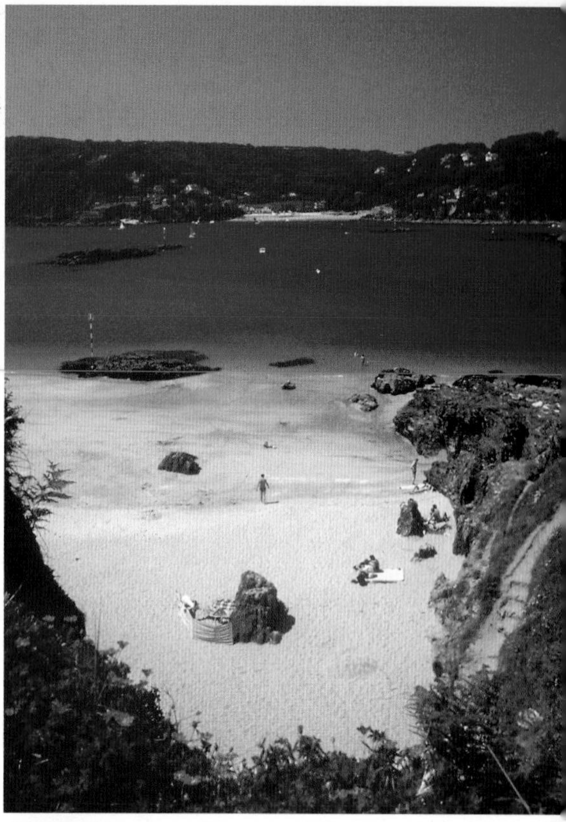

▲ Salcombe, Devon

Plymouth

Dartmoor Wildlife Park *Plymouth* More than 1000 creatures in 12 ha (30 acres) of Devonshire countryside. 01752 837645 www.dartmoorwildlife.co.uk **11 D7**

National Marine Aquarium *Plymouth* Sharks, seahorses, deep reef displays etc. The aquarium has created a new offshore reef for animals to colonise by sinking the frigate *Scylla*. 01752 600301 www.national-aquarium.co.uk **10 F4**

Somerset

Alstone Wildlife Park *Highbridge* 01278 782405 **47 B6**

Animal Farm Adventure Park *Burnham on Sea* Farm animals, pets' corner and play areas. 01278 751628 www.animal-farm.co.uk **45 F6**

Cricket St Thomas Wildlife Park *Chard* Famous country estate where animals and birds live naturally. Safari trains and walks. 01460 30111 www.cstwp.co.uk **36 E5**

Exmoor Falconry and Animal Farm *Allerford* Animal handling, flying displays, falconry days, and riding. 01643 862816 www.exmoorfalconry.co.uk **45 B5**

Ferne Animal Sanctuary *Chard* Home to 300 abandoned animals, set in 20 ha (50 acres) of countryside. 01460 65214 www.ferneanimalsanctuary.org **36 E3**

Heaven's Gate Farm Animal Rescue Centre *Henley* Rehoming centre for variety of animals and fowl. 01458 252656 www.nawt.org.uk/heavengate.htm **47 E8**

Home Farm *Carhampton* Small livestock farm. 01984 640817 www.homefarmblueanchor.co.uk **45 B7**

Tropiquaria *Minehead* Indoor tropical rain forests. Exotic creatures, farm animals, pirate ship adventure playground, trampolines etc. 01984 640688 www.tropiquaria.co.uk **45 B8**

Swindon

Roves Farm Visitors Centre *Swindon* Bottle feed and see a variety of farm animals. 01793 763939 www.rovesfarm.co.uk **65 E9**

Torbay

Brixham Sea Aquarium *Brixham* 01803 882204 **15 D6**

Living Coasts, *Torquay* Local and exotic marine life. 01803 202470 www.livingcoasts.org.uk **15 C6**

Paignton Zoo and Environmental Park *Paignton* One of England's largest zoos with more than 1300 animals, and more than 300 species within 30 ha (75 acres). 01803 697500 www.paigntonzoo.org.uk **15 D5**

Seashore Centre *Goodrington* Walk-in rock-pools etc 01803 528841 **15 D5**

Wiltshire

Bush Farm Bison Centre *West Knoyle* Herds of bison, wapiti and red deer. Gallery of North American wildlife and artifacts. 01747 830263 www.isonfarm.co.uk **49 C8**

Farmer Giles Farmstead *Teffont* Working dairy farm. Pets' corner and adventure play area. 01722 716338 www.farmergiles.co.uk **50 E4**

Longleat *Warminster* Safari park. Adventu castle, King Arthur's Mirror Maze, safari boats, Longleat railways, butterfly gardens, world's longest hedge maze and pets' corner. 01985 844400 www.longleat.co.uk **50 C2**

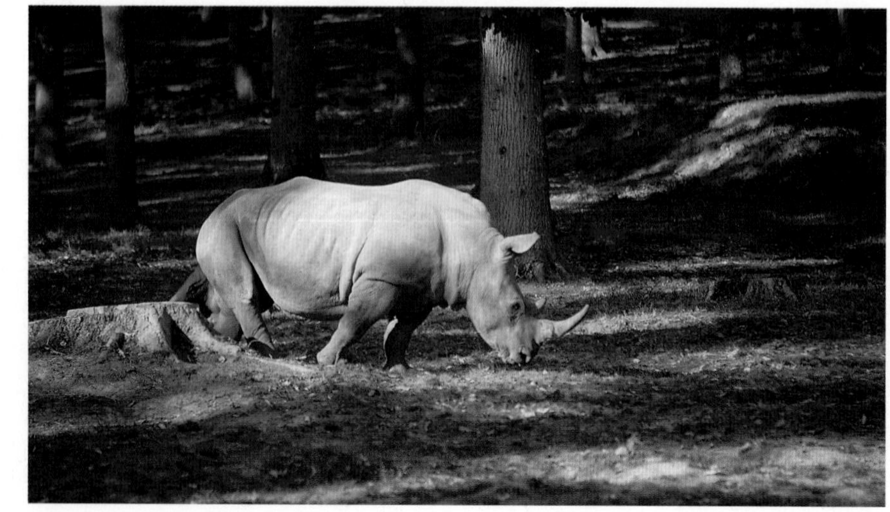

◀ Longleat safari park, Wiltshire

Beaches and resorts

Cornwall

Bude *Bude* Small unspoilt resort town. Popular beaches for families and surfers. Annual jazz festival. www.bude.co.uk **30 E4**

Carbis Bay Sheltered bay ideal for families and surfers. **3 C6**

Constantine Bay *Constantine* Wide beach with pale sands. **16 F2**

Crackington Haven Coastal village with good beach and cliff walks. Cornwall's highest coastal point. **17 A7**

Crantock Long, peaceful sandy beach backed by sand dunes. Good for surfing. **7 C6**

Crinnis, Carlyon Bay *Nr St Austell* Popular sandy beach backed by cliffs. **8 E4**

Duporth Shingle and rocky beach in a sheltered bay. **8 E3**

Fistral Beach *Newquay* Sandy beach partly sheltered by dunes. One of the top surfing spots in Europe. **7 C6**

Godrevy *St Ives* Extensive sandy beach to east of St Ives Bay, lighthouse island featurec in Virginia Woolf's 'To the Lighthouse'. **3 B6**

Great Western *Newquay* Popular family beaches in sheltered coves. **7 C7**

Gyllyngvase *Falmouth* Main resort beach for Falmouth. Small, wide sandy beach. **4 D**

Holywell Bay *Newquay* Sandy beach with dunes. Good surfing. **7 D6**

Kennack Sands *Nr Coverack* Two sheltered sandy beaches. Part of National Nature Reserve. **5 G2**

Kynance Cove (NT) *Lizard* Famed beauty spot. Sheltered sandy coves and caves at low tide. **5 H1**

lendreath *Looe* Lively beach resort. **9 E8**

ther Ivey's Bay *Padstow* Isolated rural ch accessible by coastal path. **16 D4**

wquay Cornwall's most popular and lively day resort. 11 km (7 miles) of beautiful dy beaches. UK's main centre for surfing. 7

r Sands *Nr St Austell* Extensively sandy ches. **8 E3**

ıdower *Roseland* Long sandy beach. fs and rock pools. **5 C6**

rranporth Lively beach resort. Village l beach and Penhale Sands are both sandy ches with good surfing in places. **7 E6**

th Joke *Newquay* Attractive bay with dy beach. **7 C6**

thpean *Nr St Austell* Safe, sandy cove. pular with families. **8 E3**

rthtowan *Porthtowan* North coast rural nily resort. **6 F4**

rtwrinkle *Nr Torpoint* Sandy beach with ks in a rural setting. Popular with surfers. E3

ves Bay *St Ives* 6 km (3¾ miles) of golden dy beaches bordered by fishing resort St Ives. The best stretches include Carbis y and Porthminster Beach, with Godrevy hthouse. **3 B6**

anpool *Falmouth* Small sand and pebble ach. **4 D4**

carne *Newquay* One of Newquay's most pular beaches, close to the town centre. 7

eyarnon Bay *Treyarnon* Wide sandy bay an Area of Outstanding Natural Beauty. F2

ult Beach *Gorran Haven* Gently shelving ndy beach on National Trust land. Good families. **5 B8**

atergate Bay *Watergate* 3 km (1¾ miles) golden sands. Lots of activities and rival to tral Bay for surf. **7 B7**

idemouth Sand *Widemouth Bay* rge sandy beach with low cliffs and rock mations. Good surfing due to reef. **30 F3**

evon

ntham Sandy beach backed by sand nes. Popular with surfers. **12 D4**

gbury-on-Sea Sandy beach at the mouth the South Devon Avon. Connected to Burgh and by a causeway at low tide; at high tide a a tractor transports passengers. **12 D4**

ackpool Sands *Blackpool* One of the most turesque beaches in Devon. Crescent nds backed by cliffs and fields. European e flag award and Seaside awards. **15 F5**

allaborough Sheltered sandy cove; rock ols at low tide. **12 C3**

oyde Beach *Croyde* One of the best rfing beaches in the country. **42 D3**

mouth Beach *Exmouth* Exmouth has mained a popular resort since its Victorian yday. The sandy beach is backed by a wide omenade. **22 D2**

ope Cove *Nr Salcombe* Sandy beach. Safe imming area. **12 E4**

racombe (Tunnels) Beach *Ilfracombe* ey sand and shingle backed by cliffs with nall bays and rock pools. Swimming and uba diving. **42 B5**

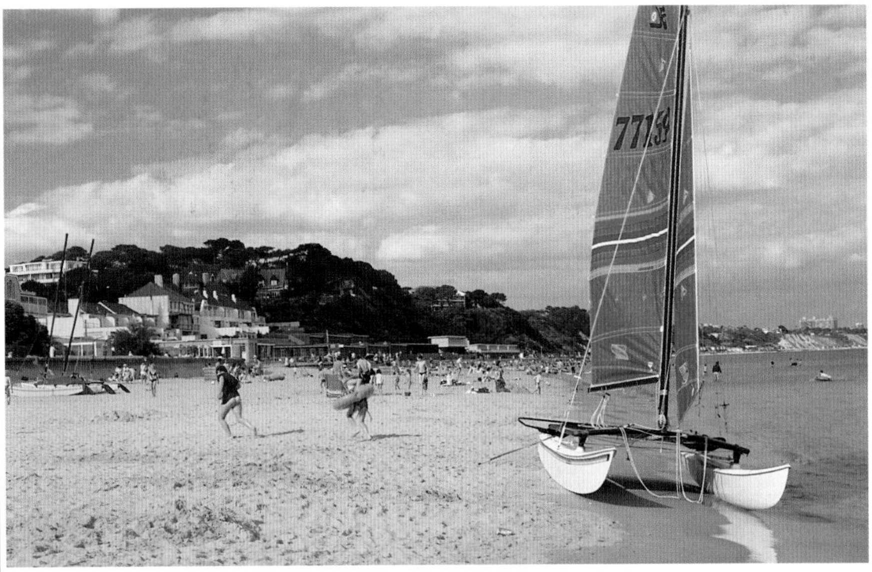

▲ **Golden sands at Poole, Dorset**

Ness Cove *Shaldon* Sandy cove backed by red sand cliffs. **15 A6**

Putsborough Beach *Putsborough* 5 km (3 miles) of golden sands. Excellent surfing towards the two headlands. **42 C3**

Salcombe North and South Sands *Salcombe* Sandy, family beach. **13 E5**

Saunton Sands *Saunton* Superb beaches with miles of sand dunes. **42 D3**

Slapton Sands *Slapton* Long, straight shingle beach backed by Slapton Ley freshwater lake (NT). **13 D7**

Thurlestone North and South *Thurlestone* Owned by the National Trust. Popular sandy beach. **12 D4**

Wembury Small cove surrounded by low cliffs. **11 F6**

Woolacombe Village Beach *Woolacombe* 3.6 km (2¼ miles) of golden sands backed by hills and downs. Water sports. Regular surfing competitions. Woolacombe Sands is within the Heritage Coastline and is backed by National Trust land. **42 C4**

Dorset

Bournemouth One of the most popular resorts in the south. Bournemouth town has lots to do and has numerous sandy beaches. See 'Museums and Galleries', 'Religious Buildings' and 'Sports' for things to do in Bournemouth. **28 B1**

Charmouth Ideal for family holidays. Sandy beach with café and beach huts nearby, as well as Heritage Coastal Centre. Famous worldwide for its fossils. **24 B2**

Christchurch Friars Cliff and Highcliffe Castle *Christchurch* Sand and gravel beaches. Backed by promenade and beach huts. **28 B4**

Church Ope Cove *Portland* Sheltered beach with limestone pebbles. Private beach huts. **26 D3**

Durdle Door *Nr Wareham* Famous for Durdle Door Arch, a naturally formed arch in the headland. The beach is narrow and shingly. **26 D3**

Kimmeridge Bay *Kimmeridge* Sandy beach with fossil-bearing shale. Popular with surfers. **27 E5**

Lyme Regis Known as the Jurassic Coast due to number of fossils. Site from which ships sailed to meet the Spanish Armada. **24 B1**

Shell Bay *Studland* Beautiful beach on tip of Studland Peninsula. Part of Purbeck Heritage Coast. **27 D7**

North Somerset

Weston-Super-Mare Resort with wide sandy beach. **55 D6**

Poole

Sandbanks, Harbour Lake *Poole* Popular sandy beaches. **27 C7**

Somerset

Burnham-on-Sea Traditional family resort. 11 km (7 miles) of sandy beaches with sand dunes. **47 B6**

Dunster Beach *Dunster* Quiet sandy beach. Safe for children. **45 B7**

Minehead Boasts a sandy beach and seafront. Varied choice of entertainments and shopping facilities nearby. **45 B6**

Torbay

Goodrington Sands *Goodrington* Long sandy beach. **15 D5**

Meadfoot *Torquay* Sandy beach to the east of Torquay in the middle of popular resort. **15 C6**

Oddicombe and Maidencombe Bay *Torquay* Known as 'the English Riviera', Torquay and its surrounding coast are popular due to mild climate and golden sands. **15 C6**

Shoalstone Beach *Brixham* Gently shelving shingle beach. Open air swimming pool **15 D6**

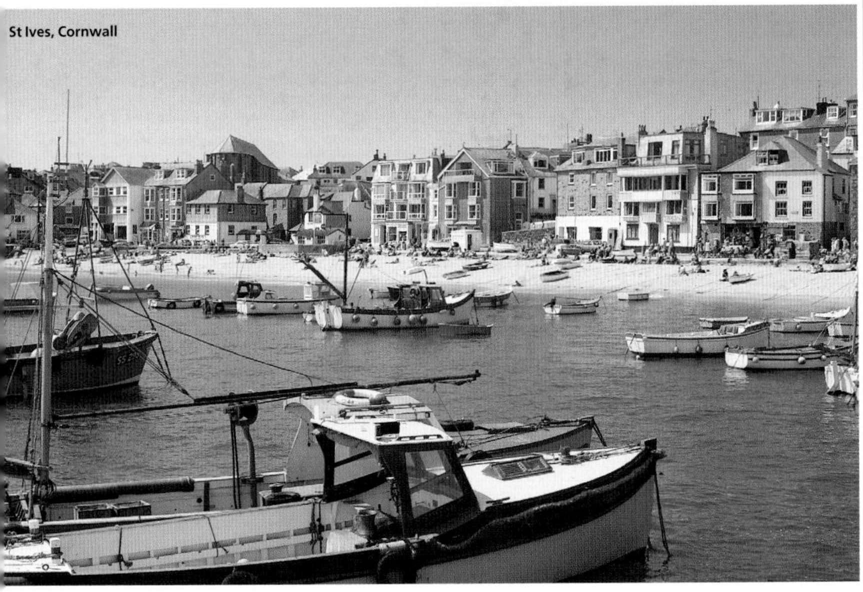

St Ives, Cornwall

Country and forest parks

Bath & NE Somerset

Avon Valley Country Park *Keynsham* Only 7.25 km (4½ miles) from the centres of both Bristol and Bath. Facilities include an outdoor adventure playground, junior assault course, pets' corner, soft-play area, boating and places for fishing. The riverside trail is way-marked with information about the plants and animals. The park itself is designed as a riverside trail, which is well marked with numbered signs providing information about the animals, birds and plants that can be seen along the way. Café. ☎0117 986 4929 🖳www.avonvalleycountrypark.co.uk **57 C5**

Cornwall

Colliford Lake Country Park *Bodmin* Set in the heart of Bodmin Moor, with trails throughout the varied moorland, wetland, lakeside, meadow and woodland habitats. There are children's play areas, farm animals (sheep and goats), red deer, as well as varied wildlife. Picnic area, cafés. ☎01208 821469 🖳www.collifordlakepark.com **17 F8**

Kit Hill Country Park *Callington* A wild, rugged granite hilltop, at 333 m (1000 ft) Kit Hill dominates the landscape for miles. As well as heathland landscape and wildlife, there are lots of interesting archaeological features such as a Neolithic long barrow, several round barrows and evidence of human activity stretching back well over 5000 years. There are several old mine shafts, some of which have been colonised by bats. The views are stunning and there are explanatory boards at the summit. ☎01579 37 00 30 🖳www.cornwall.gov.uk **10 A3**

Mount Edgcumbe Country Park *Cremyll Torpoint* The earliest landscaped park and gardens in Cornwall, Mount Edgcumbe lies in an area that has been inhabited for over 3000 years and was an important early crossing point between Devon and Cornwall. Within the park are formal gardens, garden buildings and follies, two churches, two chapels, a coastguard station, a Bronze Age barrow, a grotto and deer. The South West Coastal Path runs through the park and the 'zig zag' paths criss-cross the steep cliffs. Restaurant. ☎01752 822236 🖳www.mountedgcumbe.gov.uk **10 E5**

Northam Burrows Country Park *Northam* This country park is on a coastal plain within an Area of Outstanding Natural Beauty and SSSI that forms part of a designated United Nations Biosphere Reserve. Habitats include unimproved coastal grassland, sand dunes and fragile salt marsh, providing refuge for a wide variety of wildlife. Access to Westward Ho! beach, visitor centre (summer). ☎01237 479708 🖳www.torridge.gov.uk **42 E3**

Tehidy Country Park *Camborne* Covering 100 ha (250 acres), the Tehidy estate was purchased by Cornwall County Council in 1983 and turned into a recreational country park. It has a mixture of old formal landscaped gardens, woodland with a spring carpet of bluebells, grassland near the cliffs (from where visitors can get spectacular views) and wilder areas. The remnants of the headgear of South Crofty mine, the last working tin mine in Cornwall, can be seen, as can a number of granite engine houses. The area near the lake is popular for picnics, while Oak Wood and the path beside the Tehidy river are good places for walking. The wildlife here includes badgers, weasels and bats, as well as birdlife on the lake and river. Visitor centre and café. ☎01872 322 257 🖳www.cornwall.gov.uk **3 B8**

Devon

Stover Country Park *Heathfield* Stover Country Park's 46 ha (114 acres) include a variety of grassland, heathland, lake, marsh and woodland, giving it a wide range of wildlife including roe deer, otters, dormice, dragonflies, adders, wildfowl and breeding birds such as nightjar, spotted flycatcher and tawny owl. The history of the development of the area, particularly the industrialisation of the 18th century, is explained on the waymarked Heritage Trail that passes through the park. ☎01626 835236 🖳www.devon.gov.uk/stover_country_park.htm **21 E6**

Dorset

Durleston Country Park *Swanage* Set in the beautiful Isle of Purbeck, a World Heritage Site, Durlston has 113 ha (280 acres) of spectacular countryside – limestone downland, hay meadows, sea-cliffs for spectacular views and woodland. There is a huge variety of wildlife, including the colonies of breeding seabirds on the cliffs in summer, peregrines and ravens, bottlenose dolphins offshore, large numbers of migrating birds in spring and autumn and a wide variety of insect life, including 34 species of butterfly. The visitor centre has video links to the seabird colonies. The area's geology and history can be seen in the landscape, with two quarries, a visible Saxon field system, the folly of Durlston Castle and the Great Globe, a monument in Portland limestone showing the Victorian view of the world in the 1880s. Guided walks with rangers, boat trips and way-marked trails. Visitor centre, shop and café. ☎01929 424443 🖳www.durlston.co.uk **27 E7**

Moors Valley Country Park *Ashley Heath* A 300-ha (750-acre) country park with a broad range of habitats and wildlife, as well as a wide variety of facilities including a woodland adventure play area for older children, a castle and sand area for toddlers. A narrow-gauge steam railway runs alongside the lake, and there is an 18-hole golf course. Miles of footpaths, way-marked walks and cycle trails allow visitors to explore much of the valley. Visitor centre, restaurant, shop, wildlife events, cycle hire. ☎01425 470721 🖳www.moors-valley.co.uk **40 E5**

Gloucestershire

Cotswold Water Park *South Cerney* A vast complex of lakes created by gravel extraction. Activities on offer include walking, cycling, angling, sailing, canoeing, kayaking, horse riding, watersking, wind surfing and horse riding. Three of the lakes are designated nature reserves and have bird hides. The complex of parks includes Neigh Bridge Country Park and Keynes Country park ☎01285 861459 🖳www.waterpark.org **65 C5**

Forest of Dean Forest Park *near Cinderford* Formerly a royal hunting forest, this 90-km (35-mile) square area is a tranquil place. There are walking trails, way-marked cycling trails and a sculpture trail. There is a wide variety of wildlife and fallow deer can sometimes be seen. Visitor centre, café. ☎01594 833057 🖳www.forestry.gov.uk **69 E6**

Robinswood Hill Country Park *Gloucester* Surprisingly close to the centre of Gloucester, this park has 100 ha (250 acres) of country-side with pleasant walks and views. There are way-marked geology, nature and riding trails. There is also a rare breeds farm. Gift shop. ☎01452 304779 🖳www.gloucestershire.gov.uk **70 E2**

Poole

Upton Country Park *Poole* This park consists of roughly 40 ha (100 acres) of parkland, gardens and woodland on the shores of Poole Harbour. The Italianate house was built in about 1818. Visitor centre, tearooms. ☎01202 672625 🖳www.boroughofpoole.com **27 B6**

Swindon

Barbury Castle Country Park *Chiseldon* The park, on the northern edge of the Marlborough Downs and within the Wessex Downs Area of Outstanding Natural Beauty, surrounds the Iron Age hillfort after which it is named. The hillfort lies next to the Ridgeway ancient track and the views over the Downs from the top are breathtaking. The area is also a local nature reserve. The unimproved chalk grassland is rich in flowers, grasses and insects in summer. ☎01793 490150 🖳www.swindon.gov.uk/leisuresport/parksandgardens/barbury.htm **59 A8**

Trails

Cornwall and Devon

Tamar Valley Discovery Trail *Cornwall and Devon* The Tamar river forms the historic boundary between Devon and Cornwall and this route follows the river valley for 48 km (30 miles) between Plymouth and Launceston. The landscape varies from the broad Tamar estuary to the quiet woodland higher up the valley. The route passes through a few quiet places, such as Bere Alston and Milton Abbot. Towards the end of the route, the river can be crossed by either the ferry or the train. www.devon.gov.uk

Two Castles Trail *Cornwall and Devon* This route runs 39 km (24 miles) west between Okehampton and Launceston. In the east it crosses open moorland while in the west it passes through peaceful valleys. There are a number of historic sites, including the Norman castles at Okehampton and Launceston, and several small villages. www.devon.gov.uk

West Devon Way *Devon* This 58-km (36-mile) trail runs along the western edge of Dartmoor between Okehampton and Plymouth. It passes across moorland and through river valleys, picturesque farmland, a number of small villages and Tavistock. www.devon.gov.uk

Cornwall, Devon, Dorset and Somerset

South West Coast Path *Cornwall, Devon, Dorset and Somerset* This is Britain's longest National Trail, which runs from Minehead in Somerset to South Haven Point near Poole in Dorset, via the spectacular Devon and Cornwall coastlines and the entire length of the Jurassic Coast World Heritage Site. 01392 383560. www.southwestcoastpath.com/

Dorset

Castleman Trailway *Dorset* This 26-km (16-mile) route follows the line of the former Southampton and Dorchester railway from Upton Park to Ashley Twinning. Linear route following the former Southampton and Dorcester railway line from Upton Park and Holes Bay skirting Poole to the River Avon at Ashley Twinning. There is a connection with the Stour Valley Way at Wimborne Minster. www.dorsetforyou.com

Jubilee Trail *Dorset* This 145-km (90-mile) trail was created by local ramblers to celebrate the Ramblers' Associations 60th anniversary. It winds through wooded valleys and across rolling hillsides in the quietest areas of Dorset, from Forde Abbey in the west to Bokerley Dyke in the east. www.ramblers.org.uk/info/paths/jubileedorset.html

Stour Valley Way *Dorset* This 37-km (23-mile) gentle footpath follows the Stour from Christchurch to Sturminster Marshal through picturesque countryside in southeast Dorset, avoiding the busier towns, and passing such sites as Hengistbury Head. www.dorsetforyou.com

Dorset, Gloucestershire, Somerset and Wiltshire

The Monarch's Way *Dorset, Gloucestershire, Somerset and Wiltshire* This 990-km (615-mile) walk from Worcester to Shoreham (West Sussex) closely follows the trail of Charles II after the Battle of Worcester in 1651. In the southwest, it passes south through or near Chipping Campden, Moreton-in-Marsh, Stow-on-the-Wold, Cirencester, Chipping Sodbury, Keynsham, Abbots Leigh, Compton Martin, Wells, Castle Cary, South Cadbury, Ham Hill, Crewkerne and Charmouth before heading back north towards Yeovil and and then east via Bridport, Winyard's Gap, Wincanton, Mere, Hindon, Great Wishford and Middle Winterslow, and from there to Shoreham. www.monarchsway.50megs.com

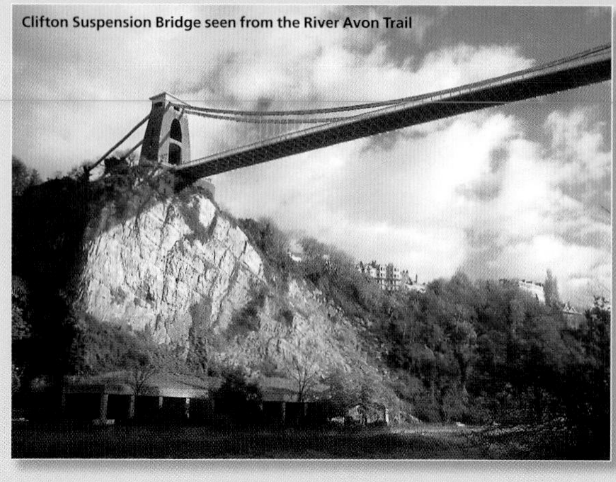

Clifton Suspension Bridge seen from the River Avon Trail

Gloucestershire

Thames Path *Gloucestershire* The Thames Path in its entirety is 296 km (184 miles) long, but the western reaches are among the most pleasant landscape from the lower slopes of the Cotswolds at Thameshead near Kemble, it passes southeast through the Cotswold Water Park and then strikes east via Cricklade until it leaves the region at Lechlade. 01865 810224 www.nationaltrail.co.uk

The Wysis Way *Gloucestershire* The Wysis Way runs for 88.5 km (55 miles) from Monmouth to Kemble through the Forest of Dean, the Leadon and Severn Vales, via Gloucester, and the Cotswolds. It links the Wye and the Thames and joins the Offa's Dyke and Thames paths.

N Somerset, Bristol, Bath & NE Somerset

River Avon Trail *Pill to Bath* This 37-km (23-mile), mainly off-road, trail runs from Pill Harbour, via Clifton and Bristol to Pulteney Bridge in Bath. Sights along the way include the Avon Gorge, the Clifton Suspension Bridge, Leigh Woods and Hanham Weir. The Trail is nearly all level and on good surfaces although it may be muddy in one or two places after wet weather. The path is off-road except for a couple of short sections in the centre of Bristol. You can quite easily link up with the Bristol and Bath Railway Path from the River Avon Trail at Hanham Weir to continue along the Avon Valley to Bath. 0117 922 4325 www.riveravontrail.org.uk

Somerset

Coleridge Way *Somerset* A 58-km (36-mile) trail between Nether Stowey and Porlock. It crosses the Quantock Hills, then dips down before climbing up to cross the northern parts of Exmoor.

Mendip Way *Somerset* An 80.5-km (50-mile) path that travels the entire length of the Mendips from the Roman port of Uphill near Weston-super-Mare to Frome, passing by Wookey Hole, Cheddar Gorge, Ebbor Gorge Nature Reserve and historic towns such as Wells and Shepton Mallet. including the broad vale of the Western Mendips, the high plateau of the central part and the wooded valleys of the eastern end. Includes some steep climbs. www.mendipsociety.org.uk

River Parrett Trail *Somerset* This 80.5-km (50-mile) trail runs north from the Dorset/Somerset border near Crewkerne, roughly following the course of the River Parrett, which finally reaches the sea near Burnham on Sea. As well as the hills of the Dorset/Somerset border, it travels across the beautiful Somerset Levels and Moors and passes through several pretty villages. 01935 845946 www.riverparrett-trail.org.uk

Wiltshire

The Ridgeway National Trail The whole of this ancient path is 140 km (87 miles) long, although only the very end lies within southwestern England. This section is on the Marlborough Downs and starts at the Sanctuary, runs close to Silbury Hill, Avebury and Barbury Castle, before heading off the Downs and east through Oxfordshire and Berkshire. www.nationaltrail.co.uk

The White Horse Trail *Wiltshire* This 145-km (90-mile) walking route connects Wiltshire's eight white horses at Alton Barnes, Broad Town, Cherhill, Hackpen, Marlborough, Pewsey, Westbury and the new Millennium Horse at Devizes. The trail uses several of the ancient trackways that criss-cross the high downs. 01980 623255

Coate Water Country Park Two reservoirs, the smaller of which forms the heart of a nature reserve and SSSI with woodland and wildflower meadows. Facilities and activities on offer include pitch and putt, orienteering, fishing, cycle hire, mini golf, a paddling pool and birdwatching. Ranger centre, café. 01793 490150 www.swindon.gov.uk/leisuresport/parksandgardens/leisure-parkscoatewater.htm **65 F9**

Torbay

Berry Head Country Park *Brixham* See under 'Nature Reserves' **15 D6**

Wiltshire

Brokerswood Country Park *Westbury* Set in remnant ancient forest, this park has a strong emphasis on conservation with a Woodland Heritage Centre, as well as amusements including a woodland railway, fishing, an undercover play area for toddlers, and an adventure play area and play trails for older children. 01373 822238 www.brokerswood.co.uk **50 A1**

Nature reserves, national parks and conservation areas

Bath & NE Somerset

Chew Valley Lake (Avon Wildlife Trust) *Chew Magna* 83.5 ha (207 acres) of the extensive reed beds at the southern end of the large Chew Valley Reservoir, providing habitat for songbirds and wildfowl in summer, spring and autumn migrants and wintering wildfowl and waders. Osprey may sometimes be seen on migration. There are bird hides (permit needed) and a visitor centre. 0117 9177270 www.wildlifetrusts.org **56 D3**

Folly Farm (Avon Wildlife Trust) *Bishop Sutton* An unspoilt 17th-century farm of 101 ha (250 acres), with flower meadows and woodlands (meadows and Dowlings Wood are SSSI). In summer the meadows are full of traditional wild plants and butterflies. Much of Dowlings Wood is old coppiced hazel and the floor is carpeted with spring flowers. Buzzard, great spotted woodpecker and tawny owl may be seen (or heard). 0117 9177270 www.wildlifetrusts.org **56 E3**

Cornwall

Golitha Falls NNR (EN) *Liskeard* The 18-ha (44½-acre) reserve is a relic of ancient oak and ash woodland occupying a steep-sided gorge on the southern edge of Bodmin Moor, with the River Fowey flowing through it in a series of spectacular cascades. The area is rich in mosses, lichens and liverworts as well as plants typical of valleys and meadow areas. Noctule, brown long-eared and lesser horseshoe bats roost in the old mine workings and some 30 species of birds breed here. There are more than 80 moth species and a good variety of butterflies. 01872 265710 www.english-nature.org.uk **9 B7**

Goss Moor NNR (EN) *St Colomb* This 482-hectare reserve is situated in a broad, flat valley basin and has wetland habitats (resulting from tin mining and gravel extraction) and dry heathland, both with a wide variety of plant species. Insects found at the site include some rarities such as the double line moth and the small red damselfly. Nightjars, reed buntings and spotted flycatchers are among the less common birds that breed here, while great grey shrikes, hen harriers and hobbies may be present in winter. 01872 265710 www.english-nature.org.uk **8 C2**

Hayle Estuary (RSPB) *Hayle* The estuary is an important location for over-wintering ducks and a good place to watch birds in autumn and winter. 01736 711682 www.rspb.org.uk **3 C7**

Marazion Marsh (RSPB) *Marazion* Cornwall's largest reedbed with rare breeding warblers, and a large variety of plants and insects. Rare summer migrants include the spotted crake and aquatic warbler, while bitterns overwinter. 01736 711682 www.rspb.org.uk **3 D6**

North Predannack Downs (Cornwall Wildlife Trust) *Helston* Set within an SSSI among the beautiful landscape of the Lizard peninsula, this reserve has 40 ha (99 acres) of heathland, wet willow woodland and pools. As well as being home to important plants, there are often dragonflies near the pools and in April and May. Emperor moths can be seen on sunny days. 01872 273939 www.wildlifetrusts.org **5 G1**

Redmoor (Cornwall Wildlife Trust) *Bodmin* An SSSI and mixed reserve of 95 ha (235) with dry heath, peat bog and open water, mixed woodland and scrub. As well as a mix of plants it has large numbers of dragonflies in the wet areas, and birds such as sparrowhawk, tree pipit and willow tit. Grazing rare breeds of ponies and sheep are used to manage the heath. 01872 273939 www.wildlifetrusts.org **8 C4**

Tamar Estuary (Cornwall Wildlife Trust) *Saltash* An SSSI and nationally and internationally important area for wintering wildfowl and waders, including nearly 405 ha (1000 acres) of wetland. Birds that may be seen in winter include a large population of avocets, black-tailed godwit, curlew and whimbrel. Otters are known to be in the area. 01872 273939 www.wildlifetrusts.org **10 C4**

The Lizard NNR (EN) *Helston* The Lizard NNR is a complex of isolated coastal grasslands and heaths and inland heaths: Mullion and Predannack Cliffs are good for early summer flowers and birdlife; Caerthillian is an area of maritime grassland between Kynance and Lizard Point that holds rare clovers; Kynance cove itself has a wide range of rare plants; Goonhilly Down has expanses of heather and gorse as well as adders, buzzards, lizards, owls and many species of dragonfly: Gwendreath and Kennack Sands near Kuggar is a good place to look at the local geology and, sometimes in summer, basking sharks; and Main Dale south of St Keverne has plentiful heathers and orchids. 01872 265710 www.english-nature.org.uk **5 G2**

Devon

Axmouth to Lyme Regis Undercliffs NNR (EN) *Axmouth/Lyme Regis* This whole area has been shaped by repeated landslides and cliff falls. The site is also part of Sidmouth to West Bay Special Area of Conservation and of the East Devon Area of Outstanding Natural Beauty. The site's importance lies in its geology, fossils and a mosaic of different habitats. 01392 889770 www.english-nature.org.uk **23 C7**

Aylesbeare Common (RSPB) *Aylesbeare* A small area of heathland in East Devon that provides good habitat for rare Dartford warblers, nightjars and stonechats. There are also good numbers of butterflies, damselflies and dragonflies. 01395 233655 www.rspb.org.uk **22 B3**

Bystock Budleigh (Devon Wildlife Trust) *Salterton* An area of heathland, grassland, woods, bogland and a small lake forming part of an SSSI. The heathland is gradually being reclaimed from scrub. It is home to a variety of heathland birds and flowers, damselflies and dragonflies as well as rare reptiles. 01392 279244 www.wildlifetrusts.org **22 D2**

Chudleigh Knighton Heath (Devon Wildlife Trust) *Bovey Tracey* An SSSI and nature reserve of 42 ha (104 acres) of wet and dry heathland, scrub and small ponds. Insects include wood ants and narrow-headed ants, dragonflies, glow worms and some rare butterflies. There is a good variety of heathland birds and all 9 of Devon's reptile and amphibian species may also be found here. 01392 279244 www.wildlifetrusts.org **21 E6**

Dart Valley (Devon Wildlife Trust) *Ashburton* This reserve covers more than 290 ha (716 acres) of upland moor and wooded valley, and lies within an SSSI. It has a rich range of wildlife, including three species of woodpecker, diper, several rare species of butterfly, the extremely rare blue ground beetle and otters. 01392 279244 www.wildlifetrusts.org **14 A1/2**

Dartmoor National Park *Dartmoor* Designated a National Park in 1951, Dartmoor NP covers 954 sq km (368 sq miles) of primarily moorland, together wit farmland, forest and woodland. There are over 720 km (nearly 450 miles) of accessib roads, tracks and paths. It is characterised by the granite of its tors and its high open moorland, dotted with more than 10,000 menhirs, tombs and other ancient monuments. There are several nature reserves and SSSIs within the park. It is hor to a wide range of otherwise rare plants and animals. However, its best-known inhabitants are the ponies. 01822 89041 www.dartmoor-npa.gov.uk **20 D2**

Dawlish Warren NNR *Dawlish Warren* This important site is jointly owned and managed by the Teignbridge District Counc and the Devon Wildlife Trust. It has a wide range of habitats, from mudflats where thousands of waders feed, to sand dunes. I is internationally important for its winterinc bird populations. Its vast list of plant specie includes the endemic Warren crocus. It is a Special Area of Conservation and a Ramsar site as part of the Exe Estuary. 01392 279244 www.wildlifetrusts.org **22 E1**

Dunsdon (Devon Wildlife Trust)* *Holswor* Dunsdon contains a type of pasture known locally as culm grassland, a marshy vegetati that grows well over the slates and shales of the area. There are nearly 200 species of flowering plant, liverworts and mosses, 26 butterfly species, a wide variety of moth damselflies and dragonflies. More than 50 bird species have been recorded, including breeding herons, buzzards, rare songbirds, wintering snipe, owl, woodcock and curlew. Mammals include roe deer, badgers and dormice. 01392 279244 www.wildlifetrusts.org **31 E5**

Dunsford (Devon Wildlife Trust) *Dunsford* Part of a larger SSSI and lying within the Dartmoor National Park, this reserve consis of 57 ha (140 acres) of river valley woodlanc flood plain, scrub and heathy rocky slopes. This variety of habitats means that there is a huge number of different plants. In spring there is a spectacular display of wild daffodils on the floodplain. Animals that ca be seen include many species of butterflies, dragonflies, wood ants and wood crickets, woodland birds, fallow deer, otter and dormice, as well as mink. 01392 279244 www.wildlifetrusts.org **21 C5**

East Dartmoor Woods and Heaths NNR (EN) *Bovey Tracey* Yarner Wood, Trendlebere Down and the Bovey Valley Woodlands make up an internationally important western oakwood. The heathlands at Yarner Wood and Trendlebere Down add diversity. Birdlife the latter includes nightjars, Dartford warble and stonechats. The Bovey Valley Woodland are home to a number of rare butterflies and the River Bovey has dippers, dragonflies and otters. 01392 889770 www.english-nature.org.uk **21 E5**

Haldson (Devon Wildlife Trust) *Dolton* A handsome reserve of 57 ha (140 acres) of valley woodlands, meadows and marsh and a stretch of the River Torridge. It is an SSSI. In spring the mixed woodland floors are a carpet of flowers. The real attraction, however, is the otters. 01392 279244 www.wildlifetrusts.org **32 D4**

Hawkswood (Devon Wildlife Trust) *Honito* Around 4 ha (10 acres) of north-facing mosaic of heath and grassland with areas of birch scrub. There are also small plantations of beech and rhododendron hedge. The lower areas have a good variety of bog plan and there is a particularly rich variety of fungi. In summer, there is a good populatior of butterflies. 01392 279244 www.wildlifetrusts.org **23 A5**

Little Bradley Ponds (Devon Wildlife Trust) *Bovey Tracey* Two ponds in old clay workings, surrounded by 4 ha (10 acres) of mainly grassland. This reserve is particularly noted for its insects including two species of water scorpion, 20 species of dragonfly, grasshoppers, bush crickets and rare butterflies. Keep to the rights of way. 0139 279244 www.wildlifetrusts.org **21 E6**

Lundy NNR (Landmark Trust) *Bristol Channel* Access is by boat from Bideford or Ilfracombe. The island boasts a wide variety of migratory seabirds, Lundy ponies and a spectacular landscape. Lundy Marine Nature Reserve (MNR) was the first designated Marine Nature Reserve. It encompasses the shores and sea around Lundy and contains spectacular marine plants and animals, including seals. 01271 863636 www.lundyisland.co.uk **42 B2**

North Devon Voluntary Marine Conservation Area (Devon Wildlife Trust) *Combe Martin* The area stretches Hangman Point in the east to Down End in Croyde in

e west, covering a 34-km (21-mile) long p from the cliff base out to the 20 m depth ntour. Wildlife includes corals, rockpool ecies and in summer, basking sharks. 1392 279244 www.wildlifetrusts.org D3/ 43 B6

ckenford and Knowstone (Devon ldlife Trust) *Knowestone* An important a of culm grassland with a rich mix of g, heath, wet grassland and scrub, which particularly important for butterflies. It is mmon land and the grazing cattle should t be disturbed. Birds include curlew, nechat and whinchat, and jack snipe, pe and woodcock in winter. There are also d and roe deer. 01392 279244 www. ldlifetrusts.org **34 B1**

iggadon Middlepark (Devon Wildlife ust) *Trisham* This 3.1-ha (7½-acre) reserve nsists of sloping wildflower meadow, wet ass-land and a copse of mainly oak, the or of which is carpeted with flowers in ring. There are good numbers of butterflies d woodland birds, as well as badgers and er. 01392 279244 www.wildlifetrusts. g **21 D7**

anniclift Copse (Devon Wildlife Trust) *ristow* An ancient coppiced woodland of 8 (20 acres) that lies on a steep slope in the ign valley. Keep to the circular path. Tree d shrub species include ash, blackthorn, ech, hazel, holly, hornbeam and coppiced ak The flowers that can be seen at various nes include bluebells, wood anemones, ld garlic, sweet woodruff and enchanter's ghtshade. Insects include fritillaries, and re beetles. There is also a good range of eeding woodland birds, including, in some ars, redstarts. 01392 279244 www. ildlifetrusts.org **21 C6**

apton Ley NNR (Field Studies Council) *apton* This reserve is an important stopping-f point for migrating and wintering birds it includes a large freshwater lake, which separated from the sea by a shingle bar. nusual plants here include strapwort and ere is an enormous range of fungi, some of hich appear to be unique to the area. Birds clude the rare Cetti's warbler. This reserve managed by the Field Studies Council on ehalf of the Whitley Wildlife Conservation ust. 01548 580685 www.field-studies-ouncil.org **13 D7**

tapleton Mire (Devon Wildlife Trust) *ibb Cross* A rich area of culm grassland nd wet and dry woodland. There is a wide ariety of butterflies, wintering woodcock nd snipe may be seen and roe deer are resent throughout the year. 01392 279244 www.wildlifetrusts.org **32 D1**

towford Moor (Devon Wildlife Trust) *ast Putford* Stowford Moor is an important rea of 19 ha (47 acres) of culm grassland. is a nationally important site for heath potted orchids, as well a rich in other plants. n summer, there are plenty of butterflies, mong other insects. Mammals include roe eer and several species of bats. 01392 79244 www.wildlifetrusts.org **31 C7**

enn Ottery (Devon Wildlife Trust) *Venn Ottery* This reserve is part of the East Devon ebblebed Heaths, which are an SSSI and pecial Area of Conservation. It has large reas of wet and dry heathland, some raised og, patches of birch and willow scrub, allow carr and wet woodland. There is a ange of plant species, including butterwort nd oblong-leaved sundew (both of which re insect-eaters) in the raised bog. There are everal species of dragonflies and butterflies, ne birdlife includes stonechat and Dartford varbler and mammals include muntjac deer nd dormice. 01392 279244 www. vildlifetrusts.org **22 B3**

Warleigh Point (Devon Wildlife Trust) *lymouth* A beautiful area of coastal oak voodland overlooking the Tamar estuary, vith a mixture of trees and shrubs and lowers. The short-winged conehead (a ery uncommon species of cricket) is a peciality. Among the birds, little egret can ometimes be seen. 01392 279244 www. vildlifetrusts.org **10 C4**

Velcombe and Marsland (Devon Vildlife Trust) *Welcombe* Welcombe and Marsland is a very large reserve on the northern border of Devon and Cornwall. Occupying two adjacent valleys and xtending several kilometres inland from a dramatic coastline, this inspiring site offers something for everyone. Animals include dormice, butterflies in the sunnier areas, and damselflies and dragonflies in the wet areas. Otters may be in the area. Keep to the public rights of way. 01392 279244 www. vildlifetrusts.org **30 C4**

Wembury Voluntary Marine Conservation Area (Devon Wildlife Trust) *Wembury* A length of 6.4 km (4 miles) of shore and adjacent coastal waters with a variety of wildlife habitats. Specialities include the bloody-eyed velvet swimming crab and other rockpool species. There are interactive displays in the Wembury Marine Centre. 01752 862538 01392 279244 www.wildlifetrusts.org **11 F6**

Dorset

Brownsea Island (Dorset Wildlife Trust) *near Poole* A 100-ha (250-acre) island reserve and SSSI, with Scots and maritime pine woodlands, lakes with reedbeds and some wetland carr with sallow and alder; and a brackish lagoon. It is particularly well known for its red squirrel population, but also has breeding colonies of common and sandwich terns, a large heronry and thousands of wintering wildfowl and waders. Access, which is limited by numbers, is by ferry, via the National Trust land, for guided or self-guided tours. 01305 264620 www. wildlifetrusts.org **27 C7**

Fontmell Down (Dorset Wildlife Trust) *Fontmell Magna* An SSSI and reserve consisting of 58 ha (145 acres) of chalk downland, scattered scrub and woodland. It is rich in typical downland flowers and butterflies. 01305 264620 www. wildlifetrusts.org **39 C7**

Hambledon Hill NNR (EN) *Blandford Forum* The hilltop is encircled by an Iron Age earthwork and there are also several Neolithic features. The chalk grassland's thin infertile soils support a variety of typical grasses, sedges and flowers, particularly on the steep south and west facing slopes. Butterflies include the chalkhill blue and the even rarer adonis blue. 01929 557450 www.english-nature.org.uk **39 D6**

Hartland Moor NNR (EN) *Wareham* Hartland Moor NNR (243 ha/600 acres) is a superb example of an extensive heathland site. The NNR covers an entire drainage basin and is unique in having a Y-shaped bog system which includes both acid and alkaline drainage systems. Heathland is a rare and threatened habitat, and many of the species of plants and animals found on Hartland are equally rare. Typical plants found on site are ling, cross-leaved heath, bell heather, bog asphodel, white beak sedge, western gorse, and rarities such as Dorset heath, marsh gentian and bog orchid. Heathland insects include rare heath and large marsh grasshoppers, and the site supports birds such as Dartford warbler, hobby, meadow pipit, stonechat, nightjar and hen-harrier. 01929 557450 www.english-nature. org.uk **27 C6**

Chalk carvings

Figures cut into chalk hillsides are a well-known feature of the south-western landscape.

Dorset

Cerne Abbas Giant (NT) *Just to the N of Cerne Abbas* 55-m (180-ft) chalk figure of a man, which some believe dates back to 1500 BC but is not mentioned in historical records until the late 17th century. **38 F3**

Wiltshire

Alton Barnes *On Walker's Hill, 1.2 km (¾ mile) N of Alton Barnes* Horse figure cut in 1812. **59 D7**

Broad Town *0.8 km (½ mile) NE of Broad Town* Horse figure thought to have been cut in 1864 but may be older. **59 A7**

Cherhill *Cherhill Down, nr Oldbury Castle hillfort* Horse cut in 1780. At various times the eye was formed from old glass bottles but is currently made of concrete. **59 C5**

Devizes *Nr Oliver's Castle hillfort, N of Devizes* Horse carved in 1999 as a mirror image of one cut in 1845 which is no longer visible. **58 D5**

Fovant Chalk Badges *On Fovant Down, 1.2 km (¾ mile) SE of Fovant* Regimental badges carved by solders camped in the area during WWI, 1914-1918. **50 F5**

Hackpen Hill *2.4 km (1½ miles) SE of Broad Hinton* Horse figure cut in 1838, probably to mark the coronation of Queen Victoria. **59 B7**

Marlborough *Off the A345 Granham Hill SW of Marlborough* Horse cut in 1804 by pupils from a local school. **59 C8**

Pewsey *On Pewsey Hill, 2 km (1¼ miles) S of the town* Horse figure cut 1937 to close to the site of an earlier one cut in 1785 which is no longer visible. **59 E8**

Westbury *On Westbury Hill, close to Bratton Camp hillfort* A horse carved in the late 17th-century, no longer truly a chalk figure as it has been concreted over. **50 A2**

Higher Hide Heath (Dorset Wildlife Trust) *Wareham* An area of 40 ha (100 acres) of Dorset lowland heath and old sand and gravel workings. It is an SSSI. Plants include bog mosses, sundews and pale butterworts in the wet heath (the last two are carnivorous), and the dry heath is dominated by heathers and heaths. Insects include dragonflies, damselflies, emperor moths, butterflies and bog bush crickets. Sand lizards and smooth snakes are sometimes seen. Nightjars and Dartford warblers nest. 01305 264620 www.wildlifetrusts.org **26 B4**

Hog Cliff NNR (EN) *Maiden Newton* A chalk downland reserve made up of three separate sites. The grassland supports a wide range of grasses, herbs and flowering plants as well as fungi, and butterflies. 01929 557450 www.english-nature.org.uk **25 A7**

Holt Heath NNR (EN) *Ferndown* This is one of Dorset's largest remaining areas of lowland heathland. Holt Forest and Holt Wood are also part of the reserve. A mixture of habitats includes dry heath, wet heath and mire and sundews are among the rarer plants. It is a good area for Dartford warbler, nightjar and stonechat, and for breeding curlews. All six of Britain's reptile species are found here. 01929 557450 www.english-nature.org.uk **40 F4**

Lodmoor (RSPB) *Weymouth* A grazing marsh with ditches, shallow pools and reedbeds. It is a prime site for watching autumn migrants, such as swallows, departing, in winter there are good numbers of wildfowl and waders, including bitterns. There is a large breeding colony of common terns and bearded tits and Cetti's warblers are present all year. 01305 778313 www.rspb.org.uk **25 D7**

Morden Bog NNR (EN) *Wareham* A large valley bog that lies within the pine plantations of Wareham forest. The bog has rare plants, including sundews and bladderworts, which prey on the smaller insects, and many dragonflies. The dry heathland to the north has typical birds and reptiles such as sand lizard and smooth snake. 01929 557450 www.english-nature.org.uk **27 B5**

Radipole Lake (RSPB) *Weymouth* In the centre of Weymouth, this reserve has reedbeds, open water and flood meadows. In autumn there are large numbers of migrant birds, wildfowl are around in winter and there is a variety of songbirds in summer. 01305 778313 www.rspb.org.uk **25 D8**

Stoborough Heath NNR (EN) *Wareham* The habitat is made up of dry heath, mire and acid grassland which management is helping to revert to heath. Plants found here include the rare bog orchid, while insects include the wartbiter cricket and a range of dragonflies. In spring and summer skylarks fill the air with song. 01929 557450 www.english-nature.org.uk **27 C5**

Studland and Godlingston Heath NNR (NT) *Studland* The reserve includes 5 km (3 miles) of sandy beaches, as well as bogs, a freshwater lake (Little Sea), heathland, scrub, woodland and sand dunes. In summer all 6 British reptile species can be found here and in winter there are large wildfowl and wader populations. Godlingston Heath has large numbers of Dartford warblers, nightjars and all 6 British reptile species. Wintering waders feed at low tide and rest at the north end of Studland beach at high tide. Little egrets are present all winter. The heathland is also home to bees, dragonflies, grasshoppers and wasps. 01929 450259 www. nationaltrust.org.uk. **27 D7**

The Valley of Stones NNR (EN) *Littlebredy* The chalk grassland slopes are rich in butterflies such as adonis blue, and wild flowers such as autumn gentian. The stones after which the valley is named support many lichens, some of them very rare. 01929 557450 www.english-nature.org.uk **25 C6**

Gloucestershire

Ashleworth Ham and Meerend Thicket (Gloucestershire Wildlife Trust) *Ashleworth* A good site for birdwatchers with 41 ha (101 acres) of meadow in the Severn's floodplain and a steep wooded bank. The meadow forms part of an SSSI. In winter thousands of mallard, teal and wigeon may be seen here, as can Bewick swans, fieldfares, goldeneye, great crested and little grebes, peregrines, pintail, pochard, shoveler and tufted duck. Migrants include snipe, which also nest here, together with curlews, lapwings and redshank. 01452 383333 www.wildlifetrusts.org **70 B2**

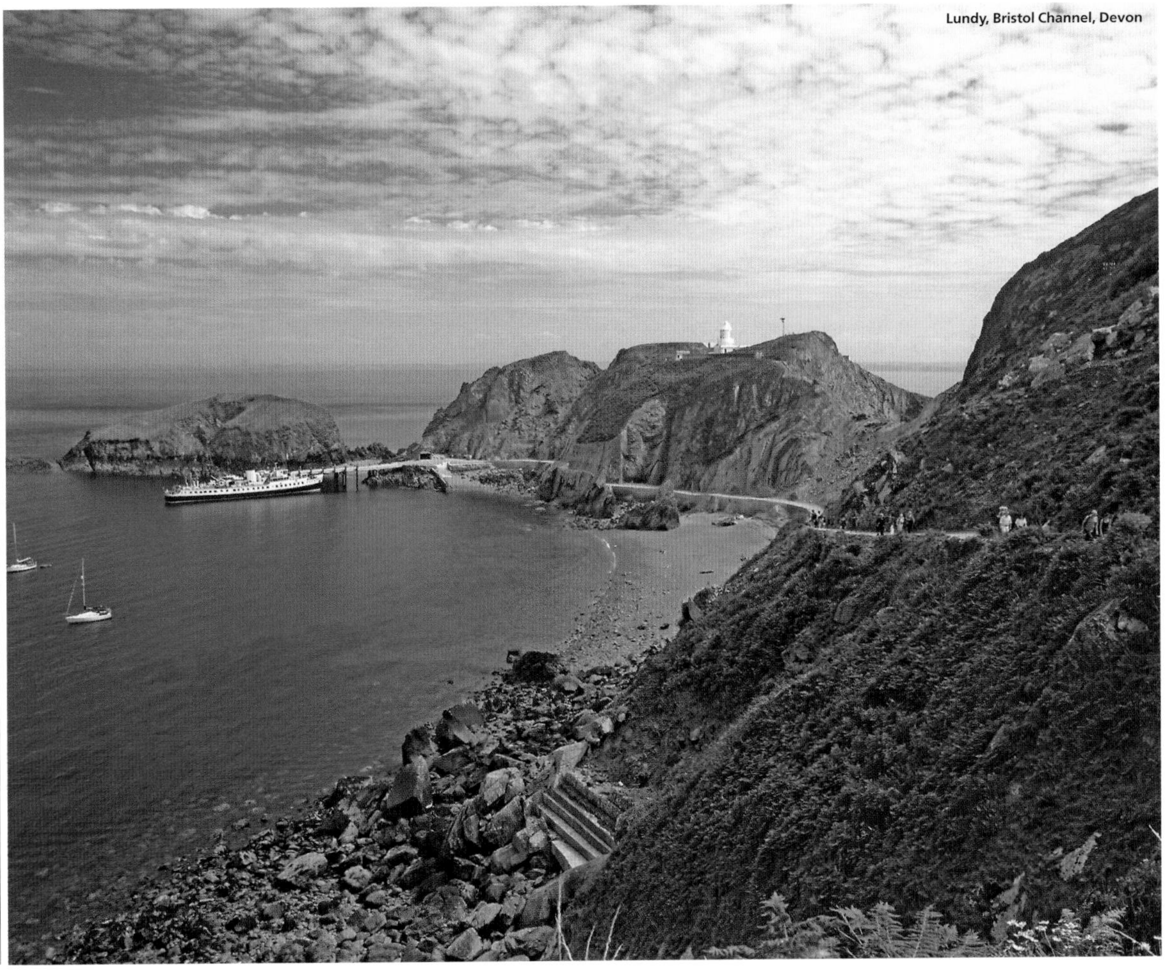

Lundy, Bristol Channel, Devon

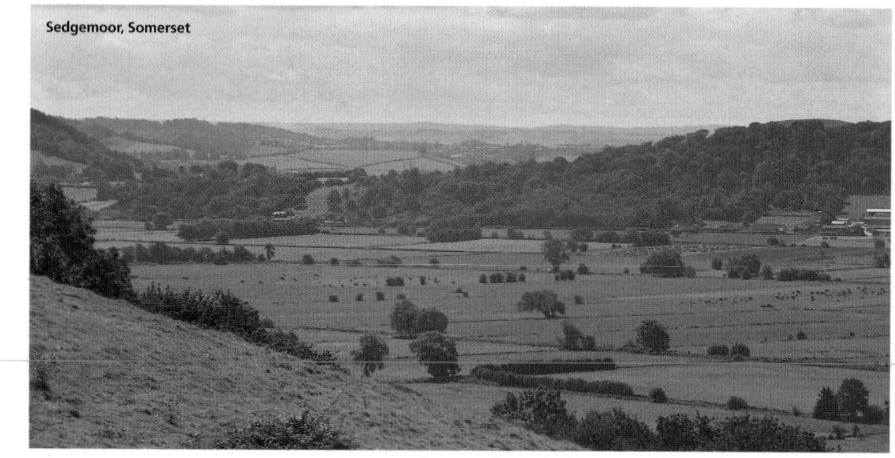

Sedgemoor, Somerset

Betty Daw's Wood (Gloucestershire Wildlife Trust) *Four Oaks* An ancient sessile oak wood, best known for its spectacular spring show of wild daffodils, wood anemone, bluebells and primroses. A box scheme has encouraged marsh tits, nuthatches and treecreepers and pied and spotted flycatchers to nest. Nightingales are sometimes heard. 01452 383333 www.wildlifetrusts.org **69 B7**

Chedworth (Gloucestershire Wildlife Trust) *Chedworth* A fragment of ancient Cotswold beechwood around a section of disused railway track, next to the Roman villa (see under 'Ancient Monuments'). Plants include autumn gentian, bluebell, primrose, wayfaring tree and wood spurge. There are also butterflies and moths typical of limestone grassland areas. Blackcap, woodcock and wood warblers are among the birds that can be seen, as can adders, bats, dormice, fallow deer, lizards and Roman snails. 01452 383333 www.wildlifetrusts.org **71 E7**

Chosen Hill (Gloucestershire Wildlife Trust) *Churchdown* The reserve lies on the edge of the Cotswold scarp and contains areas of ancient woodland with ash, field maple hazel and oak, conifers, grazed grassland and scrub. The woodland floor has a spectacular show of bluebells each spring. The grassland has a small colony of bee orchids. Birdlife includes linnets and little owls. 01452 383333 www.wildlifetrusts.org **70 D3**

Clarke's Pool Meadows (Gloucestershire Wildlife Trust) *Blakeney* An SSSI and reserve, this is one of the finest surviving traditional hay meadows in the county. There are thousands of green-winged orchids in May, together with adder's tongue, common twayblade cowslip and pignut. In late summer the plants include fairy flax, field scabious quaking-grass and yellow-rattle. Keep to the edge of the meadow. 01452 383333 www.wildlifetrusts.org **63 A5**

Cotswold Commons and Beechwoods NNR (EN) *Whiteway* The reserve contains some of Britain's finest beechwoods and comprises three main sites: Buckholt Woods, Cranham Common and Edge Common. There is also a variety of other broad-leaved trees and a range of under-storey species, as well as typical insects and bird species. 01531 638500 www.english-nature.org.uk **70 E4**

Elliott (Swift's Hill) (Gloucestershire Wildlife Trust) *Stroud* A typical limestone grassland area which is renowned for its orchids and geology. Eleven orchid species regularly occur including autumn lady's-tresses, bee, fragrant and pyramidal, among many other flowers. Butterflies such as the dingy skipper and green hairstreak may be seen as can some rare grasshoppers. Reptiles include common lizards and slow worms. Breeding birds include green woodpeckers, meadow and tree pipits, skylarks and swifts. The old quarry is rich in fossils and is a SSSI for Middle Jurassic geology. 01452 383333 www.wildlifetrusts.org **64 A2**

Midger (Gloucestershire Wildlife Trust) *Lower Kilcott* An ancient woodland in a hidden valley, with typical plants such as bluebell, herb paris, spindle and wood anemones. Dormice are present, as are grey wagtails, nutches, treecreepers and great spotted woodpeckers. Good for fungi in autumn. 01452 383333 www.wildlifetrusts.org **63 E7**

Nagshead (RSPB) *Parkend* A small woodland reserve that is primarily know for its breeding pied flycatchers. Buzzards, hawfinches, ravens and wood warblers are among the other species that may also be seen. 01594 562852 www.rspb.org.uk **69 F7**

Slimbridge (Wildfowl and Wetlands Trust) *Slimbridge* On the shores of the Severn Estuary, this is a vital wintering area for thousands of geese and other wildfowl, such as Bewick's swans. It is also the headquarters of the Wildfowl and Wetlands Trust, and has a large visitor centre. 01453 890333 www.wwt.org.uk **63 B6**

Strawberry Banks (Gloucestershire Wildlife Trust) *Chalford* The limestone grassland reserve has been an SSSI since 1993 and includes plants such as the bee, common spotted and greater butterfly orchids, as well as wild columbine, while in late summer , autumn gentians and pyramidal orchids can be seen. Buteflies include the small blue, green hairstreak, the rare chalkhill blue and silver-washed fritillary. 01452 383333 www.wildlifetrusts.org **64 B3**

Whelford Pools (Gloucestershire Wildlife Trust) *Fairford* A wetland site of 12.3 ha (31 acres) of old gravel pits. In winter the lakes are a haven for wildfowl, and in summer eleven species of dragonflies and damselflies breed here. 01452 383333 www.wildlifetrusts.org **65 B8**

North Somerset

Leigh Woods NNR (NT) *Bristol* The site comprises two main habitats – mixed, previously coppiced, broad-leaved woodland and dry limestone grassland. There are some rare trees in the woodland and a wealth of fungi. The grassland supports a wide variety of plant species, while ravens and peregrines nest in the gorge. 0177 9731645 www.nationaltrust.org.uk. **56 B3**

Walborough (Avon Wildlife Trust) *Weston-super-Mare* A mixed reserve consisting of mudflats bordering the River Axe, which provides feeding and roosting habitats for wildfowl and waders. The saltmarsh area is rich in flowers and bird- and insectlife. The wet grassland and scrub are good hiding places for wintering birds and the limestone turf of Walborough Hill is rich in lime-loving wild flowers and butterflies, including the chalkhill blue. 0117 9177270 www.wildlifetrusts.org **55 E6**

Weston Big Wood (Avon Wildlife Trust) *Portishead* Avon's largest remnant of ancient woodland at 38 ha (94 acres); it is an SSSI. It has a broad range of trees and flowers. The open areas of ride are good for butterflies in summer and there is a wide range of woodland birds. Bats and badgers are also found here. Keep to the ride or paths and avoid the quarry wall. 0117 9177270 www.wildlifetrusts.org **56 A1**

Somerset

Bridgwater Bay NNR (EN) *Cannington* This is a large (2559-ha/6323-acre) reserve on the north Somerset coast covering the river Parrett's lower reaches and estuary, as well as the coast between Burnham-on-Sea and Lilstock. It is also a Special Protection Area and Ramsar site and part of the area may be given Special Area of Conservation status. The reserve's intertidal mudflats, saltmash, sandflats and shingle provide feeding, nesting and roosting sites for nearly 200 species of birds. 01823 283211 www.english-nature.org.uk **46 B5**

Catcott Heath and Lows (Somerset Wildlife Trust) *Burtle* The Lows, restored to wet grassland in 1991, flood in winter and harbour thousands of wildfowl and waders. Marsh harrier are often present. Catcott Heath has areas of carr woodland, bog myrtle scrub and tall fen and purple moor grass. There is an interesting range of flowers in the areas that are now managed. The pools have great crested newts and raft spiders. 01823 652400 www.wildlifetrusts.org **47 C8**

Dunkery and Horner Woods NNR (NT) *Porlock* Horner Woods is an ancient oakwood with a range of ferns, lichens, liverworts and mosses. 14 of the UK's 16 bat species occur, as well as a wide range of woodland birds. The upland area has rare plants; lots of insect life, including heath fritillaries; and its birdlife includes curlew, ring ouzel, stonechat and whinchat. 01643 862452 (Holnicote Estate office) www.nationaltrust.org.uk **44 C4**

Ebbor Gorge NNR (EN) *Wells* This reserve is part of the Mendip Woodlands Special Area of Conservation and sits on a scarp that is cut by two valleys: Hope Wood valley and the dry limestone gorge of Ebbor Gorge itself. Most of the reserve is ancient and secondary woodland but there are also areas of limestone grassland. Hope Wood Valley has large numbers of ferns, fungi, lichens, liverworts and mosses. The grasslands have a good range of wild flowers while the gorge provides roosting sites for greater and lesser horseshoe bats. 01823 283211 www.english-nature.org.uk **48 B2**

Exmoor National Park Designated a National Park in 1954, Exmoor covers 693 sq km (267 sq miles). About a quarter of the land remains as open heath and moorland with much of the rest having been turned into arable or grazing land. It is home to more than 30 native mammals, including fallow, red and roe deer and Exmoor ponies. Nearly 250 species of birds have been recorded, of which more than 100 breed here, and there are more than 1000 types of flowers and grasses as well as more than 1750 insect species. The moor has been exploited by humans for some 10,000 years, and there are over 4000 archaeological sites, including Neolithic standing stones and Iron Age hillforts. As well as moorland, there are some patches of ancient woodland, spectacular coastal cliffs and more than 480 km (300 miles) of rivers, which near the coast flow through deep wooded valleys known locally as combes. 01398 323665 www.exmoor-nationalpark.gov.uk **44 C2**

Ham Wall NNR (RSPB) *Meare* In the area known as the Avalon Marshes within Somerset Levels and Moors, this internationally important 190-ha (470-acre) wetland has been specially created from old peat diggings. Species that have colonised include marsh harrier, garganey, reed bunting and in winter bitterns. Water voles and otters may sometimes be seen. 01458 860494 www.rspb.org.uk **49 D9**

Hurscombe (Somerset Wildlife Trust) *Brompton Regis* This 19-ha (46-acre) reserve lies within the boundaries of the Exmoor National Park and consists of scrub, marsh, rough grass and old and new woodland bordering Wimbleball Lake reservoir. The reserve has a variety of more than 100 flowers, with the grassland being particularly rich. There are 30 species of butterfly and breeding birds include ravens, buzzards, tawny owls, all three British woodpeckers pied flycatchers and whinchats. In winter the lake provides a refuge for a variety of wildfowl. 01823 652400 www.wildlifetrusts.org **45 E6**

North Meadow Special Area of Conservation (part EN) *Cricklade* One of the finest traditionally managed lowland hay meadows in Europe, North Meadow has a great variety of wildflowers, including Britain's largest population of wild snake's head fritillaries. In spring and summer the meadow is alive with flowers, insects and birds. During winter, when the meadow usually floods, it is a haven for wildfowl. 01380 726344 www.english-nature.org.uk **65 D6**

Shapwick Heath NNR (EN) *Shapwick* This reserve is a major wetland forming a large part of the Avalon Marshes. Its habitats include traditionally managed grassland, reedbeds in old peat-extraction sites, open water, ferny wet woodland, fen and scrub. The water levels are controlled and the grassland grazed to benefit the plant- and wildlife, which includes otters, bitterns, dragonflies. Remnants of a Neolithic track – the Sweet Track – survive. 01458 860120 www.english-nature.org.uk **47 D8**

West Sedgemoor (RSPB) *Fivehead* This reserve is within the Somerset Levels and Moors. Large numbers of waders breed and in winter the area is populated by thousands of wildfowl and waders. 01458 252805 www.rspb.org.uk **36 B5**

Torbay

Berry Head to Sharkham Point NNR *Brixham* The two areas of the reserve are on the south side of Torbay and are separated by St Mary's Bay. Caves quarried in the limestone of Berry Head provide breeding roosts for both greater and lesser horseshoe bats, while the seacliffs house a guillemot colony and scrubby areas behind the cliffs are home to breeding cirl buntings and whitethroat, among others. There are many rare plants here, including orchids. Common dolphin and harbour porpoise can sometimes be seen offshore. The reserve is owned by the Torbay Coast and Countryside Trust. 01803 883262 www.countryside-trust.org.uk **15 D6**

Wiltshire

Coombe Bissett Down (Wiltshire Wildlife Trust) *Salisbury* This chalk grassland reserve of nearly 35 ha (90 acres) is tucked away in a quiet secluded valley on the downs south of Salisbury. It is basically a chalk downland reserve with species-rich chalk banks and flat areas caused by ancient ploughing. There are also small areas of scrub and a beech woodland. This is one of the best sites in Britain for the burnt orchid; other scarce plants include dwarf sedge. Adonis blue, chalkhill blue, small blue and brown argus butterflies are seen here. 01380 725670 www.wildlifetrusts.org **40 A5**

Fyfield Down NNR (EN) *Marlborough* Part of a World Heritage Site because of its archaeological links – particularly its sarsen stones, which were brought here by glaciers – Fyfield Down is on a high plateau of chalk grassland. Keep to the public rights of way. 01380 726344 www.english-nature.org.uk **59 B7**

Langley Wood NNR (EN) *Redlynch* An extensive tract of ancient, mainly oak, forest with several very rare tree species. Dormice, and five species of deer may be seen and there is a good range of woodland birds. 01380 726344 www.english-nature.org.uk **41 B7**

Pewsey Downs NNR (EN) *Pewsey* On the southern edge of the Marlborough Downs overlooking the Vale of Pewsey, this reserve includes three hills: Milk, Walkers and Knap and it is also a Special Area of Conservation because it is on of the best areas of chalk downland in England, with a wide range of typical chalkland plants and butterflies. 01380 726344 www.english-nature.org.uk **59 D6**

Smallbrook Meadows (Wiltshire Wildlife Trust) *Warminster* These water meadows were created two or three centuries ago – using a system of sluices from the nearby streams they were flushed with warm, silty water to promote an early growth of spring grass for sheep grazing. The reserve has plants that are now generally rare, such as water avens and ragged robin. In spring there are marsh marigolds, yellow flag and then great willow herb. In summer, area is shoulder-high with meadowsweet, which attracts butterflies. There are many dragonflies and damselflies. The damp willow woodland is full of mosses and lichens and ferns. 01380 725670 www.wildlifetrusts.org **50 C2**

Other natural features

Cornwall

Land's End *Sennan* The westernmost point of England, this is an 18-m (60-ft) cliff with beautiful cliff-top walks to both north and south. On a clear day, the views extend almost 40 km (25 miles). **2 E2**

Lizard and Kynance Cove (NT) *Lizard* A dramatic stretch of south Cornwall's coast As well as cliff-top walks, rare wildflowers, Looe Pool and the beautiful Kynance Bay, the area is home to Britain's rarest breeding bird, the chough. 01326 561407 www.nationaltrust.org.uk **5 H1**

▼ **Land's End, Cornwall**

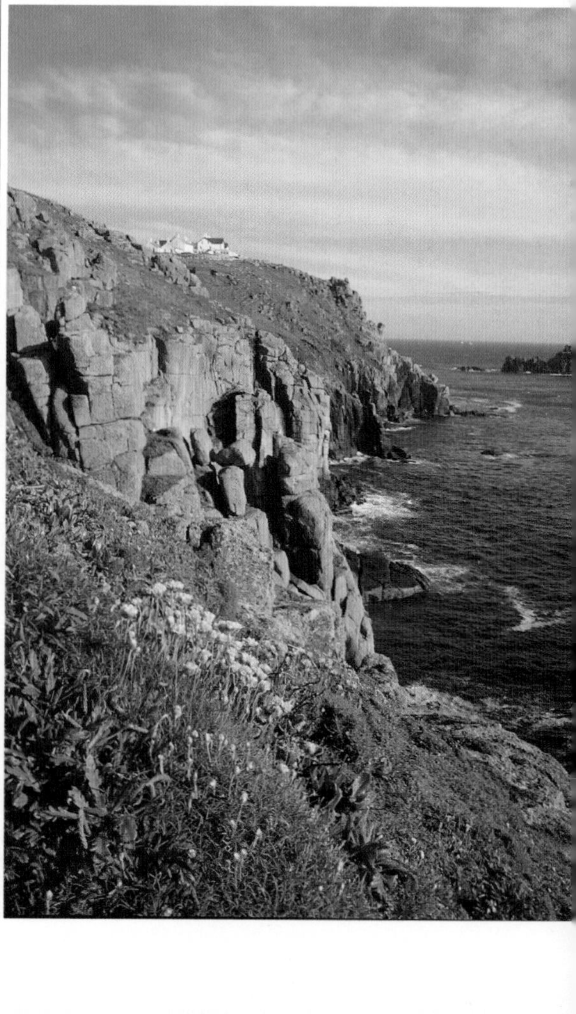

evon and Dorset

urassic Coast *Devon and Dorset* The assic Coast World Heritage Site stretchs om Orcombe Point in the west to Swanage the east. It is an area rich in geology and ldlife and has some of the south coast's ost spectacular scenery. Movements in the rth's crust over millions of years mean that ck layers that originally formed on top of ch other now lay side by side with the older cks in the west and the younger rocks in the st, showing how the area's geology was rmed and, in some places, how it is being stroyed. Highlights include fossil-spotting at armouth, Lyme Regis and Kimmeridge Bay, e stark grandeur of Portland Bill, beautiful lworth Cove and the dramatic coastal enery of Ladram Bay, Durlston Head and nesile Beach. There are also good beaches d walks. www.jurassiccoast.com **22 - 27**

omerset

ren Down (NT) *Bren* This coastal headland d cliffs form a dramatic landmark. A etwork of paths lead the visitor through the ch landscape. At the bottom of a steep walk own the cliffs is Palmerston Fort. Guided alks are sometimes available. 01934 44518 www.nationaltrust.org.uk **55 E5**

heddar Gorge *Cheddar* see under 'Family ttractions' **56 F1**

lastonbury Tor (NT) *Glastonbury* A hill at dominates the Somerset levels and verlooks the Isle of Avalon and Glastonbury. ne site is linked to many legends including ng Arthur and the Glastonbury Thorn, hich was reputed to have been brought ere by Joseph of Arimithea. The views from ne summit are stunning. 01934 844518 www.nationaltrust.org.uk **48 D2**

Vookey Hole *near Wells* see under 'Family ttractions' **48 B2**

arks and gardens

lany houses and castles listed elsewhere n these pages also have fine and important ardens.

3ath & NE Somerset

otanical Gardens *Bath* Over 5000 varieties f plants. Rock garden and pond. 01225 82624 **57 C7**

laverton Manor *Claverton* The grounds f the American Museum are a copy of eorge Washington's formal flower garden t Mount Vernon. 01225 460503 www. mericanmuseum.org **57 D7**

rior Park Landscape (NT) *Bath* Beautiful nd intimate 18th-century landscaped arden. 01225 833422 www. ationaltrust.org.uk **57 C7**

Cornwall

osvigo *Truro* Enclosed and walled gardens urrounding Georgian house. 01872 75774 www.bosvigo.com **4 B4**

urncoose Gardens and Nurseries *Gwennap* 12-ha (30-acre) woodland garden. 01209 860316 www.burncoose.co.uk **B2**

aerhays Castle Gardens *St Austell* nformal woodland garden extending some 4 ha (60 acres). 01872 501310 www. aerhays.co.uk **8 E3**

Eden Project *St Austell* Specially created emperature and humidity controlled giant biomes' in an ex-china clay pit contain a wide ange of plants and fauna from different vorld regions. This spectacular centre also nas interactive displays celebrating the varied ife on our planet and show the importance of conserving it for future generations. 01726 311911 www.edenproject.com **8 E3**

Glendurgan Garden (NT) *Mawnan Smith* One of best sub-tropical gardens in the South West. 01326 250906 www.nationaltrust. org.uk **4 E3**

Longcross Victorian Garden *Trelights* Victorian garden in 1 ha (2½ acres). Maze, pet's corner. 01208 880243 **16 D4**

Lost Gardens of Heligan *Pentewan* Over 80 acres including kitchen garden, fruit houses. 01726 845100 www.heligan.com **8 F3**

Pine Lodge Gardens and Nursery *St Austell* 12 ha (30 acres) with over 6000 plants. 01726 73500 www.pine-lodge.co.uk **8 E3**

Prideaux Place *Padstow* Deer park and restored garden 01841 532411 www. prideauxplace.co.uk **16 E3**

Trebah Garden Trust *Mawnan Smith* 10-ha (25-acre) wooded ravine garden in grounds to private beach. 01326 250448 www.trebahgarden.co.uk **4 E3**

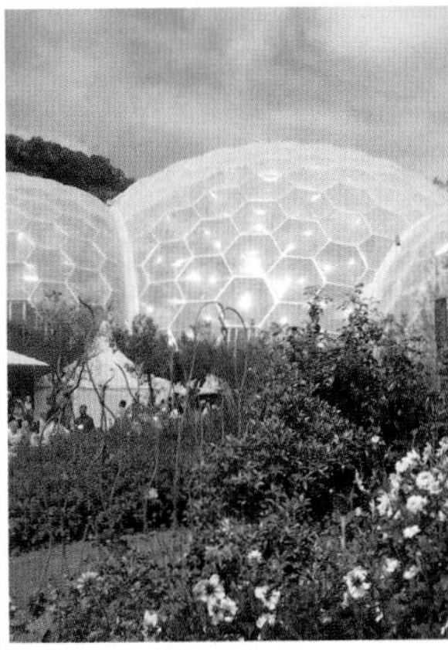

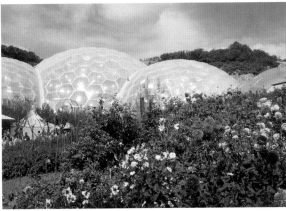

▲ **Eden Project, Cornwall**

Trelissick Garden (NT) *nr Truro* Artistically planted garden and orchard. 01872 862090 www.nationaltrust.org.uk **4 B4**

Trengwainton Garden (NT) *Penzance* Shrub and woodland garden. 01736 363148 www.nationaltrust.org.uk **3 D5**

Trerice (NT) *Nr Newquay* Summer garden, orchard. 01637 875404 www.nationaltrust.org.uk **7 C7**

Devon

Bicton Park Gardens *East Budleigh* Historic gardens. Play areas, museum and train rides. 01395 568465 www.bictongardens. co.uk **22 D3**

Burrow Farm Gardens *Dalwood* 2.8-ha (7-acre) site, part of which was created from ancient Roman clay pit. 01404 831285 www.burrowfarmgardens.co.uk **36 F2**

Dartington Hall *Dartington* Large garden of trees and shrubs. 01803 847100 www.dartingtonhall.com **14 C3**

Escot Ottery *St Mary* Wild gardens in 101 ha (250 acres) of landscaped parkland. Currently has the only otters in East Devon. Wild boar enclosures and birds of prey. 3.2 ha (8 acres) of wetlands, adventure playground. 01404 822188 www.escot-devon.co.uk **22 A4**

Lee Ford *Budleigh Salterton* 16 ha (40 acres) of parkland, formal and woodland gardens. 01395 445894 **22 D3**

Marwood Hill Gardens *Marwood* 7.2-ha (18-acre) garden, bog garden. 01271 342528 www.marwoodhillgarden.co.uk **43 D5**

Rosemoor Garden (RHS) *Great Torrington* Rose garden as well as herbaceous borders and a potager 01805 624067 www.rhs. org.uk **32 C2**

Stone Lane Gardens *Chagford* 2-ha (5-acre) landscaped arboretum and water garden. 01647 231311 **20 C4**

Dorset

Abbotsbury Sub-Tropical Gardens *Abbotsbury* Victorian walled gardens in 8 ha (20 acres) of woodland valley. Children's play area. Nature trail. 01305 871387 www.abbotsburytourism.co.uk **25 C6**

Bennett's Water Gardens *Weymouth* 2.4 ha (6 acres) of ponds, including collection of over 150 types of lilies. 01305 785150 www.waterlily.co.uk **25 E8**

Compton Acres Gardens *Canford Cliffs* Series of themed gardens over 6 ha (15 acres) of land. 01202 700778 www. comptonacres.co.uk **27 C8**

Corfe Castle Model Village and Gardens *Corfe Castle* Detailed model of the Corfe Castle and village. Old English country garden. 01929 481234 www.corfecastle. co.uk **27 D6**

Cranborne Manor Gardens *Cranborne* 01725 517248 www.cranborne.co.uk **40 D3**

Dean's Court *Wimborne Minster* 5.3 ha (13 acres) of gardens. Peacocks and monastery fish pond. 01725 517248 **27 A7**

Horn Park Gardens *Beaminster* 01308 862212 **37 F7**

Knoll Gardens *Hampreston* A nationally-acclaimed modern garden. 01202 873931 **27 A8**

Mapperton Gardens *Beaminster* Terraced hillside gardens with ancient fishponds and summerhouse. 01308 862645 www. mapperton.com **37 F7**

Minterne *Minterne Magna* Large shrub garden. Fine Japanese cherry display in spring. 01300 341370 **38 F3**

Moreton Gardens *Moreton* 1.4 ha (3.5-acre) landscaped garden. Lawrence of Arabia is buried nearby. 01929 463662 www. moretondorset.co.uk/gardens.htm **26 C3**

Stapehill Abbey Gardens *Stapehill* Award-winning gardens in grounds of restored monastery. 01202 861686 **40 F4**

Gloucestershire

Barnsley House Garden *Barnsley* Vegetable garden, herb garden and fruit trees. 01285 740000 www.barnsleyhouse.com **65 A6**

Batsford Arboretum *Moreton-in-Marsh* Established 1880s. Over 20 ha (50 acres) with 1500 different species. Waterfall. 01386 701441 www.batsarb.co.uk **72 A3**

Hidcote Manor Garden (NT) *Hidcote Bartrim* Arts and Crafts garden on a hilltop. 01386 438333 www.nationaltrust.org. uk **77 D6**

Kiftsgate Court *Mickleton* Roses. 01386 438777 www.kiftsgate.co.uk **77 D6**

Lydney Park Gardens *Lydney* Extensive gardens. Roman temple site and museum. 01594 842844 **62 B4**

Miserden Park *Miserden* Well established garden. Topiary and parterre. 01285 821303 **70 F4**

Painswick Rococo Garden *Painswick* Ponds, woodland walks, maze, kitchen garden. 01452 813204 www.rococogarden. co.uk **70 F3**

Westbury Court (NT) *Westbury-on-Severn* Formal water garden with canals and yew hedges. 01452 760461 www. nationaltrust.org.uk **69 E8**

Westonbirt – The National Arboretum *Westonbirt* 01666 880220 www. forestry.gov.uk/westonbirt **64 E2**

Scilly Isles

Tresco Abbey *Tresco* Sub-tropical gardens and remains of Benedictine priory. 01720 4241 www.tresco.co.uk/the_abbey_ garden **05 A2**

Somerset

Cothay *nr Wellington* Virtually untouched since Edward IV. Small individual gardens. 01823 672283 **35 B7**

East Lambrook Manor *South Petherton* Notable garden. Many unusual plants. 01460 240328 www.eastlambrook. co.uk **37 C6**

Hazelbury Manor Gardens *Crewkerne* 75 ha (186 acres) of which 3.2 ha (8 acres) are landscaped gardens. 01225 812088 **37 E6**

Hestercombe Gardens *nr Taunton* Formal garden. 01823 413923 www. hestercombegardens.com **36 A2**

Iford Manor *Bradford-on-Avon* Italian-style manor garden. 01225 863146 www. ifordmanor.co.uk **57 E8**

Tintinhull Garden (NT) *nr Yeovil* 17th-century house. 1.6 ha (4 acres) of formal gardens and with orchard. 01935 822545 www.nationaltrust.org.uk **37 E8**

Wiltshire

Broadleas *Devizes* 3.2 ha (8 acres) of beautiful garden and woodland. 01380 722035 **58 D5**

Stourton House Flower Garden *Stourton* Over 1.6 ha (4 acres) of flower gardens. 01747 840417 **49 E7**

The Courts Garden (NT) *Holt* English garden style at its best. Garden includes topiary, water features. 01225 782875 (opening hours), 01225 782340 (other times) www.nationaltrust.org.uk **58 D2**

River cruises and boat rides

Bath & NE Somerset

Bath Narrowboats *Bath* 01225 447276 www.bath-narrowboats.co.uk **57 C7**

Kennet & Avon Boat Trips *Bath* 01373 813957 **57 C7**

Pulteney Cruisers *Bath* 01225 312900 www.bathboating.com **57 D7**

Devon

Dart Pleasure Craft *Dartmouth* Devon Coast and river boat trips. 01803 834488 www.riverlink.co.uk **15 E5**

Exmoor Boat trips *Lynmouth* Along heritage coastline. 01598 752509 **44 B1**

Grand Western Horseboat Co *Tiverton* See 'Boat Hire' **34 D4**

Plymouth Boat Cruises *Plymouth* 01752 822797 **10 E5**

Salcombe Powerboat School *Salcombe* Offers four-day trips to the Isles of Scilly and return, as well as Channel Islands or France for three or four days. Once a year Round Britain RIB Cruise. 01548 842727 www. salcombepowerboats.co.uk **13 E5**

Stuart Line Cruises *Exmouth* 01395 279693 www.stuartlinecruises.co.uk **22 D2**

Tamar Cruising *Plymouth* 01752 822105 www.tamarcruising.com **10 E5**

Tarka Cruises *Barnstaple* Cruises on the Taw and Torridge Estuary 01237 476191 **43 E6**

Whitestrand Boat Hire *Salcombe* Cruises and self-drive boats available. 01548 843818 www.webmachine.co.uk/ whitestrand **13 E5**

Gloucestershire

Kingfisher Ferries *Tewkesbury* 01684 294088 **70 A3**

Pride of Avon Cruises *Tewkesbury* 01684 294088 **70 A3**

Tjalk of Tewkesbury *Tewkesbury* 01684 292981 **70 A3**

Towns and villages

There are many charming and fascinating towns and villages in the regions covered by this atlas. What follows is a selection of some that are particularly worth visiting.

Bath & NE Somerset

Bath Bath became a fashionable spa town in the 18th century and is famous for the Palladian elegance of its squares, terraces and crescents, all built in the local stone. Attractions include the Roman and Regency baths, the abbey, No 1 Royal Crescent, the Assembly Rooms and Guildhall, Bath Postal Museum, Bath Royal Literary and Scientific Institution, the Building of Bath Museum, the Holburne Museum of Art, the Jane Austen Centre, the Museum of Costume, the Museum of East Asian Art, the Roman Baths Museum, the Royal Photographic Society, the Victoria Art Gallery and the William Herschel Museum. Green spaces within the city include the Botanical Gardens, Prior Park Landscape Garden (NT), the Royal Victoria Park and Sydney Gardens. **57 D7**

Bristol

Bristol An old cathedral city and port with historical architecture and a 19th-century university. The city is now a vibrant centre for the arts, with reminders of its mercantile and maritime heritage. Sights include Bristol Cathedral, the Lord Mayor's Chapel, St John's on the Wall, St Mary Redcliffe, the Temple Church (EH), the New Room, the Georgian House, Goldney House, Red Lodge, Thornbury Castle, Thomas Chatterton's house and the SS *Great Britain*. Museums and galleries include the Arnolfini Arts Centre, Bristol Industrial Museum, the British Empire and Commonwealth Museum, the City Museum and Art Gallery and the Maritime Heritage Centre. **56 B4**

Cornwall

Altarnun This is a pretty village and the 15th-century church of St Nonna, known as the cathedral of the moors, is one of best churches in Cornwall. **18 D1**

Bodmin The traditional county town of Cornwall. St Petroc's is the largest medieval church in Cornwall. Other attractions in the town include the Duke of Cornwall's Light Infantry Regiment Museum and the old Bodmin Jail. Lanhydrock (NT), Pencarrow House and Restormel Castle are nearby, while the mysterious Stripple Stones are on Bodmin moor to the north of the town. **8 B4**

Boscastle Has a small disused harbour (NT), flanked by steep cliffs which provide spectacular views. Within the village is the Museum of Witchcraft and Crackington Haven is a few miles to the north. **17 B6**

Charlestown A handsome harbour village, with a good Shipwreck and Heritage Centre. Nearby attractions include Tregrehan gardens, Wheal Martyn Museum and the Eden Project. Goonhilly Earth Station is to the north. **8 E3**

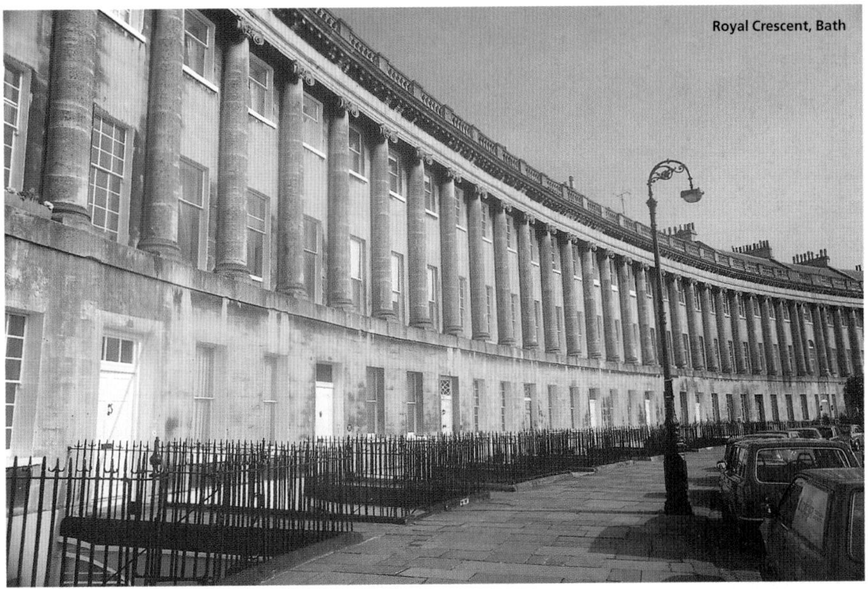

Royal Crescent, Bath

Coverack Charming place with sandy beaches and good windsurfing. **5 G3**

Fowey This former port has a charming square, medieval and Tudor cottages, cobbled streets, a Gothic church dedicated to St Finnbarus and the ruins of St Catherine's Castle (EH). **9 E5**

Launceston A pleasant town that was once capital of Cornwall and has plenty of historical architecture including the ruined Norman castle (EH), St Mary Magdalene's church and Lawrence House (NT), which houses the local museum. **18 D3**

Liskeard Picturesque ancient stannery (tin-mining) and market town on Bodmin Moor, with spacious town square, large Perpendicular church and the Thorburn Museum and Art Gallery. Nearby are St Clarus' church in St Cleer, Trethevy Quoit, King Doniert's Inscribed Stone and the Hurlers stone circles. **9 C8**

Looe Historic little port, now a popular resort and British centre for shark fishing. **9 E8**

Lostwithiel The 13th-century capital of Cornwall. Highlights include the medieval Restormel Castle (EH summer only), Fowey Bridge and Stannery Court and the Guildhall of 1740. **9 D5**

Mevagissey Attractive fishing village with cottages and fine harbour. There is a folk museum in the village and the Lost Gardens of Heligan are a few miles to the north. **5 A8**

Padstow A fishing port on the estuary of the river Camel with attractive medieval houses and a bustling harbour. On May Day the town's traditional celebrations include the 'Obby 'Orse parade. Prideaux Place has good gardens and a deer park and guided tours of the house are sometimes available. **16 E3**

Penzance One of Cornwall's most attractive towns in terms of both architecture and position, set within the curve of Mount's Bay. In the town is the National Maritime Museum Cornwall and nearby are St Michael's Mount, Trengwainton Garden and Lanyon Quoit (both NT), Chysauster Ancient Village (EH), Carn Euny Ancient Village and Men-An-Toi. **3 D5**

Polperro Picturesque fishing village with colour-washed cottages. Like many places in the area, it was renowned in past for smuggling and this is reflected in the village's Smuggling Museum. **9 E7**

Polzeath Sandy resort with Pentire Point (NT) to the north and Trebetherick and Daymer Bay to the south. St Enodoc church is situated in the middle of the local golf course. **16 E3**

St Ives A popular resort town on one of the most charming bays in England. It has thriving artistic connections, reflected in the presence of the Barbara Hepworth Museum and Sculpture Garden and Tate St Ives. Other attractions include the Barnes Museum of Cinematography and the Heritage Museum. The local church is dedicated to St Ia, while the Chapel of St Nicholas is the oldest in the area. **3 B6**

Tintagel One of the most famous places in Cornwall. Village connected with the romantic ruins of Tintagel castle and legend of King Arthur. The church is dedicated to St Materiana. The Old Post Office (NT) is actually a 14th-century manor house that served as a Post Office in the 19th century. **17 C6**

Truro Situated on the Fal river. Historically important as market centre and port, Truro became a cathedral city in the 19th century. The late 19th- early 20th-century cathedral incorporates some of the 16th-century parish church. There are good gardens at Bosvigo House and Trelissick (NT). Other attractions in the city include Cornwall County Museum and Art Gallery and the Royal Cornwall Museum **4 B4**

Devon

Barnstaple An ancient port and old trading centre with handsome old buildings and the 15th-century Long Bridge across the River Taw. Within the town are the Museum of North Devon and St Anne's Chapel and Museum, while Arlington Court (NT) and the gardens of Marwood Hill are within easy reach. **43 E6**

Chagford Quiet and charming old 'Stannary' (tin-mining) town right in the centre of Devon and set in the northern part of Dartmoor. Stone Lane Gardens and Castle Drogo are both northeast of the town. **20 C3**

Clovelly A picturesque fishing village with steep cobbled streets and pretty white cottages. The grounds of Clovelly Court provide views over the coast. **31 B6**

Combe Martin A popular north-coast resort situated at the head of a sheltered valley. The Combe Martin Motorcycle Collection is among its attractions and Arlington Court (NT) is a few miles to the south. **43 B6**

Exeter Historic cathedral city with medieval walls and the remains of Roman roads. Other buildings include the cathedral, Bowhill House, Killerton (NT), Exeter (Rougemont) Castle, the Customs House, the Guildhall and Marker's Cottage (NT). Other things to see include the Bill Douglas Centre and the Royal Albert Memorial Museum and Art Gallery. **21 B8**

Sidmouth Regency style resort situated between reddish cliffs. York Terrace has balconied Georgian houses with wrought-iron railings. Activities include the Norman Lockyer Observatory, Radway and Sidmouth Sports Centre **22 C4**

Totnes One of oldest and most handsome towns in England. It primarily consists of one main street with many Elizabethan houses. Totnes Castle (EH) is at the top of the High Street. The Guildhall is 16th–17th century and the Elizabethan House Museum was built in the 1570s and has a collection of furniture and other domestic objects. Outside the town, Berry Pomeroy Castle, Dartington Hall gardens and Bowden House are both worth visiting, especially as the latter contains the British Photographic Museum. **14 C4**

Dorset

Beaminster Set within the beautiful countryside of northwest Dorset, this is a handsome place set below the extravagantly decorated Gothic St Mary's church, Georgian buildings and picturesque 17th-century cottages. Nearby attractions include Mapperton and Horn Park Gardens. **37 F7**

Blandford Forum A market town on the Stour with some fine buildings of 1735–40 by John and William Bastard and a near-contemporary Palladian church. Within the town are Blandford Museum and the Cavalcade of Costume Museum, while Milton Abbey is to the southwest and Badbury Rings to the southeast. **39 E7**

Bridport Pleasant little maritime town with attractive main street and 18th-century Town Hall. Believed to have last thatched brewery in country. **24 B4**

Cerne Abbas Pretty village with the 15th-century gatehouse from a long-gone Benedictine monastery and a small church with a 15th-century screen and wall paintings. The village is most famous for the chalk figure of the Cerne Giant (NT) on a nearby hill. **38 F3**

Corfe Castle A pretty village clustered around the foot of a hill. Its ruined Norman castle (NT) is spectacular and holds a local museum. The water of the Blue Pool west of the village changes colour and is set within a Site of Special Scientific Interest. **27 D6**

Cranborne Set in beautiful countryside as known as 'Chaseborough' in novels of Thomas Hardy. Cranborne Manor Gardens were originally laid out by John Tradescant, one of the earliest and greatest plant-hunters. Knowlton Church and Earthworks (NT) consists of a Norman ruin set within the remains of an ancient henge. **40 D4**

Dorchester Dorset's county town. Attractions in and around the town include Wolfeton House, the Dorset County Museum, The Keep Military Museum, Hardy's Cottage (NT), Cloud's Hill (NT), Max Gate (NT) and Wolfeton House. Evidence of the areas earlier human inhabitants can be seen at Maiden Castle (EH), Maumbury Rings and Poundbury hillfort. **25 B8**

Lyme Regis A charming old resort overlooking Lyme Bay with many Regency buildings remaining from the height of its popularity. Set within the World Heritage Coast, its attractions include the Cobb (with a Marine Aquarium and Cobb History Exhibition), the Town Mill, Dinosaurland, the Philpott Museum, and the Guildhall. The beaches west of the town are popular for fossil-hunting. Lambert's Castle hillfort (NT) is in the hills north of the town and Forde Abbey is on the Somerset border. **24 B1**

Shaftesbury Picturesque old town with abbey ruins, a castle, twelve churches and four market crosses. Shaftesbury's Gold Hill looks over the picturesque Blackmore Vale of North Dorset. There is a small museum and Wardour Castle, Old Wardour Castle and White Sheet Hill are nearby. **39 B7**

Sherborne Handsome stone-built town with a magnificent Abbey Church, the ruined Old Castle, Sherborne Castle, Sherborne Museum and nearby is Sandford Orcas House. **38 C2**

Studland A charming village 4.8 km (3 miles) north of Swanage. Tiny Norman church, pretty bay and Studland National Trust nature reserve. West of the village, on the Black Down, is the Agglestone. **27 D7**

Swanage An attractive town at southern end of beautiful Studland Bay. There is a Tithe Barn Museum and Art Centre, while at nearby Langton Maltravers is the Coach House Museum of stone crafts and local history. **27 E7**

Wareham An interesting little town, on the river Frome, which was built within Anglo-Saxon earthworks and still has some Saxon walls and St Martin's church (parts of which date to 1020). The Wareham Museum includes a local items dating right back to the Iron Age and a collection of Lawrence of Arabia memorabilia. The Royal Armoured Corps Tank Museum is at Bovingdon a few miles to the northwest. **27 C5**

Weymouth An old harbour town and popular resort with late Georgian buildings. Historic buildings include Nothe Fort and the Tudor House. Weymouth Museum has items of local history. Open spaces include the Nothe gardens, Bennett's Water Gardens and the nature reserves of Lodmoor and Radipole Lake. The Isle of Portland is joined to the mainland by the shingle strip of Chesil Beach. Portland Castle (EH, summer) was built by Henry VIII. At the southern end of the island is the spectacular rocky Portland Bill. **25 E8**

Wimborne Minster A historic market town on the Allen, where it meets the Stour. It has charming narrow Georgian streets and pretty squares. The parish church is dedicated to St Cuthburga. Near to Badbury Rings and Kingston Lacy (both NT) and Deans Court Gardens. **27 A7**

Gloucestershire

Bibury One of the most popular Cotswold villages, with the beautiful Arlington Row group of stone-built cottages. St Mary's church is a mixture of Saxon, Norman and all phases of Gothic. Arlington Mill now serves as a rural museum. Barnsley House Garden is to the southwest of the town. **65 A7**

Chipping Campden Once a rich centre of the wool trade, this town has plenty of handsome stone buildings (including St James' church, the Market Hall (NT) and Woolstaplers Hall) in a picturesque High Street with styles ranging from the 14th century to the 18th. Nearby are Kifsgate Court and Hidcote Manor Garden (NT). **77 E6**

Fairford Small and attractive town on the Coln, with the late 15th-century St Mary's church and 17th- and 18th-century buildings around the market place. **65 B8**

Gloucester An interesting city with a beautiful medieval cathedral. The historic docks have been handsomely redeveloped. Other places of interest include Robert Raikes House, Gloucester City Museum and Art Gallery and the Robert Opie Collection at the Museum of Advertising and Packaging. **70 D2**

Tewkesbury Old riverside town in the cotswolds with half-timbered houses, great scenery and one of the best English Abbey churches – St Mary's. There are two museums, the Countryside Museum and the Little Museum. **70 A3**

Plymouth

Plymouth A major historical seaport and garrison at the head of Plymouth Sound. It is rich in maritime history. Buildings include St Andrew's Church, the Guildhall, the Roman Catholic Cathedral, Prysten House and the Royal Citadel (EH, guided tours in summer). On The Hoe is Smeaton's Tower – part of the third Eddystone Lighthouse. Museums include the City Museum and Art Gallery, the Merchant's House Museum, the Kathleen and May boat and museum, the Mayflower Centre and Plymouth Dome. The National Marine Aquarium is a major attraction on the water front. Attractions nearby include Saltram House (NT), Cotehele House, Anthony House and Buckland Abbey (all NT), Mount Edgcumbe, The Garden House and Mary Newman's Cotage. **10 E5**

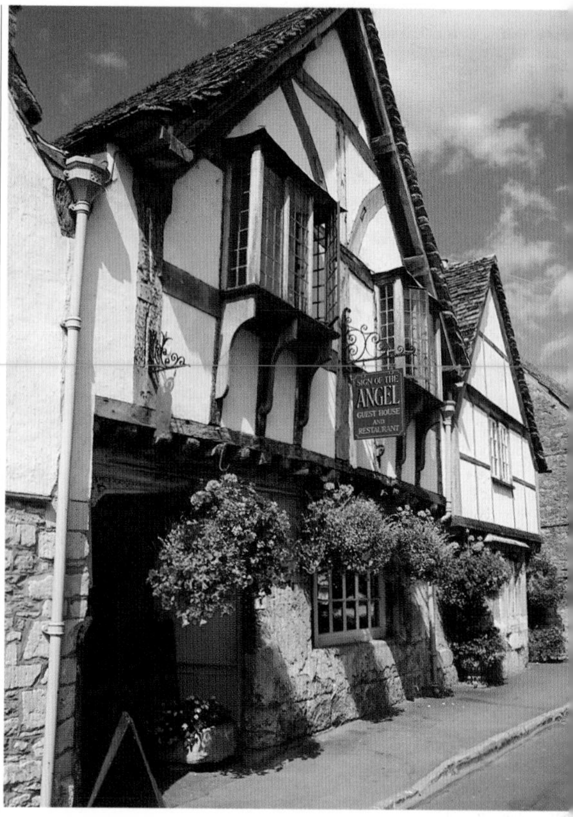

▲ **Lacock, Wiltshire**

Poole

Poole A major port set by the biggest natural harbour in Europe, Poole is particularly popular with sailors. As well as old buildings and quaint narrow streets, it has good beaches, St Osmund's church, the Waterfront Museum, tours of Poole Pottery, a small local history museum in the Guildhall and an arts centre in Poole Lighthouse. Brownsea Island is reachable from Poole Harbour. **27 B7**

Somerset

Dunster An attractive small town just inside Exmoor. Medieval buildings include the butter cross, Gallox Bridge (EH) and St George's church. Among later buildings are Dunster Working Watermill (NT), the Yarn Market (EH) and the heavily rebuilt Dunster Castle (NT) **45 C6**

Taunton A bustling county town dating back to Saxon times which lies in the pretty valley of Taunton Deane, known for its apples and cider. Attractions include St Mary Magdalene's church, Combe Sydenham Hall, Hestercombe Gardens (RHS), Somerset Cricket Museum and Somerset County Museum, which is housed in the 12th-century castle. **36 A2**

Torbay

Brixham A resort and fishing port with beaches and attractive harbour. Attractions include the Brixham Heritage Museum and, in summer, the Brixham Aquarium. There is also a good fish market. Coleton Fishacre (NT) is nearby and there are good coastal walks to the south of the town. **15 D6**

Wiltshire

Bradford on Avon A pretty little town with one of the best Saxon churches in the country, a 17th-century town bridge with a lock-up at one end, a medieval tithe barn, pretty gardens at Westwood Manor (NT) and the Hall and pleasant walks along the banks of the Avon. Farleigh Hungerford Castle is to the southwest. **57 D8**

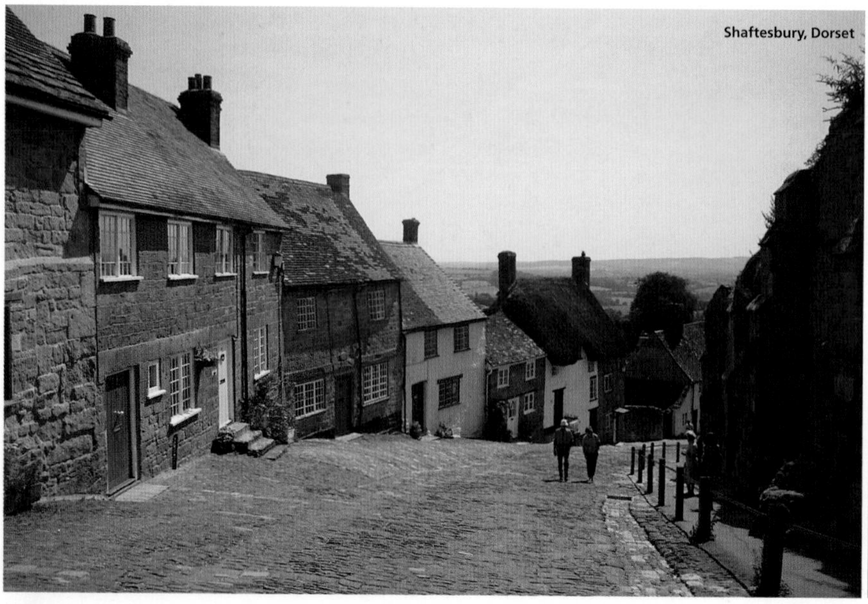

Shaftesbury, Dorset

vizes A busy market town with a pretty ırch and handsome 18th-century ldings, including the town hall and rket cross. Other places to visit include the ınet and Somerset Canal Museum and ɔadleas Gardens. The ancient monuments Avebury, Silbury Hill, Windmill Hill neolithic np, the Sanctuary and West Kennet long row are a little to the east. **58 D5**

cock Pretty village with lots of picturesque tages, very few of which date from after 00. It is often used in films and television ɔgrammes. Nearby is Lacock Abbey (NT), ich contains the Fox Talbot Museum of otography. **58 C3**

almesbury Pleasant town above the Avon. mains of Malmesbury Abbey, in which historian William of Malmesbury (1090–43) was a monk. Westonbirt Arboretum, ckington Court and Charlton Park House nearby. **64 E3**

alisbury Cathedral city with historical ildings, including Longford Castle, almesbury House, Mompesson House (NT), ilton House and the North Canonry. On lisbury Plain to the north are Old Sarum H), Stonehenge (EH) and the surrounding storic landscape including Durrington Walls T), Woodhenge (EH) and Earl's Farm Down rrows. Museums include the Salisbury and uth Wiltshire Museum and The Wardrobe. earby is Wilton House. **51 E8**

Buildings

ne places listed here are a selection of e finest houses, castles and gardens in e counties covered by this atlas. Make ıre you check opening times before isiting, as many of the places listed are pen only at limited times or seasons.

astles

ornwall

aunceston Castle (EH) *Launceston* Set the motte of a Norman castle. 01566 72365 www.english-heritage.org.uk 8 D3

endennis Castle (EH) *Falmouth* End of ıain of castles built by Henry VIII along ɔast. 01326 316594 www.english-eritage.org.uk **4 D4**

estormel Castle (EH) *Lostwithiel* One of dest and best Norman motte-and-bailey astles in Cornwall. Founded 1100. 01208 72687 www.english-heritage.org.uk **D5**

Nunney Castle, Somerset

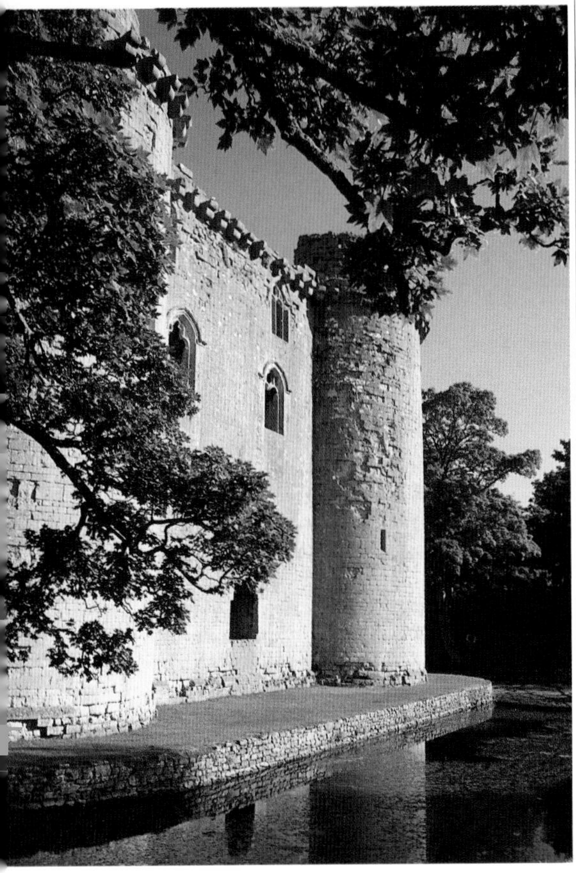

St Catherine's Castle (EH) *Fowey* Small fort built by Henry VIII. 0870 3331181 www.english-heritage.org.uk **9 E5**

St Mawes Castle (EH) *St Mawes* Built by Henry VIII. Stands in sub-tropical gardens. 01326 270526 www.english-heritage.org.uk **4 D4**

St Michael's Mount (NT) *Marazion* Spectacular castle on rocky island, dating from 14th century. 01736 710507 www.nationaltrust.org.uk **3 D7**

Tintagel Castle (EH) *Tintagel* Remains of medieval castle, thought to date from 13th century. Associated in popular legend with King Arthur. 01840 770328 www.english-heritage.org.uk **17 C6**

Devon

Berry Pomeroy Castle (EH) *Totnes* Combines medieval castle with flamboyant courtier's mansion. 01803 866618 www.english-heritage.org.uk **14 C4**

Bickleigh Castle *Tiverton* 14th-century fortified manor on site of Norman castle. 01884 855363 **34 D4**

Castle Drogo (NT) *Nr Exeter* Last castle to be built in Britain, now 20th-century home. 01647 433306 www.nationaltrust.org.uk **21 B8**

Dartmouth Castle (EH) *Dartmouth* Defensive castle. 01803 833588 www.english-heritage.org.uk **15 E5**

Exeter (Rougemont) Castle *Exeter* Started in 1068. County Court built on site in 18th century. **21 B8**

Lydford Castle (EH) *Lydford* Late 12th-century keep with rectangular bailey. Earthworks of original Norman fort are to the south. www.english-heritage.org.uk **19 D7**

Okehampton Castle (EH) *Okehampton* Ruins of largest castle in Devon with Norman motte and keep's jagged remains. 01837 52844 www.english-heritage.org.uk **20 B1**

Totnes Castle (EH) *Totnes* Superb Norman motte-and-bailey castle. 01803 864406 **14 C4**

Dorset

Christchurch Castle and Norman House (EH) *Christchurch* Built late 11th century. 01202 495127 www.english-heritage.org.uk **38 C2**

Corfe Castle (NT) *Wareham* Magnificent ruins of 1000-yr-old castle dominate Isle of Purbeck. 01929 481294 www.corfecastle.org.uk **27 D6**

Lulworth Castle (EH) *Wareham* Early 17th-century hunting lodge. 18th-century house in parkland. 01929 400352 www.english-heritage.org.uk **26 D4**

Portland Castle (EH) *Portland* One of best preserved of Henry VIII's coastal forts. Open in summer only. 01305 820539 www.english-heritage.org.uk **24 D2**

Sherborne Old Castle (EH) *Sherborne* Ruins of early 12th-century castle. 01935 813182 www.english-heritage.org.uk **38 C2**

Gloucestershire

Berkeley Castle *Berkeley* Completed 1153 at command of Henry II. Castle is now a stately home. Terraced Elizabethan gardens. 01453 810332 www.berkeley-castle.com **63 C5**

Sudeley Castle *Winchcombe* Tudor building once home of Katherine Parr. Royal relics. Fine gardens and wildlife reserve. 01242 602308 www.sudeleycastle.co.uk **71 B6**

Scilly Isles

Cromwell's Castle (EH) *Tresco* 17th-century round tower. www.english-heritage.org.uk **6 A2**

Harry's Walls (EH) *St Mary's* Incomplete 16th-century fort. www.english-heritage.org.uk **6 A3**

King Charles's Castle (EH) *Tresco* Castle remains. www.english-heritage.org.uk **6 A2**

Somerset

Daws Castle *Watchet* Site of Saxon refuge. **45 C8**

Farleigh Hungerford Castle (EH) *Farleigh Hungerford* 14th-century castle with chapel. 01225 754026 www.english-heritage.org.uk **57 E8**

Nunney Castle (EH) *Nunney* Small castle built 14th-century with moat. 0870 3331181 www.english-heritage.org.uk **49 B6**

Wiltshire

Ludgershall Castle and Cross (EH) *Ludgershall* Ruins of early 12th-century royal hunting palace with late-medieval cross. www.english-heritage.org.uk **52 A2**

Old Wardour Castle (EH) *Tisbury* 01747 870487 www.english-heritage.org.uk **50 F3**

Houses

Bath & NE Somerset

No 1 Royal Crescent *Bath* First house to be built here. Fine example of Palladian architecture. 01225 428126 www.bath-preservation-trust.org.uk **57 C7**

Bristol

Georgian House *Bristol* Georgian town house built 1790 for wealthy merchant. 0117 9211362 **56 B4**

Red Lodge *Bristol* Last surviving suite of 16th-century rooms in Bristol. Tudor-style garden. 0117 9223588 **56 B4**

Cornwall

Antony (NT) *Torpoint* Early 18th-century house in extensive grounds. 01752 812191 www.nationaltrust.org.uk **10 D4**

Cotehele House (NT) *Saltash* Medieval house. Formal gardens and valley garden. 01579 351346 www.nationaltrust.org.uk **10 D4**

Godolphin House and Garden (NT) *Helston* Tudor house. 01736 763194 www.nationaltrust.org.uk **4 E1**

Lanhydrock (NT) *Bodmin* Fifty rooms open to view. Wooded parkland and garden. 01208 265950 www.nationaltrust.org.uk **8 B4**

Mount Edgcumbe *Torpoint* House and furniture restored. Colourful 18th-century gardens. Landscaped park, woodland and coastal walks. 01752 822236 www.mountedgcumbe.gov.uk **10 D4**

Pencarrow House *Bodmin* Georgian mansion. 01208 841369 www.pencarrow.co.uk **8 B4**

Trerice (NT) *Nr Newquay* Small Elizabethan manor house with gabled facade. Pleasant gardens. 01637 875404 www.nationaltrust.org.uk **7 D7**

Devon

A La Ronde (NT) *Exmouth* c. 1796. 01395 265514 www.nationaltrust.org.uk **22 D2**

Arlington Court (NT) *Barnstaple* Noted for extensive collection of model ships and other works of art. Large collection of horse drawn carriages. Gardens and woods (not NT). 01271 850296 www.nationaltrust.org.uk **43 C7**

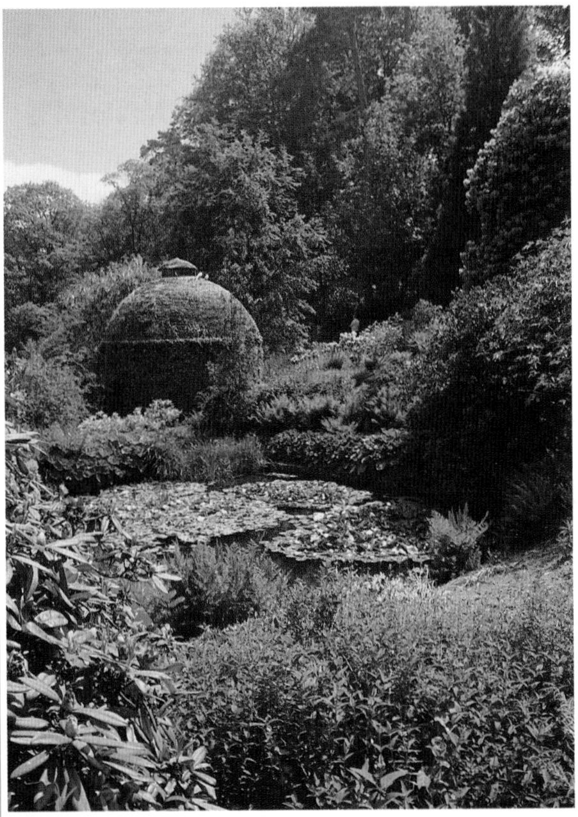

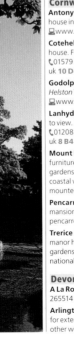

▲ **Cotehele House Gardens, Cornwall**

Bowhill House *Exeter* 15th-century Mansion. **21 B8**

Bradley (NT) *Newton Abbot* Small, 15th-century manor house. Ramparts of Berry Wood earthwork stand in the grounds. 01626 354513 www.nationaltrust.org.uk **15 A5**

Buckland Abbey (NT) *nr Tavistock* Originally Cistercian monastery, then home of Sir Francis Drake. Secret room for children. Exhibitions. Elizabethan garden. 01822 853607 www.nationaltrust.org.uk **19 F6**

Cadhay *Ottery St Mary* Elizabethan manor house. Lovely garden overlooking medieval ponds. 01404 812432 **22 A4**

Chambercombe Manor *Ilfracombe* Late 14th and early 15th century. Herb, rose and water gardens. 01271 862624 www.chambercombemanor.co.uk **42 B5**

Coleton Fishacre (NT) *Kingswear* House reflects Arts and Crafts tradition but has modern interiors. Garden has large collection of plants. 01803 752466 www.nationaltrust.org.uk **15 E5**

Compton Castle (NT) *nr Paignton* Fortified manor house. 01803 875470 www.nationaltrust.org.uk **15 C5**

Endsleigh House and Gardens *Milton Abbot* Retreat built 1811. Ornamental gardens with terraced walks. 01822 870633 www.endsleigh-house.co.uk **19 E5**

Fursdon House *Cadbury* Early manor house with Georgian alterations. Small museum. Terraced garden. 01392 860860 www.fursdon.co.uk **34 F3**

Haldon Belvedere (Lawrence Castle) *Higher Ashton* Built in 1788. 01392 833668 www.haldonbelvedere.com **21 D7**

Killerton (NT) *Exeter* Built in 1778. Collection of costumes. Hillside gardens, extensive lawns. 01392 881345 **21 B8**

Knightshayes Court (NT) *Tiverton* Completed 1874. Small woodland and terraced gardens. 01884 254665 www.nationaltrust.org.uk **34 D4**

Overbecks Museum and Garden (NT) *Salcombe* Edwardian house contains local photographs; inventions by Otto Overbeck. Secret room for children. Beautiful garden. 01548 842893 www.nationaltrust.org.uk **13 E5**

Powderham Castle *Powderham* Medieval castle built c. 1390. Georgian interiors. Gardens. 01626 890243 www.powderham.co.uk **22 D1**

Shute Barton (NT) *Shute* Important surviving non-fortified manor house from Middle Ages. 01297 34692 www.nationaltrust.org.uk **23 A7**

Tiverton Castle *Tiverton* Hexagonal castle built in 1392. Partly destroyed in Civil War. 01884 253200 www.tivertoncastle.com/tours.htm **34 D4**

Ugbrooke House *Chudleigh* House and church built c. 1200. Capability Brown landscaped the park. 01626 852179 www.ugbrooke.co.uk **21 E7**

Watersmeet House (NT) *Lynmouth* Fishing lodge. 01598 753348 www.nationaltrust.org.uk **44 B1**

Dorset

Athelhampton *Puddletown* Medieval house. Walled gardens include famous topiary pyramids. 01305 848363 www.athelhampton.co.uk **26 B1**

Chettle House *Chettle* Baroque Queen Anne house. 01258 830858 **40 D2**

Clouds Hill (NT) *Wareham* T E Lawrence's (Lawrence of Arabia) retreat. 01929 405616 www.nationaltrust.org.uk **26 B3**

Edmondsham House and Garden *Edmondsham* Tudor/Georgian manor house, 2.4 ha (6-acre) garden and 0.8 ha (2-acre) walled garden. 01725 517207 **40 D4**

Hardy's Cottage (NT) *Dorchester* Thomas Hardy born here in 1840. 01305 262366 www.nationaltrust.org.uk **25 B8**

Highcliffe Castle *Highcliffe* Completed 1835, including stonework from Benedictine abbey in Normandy. 01425 278807 www.highcliffecastle.co.uk **28 B4**

Kingston Lacy (NT) *Wimborne Minster* Completed 1665. Houses collection of Old Masters, celebrated 'Spanish Room'. 01202 883402 www.nationaltrust.org.uk **27 A7**

Max Gate (NT) *Dorchester* Designed by poet and novelist Thomas Hardy. Tours by appointment. 01305 262538 www.nationaltrust.org.uk **25 B8**

Sherborne Castle *Sherborne* 16th-century house built for Raleigh. Grounds by Capability Brown. 01935 813182 www.sherbornecastle.com **38 C2**

Wolfeton House *Dorchester* Medieval and Elizabethan house. Cider house. 01305 263500 **25 B8**

Gloucestershire

Buckland Rectory *Buckland* Oldest rectory in England. **76 E4**

Chavenage House *Chavenage Green* Elizabethan house. Medieval barn. 01666 502329 www.chavenage.com **64 C2**

Frampton Court *Frampton on Severn* Georgian stately home, dated 1732, set in beautiful gardens. 01452 740267 www.framptoncourtestate.co.uk **69 F8**

Lodge Park (NT) *Aldsworth* 17th-century grandstand. Recently restored. 01451 844130 www.nationaltrust.org.uk **72 E2**

Newark Park (NT) *Ozleworth* Tudor hunting lodge, converted into house by Wyatt. 01453 842644 www.nationaltrust.org.uk **63 D7**

Owlpen Manor *Uley* Cotswold manor house 15th–18th centuries. Terraced gardens. 01453 860261 www.owlpen.com **63 C7**

Snowshill Manor (NT) *Snowshill* Tudor manor house with early 18th-century facade. Famous for collection of musical instruments, clocks and toys. 01386 852410 www.nationaltrust.org.uk **76 F4**

Stanway House *Stanway* Jacobean manor house in 8 ha (20 acres) of landscaped grounds with 18th-century water garden and an important 14th-century tithe barn. 01386 584469 www.stanwayfountain.co.uk **71 A7**

North Somerset

Clevedon Court (NT) *nr Clevedon* Built c. 1320. One of the few complete houses of this time to have survived. 01275 872257 www.nationaltrust.org.uk **55 B8**

Tyntesfield (NT) *Wraxall* A hidden Gothic revival gem, with virtually intact Victorian decorative scheme, kitchens and family chapel. The grounds are extensive and include parkland, formal gardens and a walled kitchen garden. 01275 461900 www.nationaltrust.org.uk **7 C7**

Plymouth

Saltram (NT) *Plymouth* Former Tudor mansion. Tree and shrub garden. 01752 333500 www.nationaltrust.org.uk **10 E5**

Somerset

Brympton d'Evercy *nr Yeovil* Large mansion with late 17th-century south front and Tudor west front. Extensive formal gardens with vineyard. **37 C9**

Coleridge Cottage (NT) *Nether Stowey* Samuel Taylor Coleridge lived here 1797 to 1800. 01278 732662 www.nationaltrust.org.uk **46 D3**

Combe Sydenham Hall *Taunton* Historic house, appointment only. Parkland open to visitors. 01984 656284 **36 A2**

Dunster Castle (NT) *Dunster* House and medieval ruins framed with sub-tropical plants. 01643 821314 www.nationaltrust.org.uk **45 C6**

Forde Abbey *nr Chard* 12th-century Cistercian monastery converted into residence after Dissolution. Extensive grounds. 01460 220231 www.fordeabbey.co.uk **36 E4**

Gaulden Manor *Tolland* Small manor of great charm. Grounds include herb and bog gardens. 01984 667213 **46 E2**

King John's Hunting Lodge *Axbridge* Early Tudor merchant's house now museum. 01934 732012 **55 F8**

Lytes Cary Manor (NT) *Charlton Mackrell* Manor house and 14th-century chapel. Formal garden. 01458 224471 www.nationaltrust.org.uk **48 F2**

Midelney Manor *Drayton* 16th- to 18th-century manor house. Gardens, walks and heronry. 01458 251229 **37 B6**

Montacute House (NT) *Montacute* Late Elizabethan house. Portraits from National Portrait Gallery. Beautiful gardens. 01935 823289 www.nationaltrust.org.uk **37 C7**

Priest's House (NT) *Muchelney* Late medieval house. Occupied and furnished by tenants. 01458 253771 www.nationaltrust.org.uk **37 B6**

The Bishop's Palace *Wells* 13th-century moated palace. State rooms and gallery. Relaxing gardens surrounding the springs that gave the town its name. 01749 678691 www.bishopspalacewells.co.uk **48 B2**

Treasurer's House (NT) *Martock* Small house dating from 13th and 14th centuries. 01935 825801 www.nationaltrust.org.uk **37 C7**

South Gloucestershire

Dyrham Park (NT) *Dyrham* Built 1692–1702. Collection of Delft, paintings by Dutch masters. Formal garden, two lakes. Deer park has been here since Saxon times. 0117 937 2501 www.nationaltrust.org.uk **57 A6**

Horton Court (NT) *Nr Chipping Sodbury* 01179 372501 www.nationaltrust.org.uk **63 F6**

Swindon

Lydiard House *Swindon* Fine Georgian house in 107.6 ha (266 acres) of parkland. 01793 770401 www.swindon.gov.uk **65 E8**

Torbay

Kirkham House (EH) *Paignton* 14th-century stone house with modern furniture, pottery and fabrics. education officer: 0117 9750700 www.english-heritage.org.uk **15 C5**

Wiltshire

Avebury Manor and Garden (NT) *Avebury* Present buildings date from 16th century. Timed guided tours of house. Topiary and flower gardens. 01672 539250 www.nationaltrust.org.uk **59 C7**

Bowood House *Calne* 18th-century house designed by Adam. One of Capability Brown's most beautiful parks. Adventure playground. 01249 812102 www.bowood-house.co.uk **58 B5**

Corsham Court *Corsham* Elizabethan and Georgian house. Park and garden by Capability Brown. 01249 701610 www.corsham-court.co.uk **58 B2**

Great Chalfield Manor (NT) *Bradford on Avon* Restored 1480 moated manor house. 01225 782239 www.nationaltrust.org.uk **57 D8**

Heale House *Middle Woodford* 01722 782504 **51 D7**

Lacock Abbey (NT) *Lacock* Originally an abbey, converted into house 1540. 01249 730227 www.nationaltrust.org.uk **58 C3**

Little Clarendon (NT) *Dinton* Tudor house, altered in the 17th century, with 20th-century Catholic chapel. 01985 843600 www.nationaltrust.org.uk **50 E5**

Longleat House *Warminster* Early Renaissance house. Extensive landscaped park. See 'Outdoors: Animal attractions'. 01985 844400 www.longleat.co.uk **50 C2**

Mompesson House (NT) *Salisbury* Turnbull collection of English 18th-century drinking glasses. Walled garden. 01722 335659 www.nationaltrust.org.uk **51 E8**

Philipps House and Dinton Park (NT) *Dinton* Neo-Grecian house completed in 1820. Landscaped park . 01985 843600 www.nationaltrust.org.uk **50 E5**

Sheldon Manor *nr Chippenham* Manor house. 15th-century detached chapel. Terraced gardens. 01249 653120 www.sheldonmanor.co.uk **58 B3**

Stourhead (NT) *nr Warminster* Wilts Built in 1722 and later enlarged. Grounds are famous example of early 18th-century landscape movement. 01747 841152 www.nationaltrust.org.uk **50 C2**

Westwood Manor (NT) *Bradford on* *Avon* 15th-century manor house. 01225 863374 www.nationaltrust.org.uk **57 D8**

Wilton House *Wilton* Acres of fine lawns. 01722 746720 www.wiltonhouse.co.uk **51 E6**

Ancient monuments

Bath & NE Somerset

Stanton Drew Circles and Cave (EH) *Stanton Drew* Three stone circles, two avenues and a burial chamber. One of finest Neolithic sites in the country. www.english-heritage.org.uk **56 D3**

Stoney Littleton Long Barrow (EH) *Wellow* Neolithic burial mound. **57 E6**

Bristol

Kings Weston Roman Villa *Lawrence Weston* Possibly 3rd century AD. Bath suite, living quarters, mosaic floors, court and east wing. 0117 9223571 www.english-heritage.org.uk **56 A2**

Cornwall

Ballowall Barrow (EH) *St Just* Unusual Bronze Age chambered tomb www.english-heritage.org.uk **2 D3**

Carn Brea *Redruth* Remains of Neolithic hillfort. **4 B2**

Carn Euny Ancient Village (EH) *Sancreed* Iron Age settlement, with foundations of huts and underground passage. www.english-heritage.org.uk **2 E4**

Castle An Dinas *St Columb* Iron Age Celtic hillfort, 300–200 BC. **8 C1**

Chysauster Ancient Village (EH) *Penzance* Site of Iron Age village dating from about 1 BC to the 3rd century AD. 07831 757934 www.english-heritage.org.uk **3 D5**

Halliggye Fogou *Garras* One of several underground tunnels, linked to Iron Age villages, unique to Cornwall. **4 F2**

King Doniert's Stone (EH) *St Cleer* Two decorated pieces of 9th-century cross believed to commemorate King of Cornwall, who drowned c. 875. www.english-heritage.org.uk **9 B7**

Lanyon Quoit *Penzance* Fine cromlech consisting of capstone supported on three granite slabs. c. 1500 BC. **3 D5**

Men-An-Tol *Penzance* Holed Stone. **3 D5**

Merry Maidens *Lamorna* Circle of 19 standing stones. www.english-heritage.org.uk **2 F4**

St Breock Downs Monolith (EH) *nr Wadebridge* Prehistoric standing stone. www.english-heritage.org.uk **8 A2**

Stripple Stones *Nr Bodmin* Stone circle. **8 B4**

The Hurlers Stone Circles (EH) *Minions* Three Bronze Age stone circles in a line, some of best ceremonial standing stones in South West. www.english-heritage.org.uk **9 A8**

Tregiffian Burial Chamber (EH) *St Buryan* Neolithic or early Bronze Age chambered tomb www.english-heritage.org.uk **2 E4**

Trencrom Hill *Penzance* 2nd-century BC rampart. Hut circles and well. **3 D5**

Trethevy Quoit (EH) *St Cleer* Cromlech or prehistoric burial place. www.english-heritage.org.uk **9 B7**

Zennor Cromlech *nr Zennor* Quoit, one of largest capstones in England **2 C5**

Devon

Blackbury Camp (EH) *Southleigh* Iron Age hillfort. www.english-heritage.org.uk **23 B6**

Hound Tor (EH) *Manaton* Remains of medieval village, first occupied in Bronze Age. www.english-heritage.org.uk **20 D5**

Merrivale Prehistoric Settlement (EH) *Dartmoor* Two rows of standing stones, remains of early Bronze Age village. www.english-heritage.org.uk **19 E7**

Upper Plym Valley *Nr Yelverton* Scores of prehistoric and medieval sites covering 15.5 sq km (6 sq miles). **11 B6**

Dorset

Badbury Rings *nr Shapwick* Iron Age hillfort with evidence of Bronze Age settlement. **40 F2**

Jordan Hill Roman Temple (EH) *Preston* Foundations of Romano-Celtic temple. www.english-heritage.org.uk **25 D9**

Kingston Russell Stone Circle (EH) *Abbotsbury* Bronze Age stone circle of 18 stones. www.english-heritage.org.uk **25 C6**

Knowlton Church and Earthworks (EH) *Cranborne* Ruins of Norman church in middle of Neolithic earthworks. www.english-heritage.org.uk **40 D3**

Lambert's Castle *Lyme Regis* Iron Age hillfort. **24 B1**

Maiden Castle (EH) *nr Dorchester* Largest Iron Age hillfort in Europe. www.english-heritage.org.uk **25 C8**

Maumbury Rings *Dorchester* Originally a sacred circle of the Stone Age, the Romans later turned Rings into 'Coliseum'. **25 C8**

Poundbury Hillfort *Dorchester* Ancient entrenchment. **25 B8**

Rawlsbury Camp *Milton Abbas* Iron Age hillfort **39 F6**

The Dorset Cursus *Pentridge* Two parallel banks stretching for 6 miles. Both banks flanked with barrows. **40 C3**

The Nine Stones (EH) *Winterbourne Abbas* Remains of nine standing stones constructed about 4000 years ago. www.english-heritage.org.uk **25 B7**

White Sheet Hill *Nr Shaftesbury* Neolithic long barrow and Bronze Age barrows. Remains of Neolithic Causeway camp and Iron Age hillfort. **40 B1**

Winterbourne Poor Lot Barrows (EH) *Winterbourne Abbas,* Part of 4000-year-old Bronze Age cemetery. www.english-heritage.org.uk **25 B6**

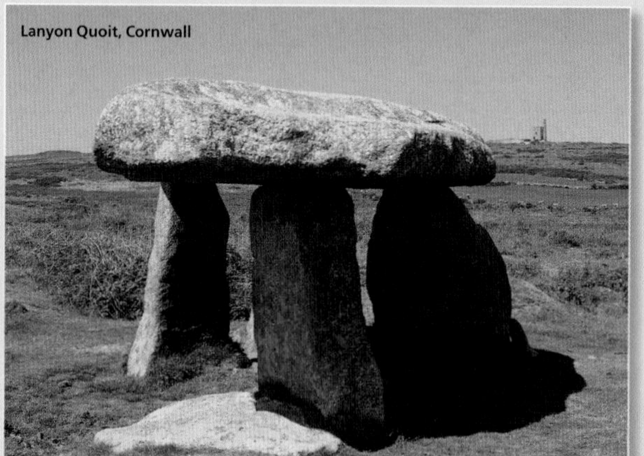
Lanyon Quoit, Cornwall

Gloucestershire

Belas Knap (EH) *nr Winchcombe* Good example of Neolithic long barrow. www.english-heritage.org.uk **71 B6**

Chedworth Roman Villa (NT) *Yanworth* One of largest Romano-British villas in country. Walls plus mosaics, bathhouses, hypocausts, water-shrine and latrine. Small museum. 01242 890256 www.english-heritage.org.uk **71 E7**

Great Witcombe Roman Villa (EH) *Great Witcombe* Built around courtyard, luxurious bath-house. 01179 750700 www.english-heritage.org.uk **70 E4**

Notgrove Long Barrow (EH) *Notgrove* A Neolithic burial mound. www.english-heritage.org.uk **71 C7**

Nympsfield Long Barrow (EH) *Nympsfield* Neolithic long barrow. www.english-heritage.org.uk **63 B8**

Uley Long Barrow (Hetty Pegler's Tump) (EH) *Uley* c. 3000 BC, Neolithic chambered burial mound www.english-heritage.org.uk **63 C7**

Scilly Isles

Bant's Carn (EH) *St Mary's* Bronze Age burial mound and Roman village. www.english-heritage.org.uk **6 A3**

Garrison Walls (EH) *St Mary's* Ramparts of walls and earthworks. www.english-heritage.org.uk **6 A3**

Innisidgen Lower and Upper Burial Chambers (EH) *St Mary's* Two Bronze Age cairns. www.english-heritage.org.uk **6 A3**

Porth Hellick Down Burial Chamber (EH) *St Mary's* Bronze Age. www.english-heritage.org.uk **6 A3**

Somerset

Cadbury Castle *South Cadbury* Iron Age hillfort (reputedly 'Camelot'). Impression of a great fortress lingers. **38 A2**

Swindon

Barbury Castle *Wroughton* Iron Age hillfort. **59 A8**

Wiltshire

Adam's Grave *Alton Barnes* Chambered long barrow. **59 D7**

Avebury Stone Circle (NT) *Avebury* Constructed 4000 years ago, originally using over 180 stones. See also West Kennet Avenue. 01672 539250 www.nationaltrust.org.uk **59 C7**

Bratton Camp and Westbury White Horse (EH) *Bratton* Large Iron Age hillfort. **50 A3**

Cley Hill *Warminster* Iron Age hillfort c. 300 BC. Single banked hill with two Bronze Age round barrows. **50 C1**

Devil's *Den Fyfield* Chambered long barrow c. 4000 BC. **59 C7**

Ethandun Memorial *At Bratton Camp, Westbury,* Sarson stone commemorating 9th-century battle. **50 A2**

Everleigh Barrows *Everleigh* 2000 BC two bell barrows, two bowl barrows and a disc barrow **59 E8**

Fyfield and Overton Downs *Fyfield* Prehistoric landscape comprising an extensive field system of banks. **59 C7**

Giant's Grave *nr Pewsey* Unchambered long barrow c. 4000 BC **59 E8**

Gopher Wood *Huish* Small Bronze Age cemetery comprising of seven bowl barrows and a disc barrow. **59 D7**

Hatfield Earthworks (EH) *Marden* Part of a Neolithic enclosure complex. www.english-heritage.org.uk **59 E6**

Knap Hill *Alton Barnes* Neolithic causewayed enclosure. **59 D7**

Marden Henge *Marden* One of largest Neolithic henge monuments in Britain. **59 E6**

Martinsell Hill *Pewsey* Iron Age hillfort enclosing 13 ha (32 acres). **59 D8**

Ogbourne Round Barrow *Ogbourne St Andrew* A round barrow in Saxon churchyard. **59 B8**

Old Sarum (EH) *Salisbury* Great earthwork with huge banks and ditch built c. 500 BC. 01722 335398 www.english-heritage.org.uk **51 E7**

Oldbury Castle *Cherhill* Iron Age hillfort **59 B5**

Oliver's Castle *Bromham* Iron Age hillfort with single bank and ditch. **58 C4**

Overton Hill *West Kennett* Bronze Age burial mounds. **59 C7**

Rybury Camp *All Cannings* Causewayed Iron Age enclosure. **59 D6**

Silbury Hill (EH) *Avebury* Largest man-made mound in ancient Europe. www.english-heritage.org.uk **59 C7**

Stonehenge (EH) *nr Amesbury* Great ancient stone circle of Stonehenge stands at centre of extensive prehistoric landscape filled with remains of ceremonial and domestic structures and round barrows. 01980 624715 www.english-heritage.org.uk **51 C7**

The Sanctuary (EH) *West Kennett* Possibly 5000 years old. Consists of two concentric circles of stones and six timber uprights indicated by concrete posts. www.english-heritage.org.uk **59 C7**

West Kennett Avenue (EH) *Avebury* Avenue of standing stones which originally ran from Avebury Stone Circle to The Sanctuary, late Neolithic. www.english-heritage.org.uk **59 C7**

West Kennett Long Barrow (EH) *West Kennett* Neolithic chambered tomb. www.english-heritage.org.uk **59 C7**

Windmill Hill (EH) *Avebury* Neolithic remains of three concentric rings of ditches. **59 B6**

Woodhenge (EH) *Durrington* Neolithic ceremonial monument 2300 BC. Entrance and long axis of the oval rings points to rising sun on Midsummer Day. www.english-heritage.org.uk **51 C7**

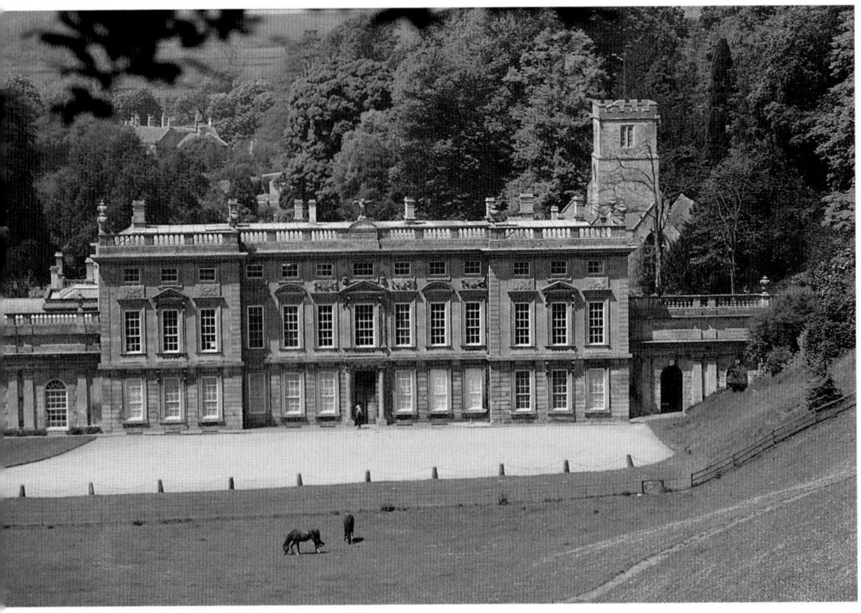

▲ **Dyrham Park, South Gloucestershire**

)ther historic buildings

ath & NE Somerset

ath Assembly Rooms (NT) *Bath* Designed
/ John Wood the Younger in 1769. ☎01225
77789 www.nationaltrust.org.uk **57 C7**

eckford's Tower *Bath* Built 1827, now a
useum. Spiral staircase and panoramic view
01225 422212 www.bath-preservation-
ust.org.uk **57 C7**

uildhall *Bath* 18th century. ☎01225
77724 **57 C7**

oman Baths and Pump Room *Bath* Baths
e fed by the only hot springs in Britain. The
ump Room is 18th-century. ☎01225 477785
www.romanbaths.co.uk **57 C7**

ristol

aise Hamlet (NT) *Henbury* Picturesque
ottages. ☎01225 833977 www.
ationaltrust.org.uk **56 A3**

lifton Observatory *Clifton* Former snuff
ill now with camera obscura. ☎0117
241379 **56 B3**

Vestbury College Gatehouse (NT)
Vestbury on Trym 15th-century gatehouse.
01225 833977 www.nationaltrust.org.
k **56 A3**

ornwall

bbot's Fish House *Meare* 14th-century
one building originally used to preserve and
ore fish for Glastonbury Abbey **47 C9**

upath Holy Well (EH) *Callington* c. 1500
nd almost complete. www.english-
eritage.org.uk **10 B3**

intagel Old Post Office (NT) *Tintagel*
4th-century stone house with thick slate
oof. ☎01840 770024 www.nationaltrust.
rg.uk **17 C6**

Vesley's Cottage *Trewint* 18th-century
ottage. Wesley stayed and preached here.
01566 86158 www.wesleycottage.
konline.co.uk **10 C1**

evon

ayard's Cove Fort (EH) *Dartmouth* A small
rtillery fort built c. 1534. www.english-
eritage.org.uk **15 E5**

**ranscombe Old Bakery, Manor Mill
nd Forge (NT)** *Seaton* ☎01392 881691
www.english-heritage.org.uk **10 E2**

ustoms House *Exeter* Oldest (1680–81)
urviving substantial brick building in Exeter.
01392 265700 **21 B8**

xeter Guildhall *Exeter* 16th-century oak
oof. ☎01392 665500 www.exeter.gov.
k **21 B8**

reenway (NT) *Galmpton* Estate on banks
f River Dart. ☎01803 842382 www.
ationaltrust.org.uk **12 D4**

oughwood Meeting House (NT)
alwood c. 1653. ☎01392 881691
www.english-heritage.org.uk **36 F2**

Aarker's Cottage (NT) *Broadclyst*
Aedieval cob house. ☎01392 461546
www.nationaltrust.org.uk **22 A1**

otnes Guildhall *Totnes* Part of Benedictine
riory. ☎01803 862147 **14 C4**

Plymouth

rysten House *Plymouth* 15th-century
riest's house. ☎01752 661414 **10 E5**

Royal Citadel (EH) *Plymouth* 17th-century fortress. Guided tours only. Open in summer. ☎01752 775841 www.english-heritage.org.uk **10 E5**

Dorset

Nothe Fort *Weymouth* Restored Victorian fort with ramparts and gun decks. ☎01305 766626 www.fortressweymouth.co.uk **25 E8**

Gloucestershire

Ashleworth Tithe Barn (NT) *Ashleworth* Stone-tiled 15th-century tithe barn. ☎01985 843600 www.nationaltrust.org.uk **70 B2**

Chipping Campden Market Hall *Chipping Campden* Built 1627. **77 E6**

Little Fleece Bookshop (NT) *Painswick* 17th-century building, restored in Arts & Crafts style in 1935. Now a bookshop. ☎01452 812103 www.english-heritage.org.uk **70 F3**

Pittville Pump Room *Cheltenham* Built between 1825 and 1830. Spa waters still available. ☎01242 523852 **71 C5**

Woolstaplers Hall *Chipping Campden* Built 1340. Now a museum. **77 E6**

Somerset

Gallox Bridge (EH) *Dunster* Stone packhorse bridge. www.english-heritage.org.uk **45 C6**

Glastonbury Tribunal (EH) *Glastonbury* Well-preserved medieval town house. ☎01458 832954 www.english-heritage.org.uk **48 D2**

Treasurer's House (NT) *Martock* c. 13th century. ☎01935 825801 www.nationaltrust.org.uk **37 C7**

Yarn Market (EH) *Dunster* 17th-century octagonal market hall. www.english-heritage.org.uk **45 C6**

Wiltshire

Barton Tithe Barn (EH) *Bradford on Avon* Medieval stone-built barn. www.english-heritage.org.uk **57 D8**

The North Canonry *Salisbury* Largest Tudor domestic building in city. ☎01722 555121 www.salisburycathedral.org.uk **51 E8**

Religious buildings

Bath & NE Somerset

Bath Abbey *Abbey Churchyard* Site dates back to 7th century. Gothic church built in 1499. After the Dissolution, the church remained incomplete until 1864. Mostly a Victorian replica interior of a Tudor design with an 1860s fan vault. Bath Abbey Heritage Vaults contain finds relating to Christianity on the site, as well as items related to the building. ☎01225 422462 bathabbey.org **57 D7**

Bournemouth

St Peter *Hinton Road and Parsonage Road* c. 1854. Tall stone tower, south aisle from earlier building. Richly restored Gothic Revival chancel and south transept. Grave of Mary Shelley. **28 B1**

St Stephen *St Stephens Road* Founded 1880. High bell-tower. Serene interior, organ loft above a vaulted chapel. Restored altar triptych. **28 B1**

Bristol

Bristol Cathedral *Deanery Road, College Green* Unique among the English cathedrals as a 'Hall church' with aisles the same height as the nave. Norman Chapter House, early English Lady Chapel. ☎0117 9264879 bristol-cathedral.co.uk **56 B3**

Lord Mayor's Chapel St Mark's *College Green* Founded c. 1230 as hospital chapel; 16th-century roof; some rebuilding; European medieval glass. ☎0117 9294350 **56 B3**

St John's on the Wall *Broad Street* Gothic church standing above gateway of old city wall. **56 B3**

St Mary Redcliffe *Redcliffe Way* 12th- to 15th-century vaulted Gothic building with twin porches; Victorian stained glass and some medieval fragments. ☎0117 9537260 **56 B3**

Temple Church *Church Street, Temple Way* Walls and tower of 15th-century church bombed in World War II. Stands on site of 12th-century church. **56 B3**

The New Room *Horsefair* Erected in 1739 as discussion room for elders of Methodism. Simple Georgian interior. Museum of Methodism. ☎0117 9264740 **56 B3**

Cornwall

Holy Trinity *St Austell* Fine Gothic tower with carved statues; Norman font. **8 E3**

Quaker Meeting House *Come-to-Good* Early 18th-century thatched chapel. Bare interior and pine furnishings. **4 B4**

St Anthony *St Anthony-in-Roseland* Victorian restoration of a 12th-century monastic church; situated by the sea. **5 D5**

St Breaca *Breage* 15th-century Cornish granite church with 15th-century mural of St Christopher and Christ. ☎01326 573 449 **3 E8**

St Buriana *St Buryan* Tall granite tower and original painted rood screen. **2 E4**

St Endelienta *St Endellion* Carved Catacleuse Gothic altar. **16 E4**

St Enodoc *St Enodoc* 13th-century church in the middle of golf course. Home and resting place of poet John Betjeman. ☎01208 802398 **16 E3**

St Germanus *St Germans* Cornwall's cathedral until c. 1409. Original church was seat of Saxon bishops, rebuilt as Norman outpost. stgermansparishes.com **10 D3**

St Ia *St Ives* Early 15th-century granite church; medieval choir stalls portray local scenes; local artist Barbara Hepworth's Madonna and Child. **3 B6**

St James *Kilkhampton* Norman south doorway and carved bench-ends. ☎01288 321314 **31 D5**

St John the Baptist *Morwenstow* Church of eccentric poet Robert Hawker. Norman and early gothic with Tudor pews. ☎01288 321314 **30 C4**

St Just in Roseland *St Just in Roseland* Gothic church situated in sub-tropical garden on Fal estuary; palm trees, cedars. stjustin-roseland.org.uk **5 C5**

St Maddern *Madron* 'Mother church of Penzance'. Contains banner made to mourn Nelson's death at Battle of Trafalgar. **2 D5**

St Mary Magdalene *Launceston* Early 16th century. Carved granite facades, 20th-century woodwork. **18 D3**

St Materiana *Church Hill, Tintagel* Well-preserved Norman church on clifftop. Copy of National Gallery's Perugino altarpiece in Blessed Sacrament Chapel. ☎01840 770315 **17 C6**

St Mellanus *Mullion* North door from 11th century, south door has dog flap for shepherd's dogs. Arts and Crafts screen. ☎01326 240325 **5 G1**

St Mylor *Mylor Churchtown* Norman details, tallest Celtic cross in Cornwall. ☎01326 374408 **4 C4**

St Neot *St Neot* Medieval windows depict lives of the saints. Panels depict medieval ship design. **9 B6**

St Nonna *Altarnun* 15th-century with tall west tower. Norman font with carvings of monsters; 16th-century benches. **18 D1**

St Petroc *Bodmin* Largest medieval church in Cornwall. Bodmin stone. Contains unique accounts listing contributors to building and St Petroc's casket (c. 1170). ☎01392 889770 st-petroc-bodmin.co.uk **8 B4**

St Probus *Probus* Cornwall's tallest tower. ☎01726 882746 **7 F8**

St Protus and St Hyacinth *Blisland* Partly Norman, with 15th-century tower, porch, aisles and transepts. blisland.com **8 A4**

St Swithun *Launcells* 15th-century woodwork and tiles, Norman font and Gothic pulpit. Bench-ends depict Bible stories. **30 E4**

St Winwaloe *Gunwalloe* 15th-century 'Church of the Storms', built half on sea, half on land. Damaged by storm. **3 F9**

Truro Cathedral *St Mary's Street, Truro* A fairly modern cathedral consecrated in 1887. Cruciform building completed 1910 to the design of J.L. Pearson RA in Early English style with strong French influence. Largely on site of 16th-century parish church, south aisle incorporated into new building as additional choir aisle. Three powerful towers. The central tower rises to 76 m (250 ft) and is a Cornish memorial to Queen Victoria. ☎01872 276782 trurocathedral.org.uk **4 B4**

Devon

Buckfast Abbey *Buckfastleigh* Built on site from the original plan of a Cistercian monastry in first half of 20th century. Remains an active monastery but welcomes visitors. buckfast.org.uk **14 B2**

Exeter Cathedral *Cathedral Yard and Cathedral Close* Built in Decorated style with three-storeyed west front and two great Norman transeptal towers. Famous for great west window with 14th-century tracery. Present building evolved from Norman building in middle of 13th century and displays much of the best in Gothic architecture. The North Tower contains an ancient astronomical clock and Peter, one of the largest bells in England. The fine West Front contains many niches filled with statues. Library contains a Exeter's copy of the Domesday Survey and other ancient documents. ☎01392 285983 exeter-cathedral.org.uk **21 B8**

Holy Cross *Crediton* Founded 12th century, mainly 15th century. Contains 20th-century works of art. Carved sedilia. ☎01363 773226 creditonparishchurh.org.uk **34 F1**

Ottery St Mary *Ottery St Mary* Copied from Exeter Cathedral by Bishop Grandisson from 1338–42. Painted roof, fan vaulted aisle. Much original woodwork. Medieval weather vane. otterystmary.org.uk **22 A4**

St Andrew *Bere Ferrers* Slate tombs and granite interior. 14th-century stained glass features in east window. Ferrers monuments. **10 C5**

St Andrew *Cullompton* 15th century. Highly decorated tower with pinnacles and gargoyles. Richly carved, panelled ceiling. Complete colourful screen. ☎01884 33249 **35 E5**

St John the Baptist *Ashton, Nr Chudleigh* 15th-century church in peaceful setting. Richly decorated north aisle chapel. South door scarred with bullet holes from Civil War. **21 E7**

St Mary *Molland* Georgian furnishings, medieval statues. **44 F3**

St Nectan *Hartland* Site of Saxon abbey founded 1050. Second tallest tower in Devon, used to attract mariners at sea. **31 B5**

St Peter *Tawstock* 14th-century church with wooden gallery from local Tawstock Court. Collection of Bourchier and Wrey monuments. **43 F5**

St Saviour *Dartmouth* Nautical town church, medieval door and carved stone pulpit. gallery of 1633 with arms of merchant families. **15 E5**

Dorset

Abbey of St Mary *Sherborne* Cathedral until 1075. 11th-century doorway at west end and four pillars survive from last Saxon church on site. South porch, crossing arch and parts of north and south transepts survive from Norman church. Remainder is 15th century. Fan vaults cover virtually whole interior. ☎01935 812452 sherborneabbey.com **38 C2**

▼ **Exeter Cathedral**

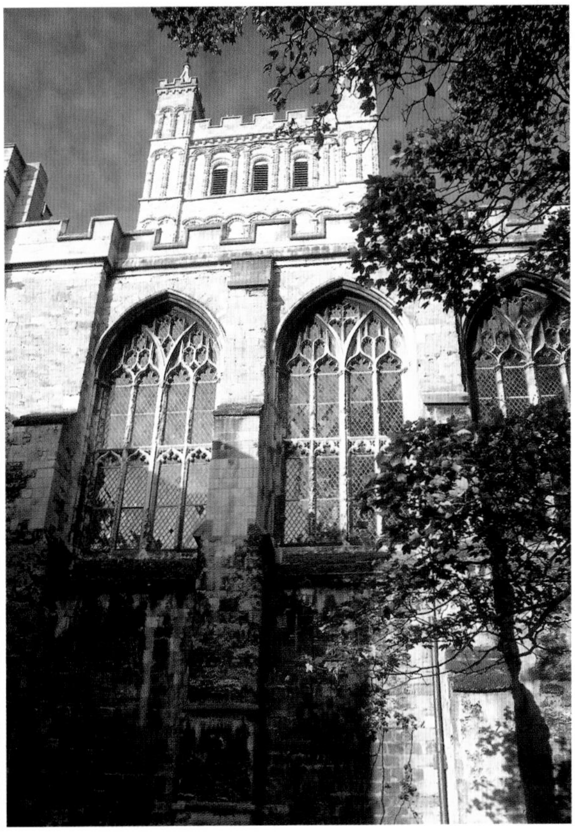

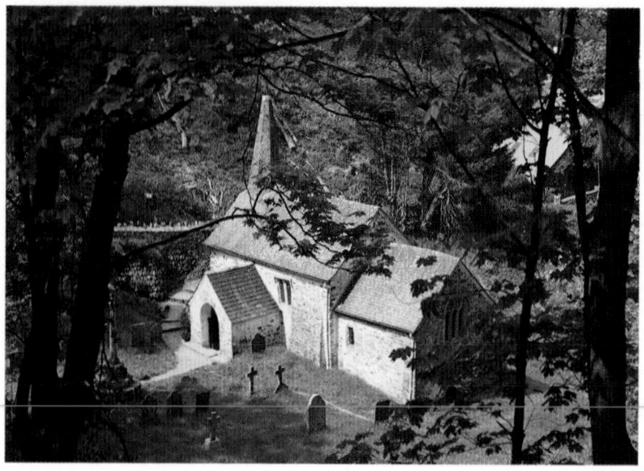

▲ **Culbone church, Somerset**

Abbotsbury Abbey Buildings (EH) *Abbotsbury* Remains of cloister building of Benedictine abbey, founded c. 1044. **25 C6**

Cerne Abbey *Cerne Abbas* Cerne Abbey, founded 987, consists of gatehouse, 987 onwards, Abbey House, the hospice or guesthouse, c. 1450, and the abbot's porch, c. 1509. 01300 341284 **38 F3**

Christchurch Priory *Christchurch* Late 15th-century tower. North porch (1300) is largest in country; monument to Shelley. Norman nave and transepts. Decorated stone reredos representing Tree of Jesse. 01202 488645 christchurchpriory.org **28 B3**

Milton Abbey *Milton Abbas* 14th-century fragment of much bigger intended building. Decorated Gothic windows. Rich altar screen of 1492. **39 F6**

St Candida (St Wite) and Holy Cross *Whitchurch Cannonicorum* Only parish church in England to retain relics and shrine of its saint. Norman font. 01297 489223 **24 A2**

St Cuthburga *Wimborne Minster* Early 16th-century Flemish glass in east window. One Norman, one Gothic tower. Norman font on Purbeck marble shafts. Early 14th-century astronomical clock. **27 A7**

St Peter and St Paul *Blandford Forum* Rebuilt 1733–9. Palladian church with square tower. Pulpit from destroyed Wren church St Antholin in London. **39 E7**

Gloucestershire

Abbey of St Mary *Tewkesbury* Biggest Norman tower in Europe. Decorated chapels at east end contrast with Norman work. Carved roof bosses portray life of Christ. Brasses, monuments and 14th-century windows of the choir commemorate Lords of Tewkesbury. Vestry door covered with metal taken from armour of knights killed at Battle of Tewkesbury. 01684 850959 tewkesburyabbey.org.uk **70 A3**

All Saints *Newland* Known as 'the Cathedral of the Forest'. Sandstone church with decorated spire. 01594 810036 **68 F5**

Gloucester Cathedral *Westgate Street, College Street* Romanesque building of 11th and 12th centuries with later 15th-century exterior. Beautiful Norman building with Perpendicular work on the exterior. Noted for fine 68.5 m (225 ft) high central tower and huge 14th-century east window. Tomb of Edward II with fine canopy and figure. Choir stalls with fine misericords. Lady Chapel with rare Norman lead font. Interesting roof bosses, including several Green Men. 14th–15th-century cloisters with some medieval glass. 01452 508210 gloucestercathedral.org.uk **70 D2**

Holy Innocents *Highnam* Founded 1849 Wall paintings cover the interior; iron screen and carved stone reredos. 01452 525567 **70 C1**

Odda's Chapel (EH) *Deerhurst* Rare Anglo-Saxon chapel attached to half-timbered farmhouse 0117 9750700 **70 B3**

St James *Chipping Campden* Reputedly houses Britain's only complete set of medieval altar hangings. **77 E6**

St John *Elkstone* Norman church. West tower built c. 1370; gargoyles. Fine woodwork. Priest's dovecote. 01242 870232 **71 E5**

St John the Baptist *Cirencester* Largest and most complex south porch in Britain. Coats of arms of patrons. Garstang chapel surrounded by 15th-century screen. Second chapel with stone screen and timber roof. Anne Boleyn cup on display. **65 B5**

St Lawrence *Lechlade-on-Thames* 1470 church built on earlier foundations. Additions in 16th century. Carvings and depictions of domestic and religious life. **66 C1**

St Mary *Berkeley* Sandstone church. Early Gothic west front. Berkeley memorials. East window memorial to Edward Jenner. **63 C5**

St Mary *Deerhurst* Former Anglo-Saxon monastery. Restored interior with much Saxon work still evident and in good condition. Wall of tower has 8th-century relief of Madonna and Child. 01452 780880 **70 B3**

St Mary *Fairford* Late 15th-century church. England's only complete set of medieval narrative windows. 01285 712611 **65 B8**

St Mary's (EH) *Kempley Norman church.* 12th to 14th-century frescoes. Roof timbers are oldest in England, c. 1120-50. 0117 9750700 **69 B7**

St Michael *Bishops Cleeve* Norman church, Jacobean musician's gallery. **71 B5**

St Peter and St Paul *Northleach* 15th-century wool church with brasses of local wool merchants. Decorated two-storey porch. 01451 860293 **71 E8**

Plymouth

Plymouth Cathedral *Cecil Street and Wyndham Street* Roman Catholic cathedral built mid-19th century in Early English style plymouthcathedral.co.uk **10 E5**

Poole

St Osmund *Poole* Built 1904–1927. Frankish turrets, Lombard arcading, Saxon patterning, Art Nouveau terracotta arch. Arts and Crafts grille. **27 B7**

Somerset

All Saints *Farley* Rare countryside example of 17th-century brick church. Built by one of Wren's master masons. **52 F1**

All Saints *Martock* 16th-century carved wooden 'quilted' ceiling. martockonline.co.uk **37 C7**

All Saints *Selworthy* Limewashed church on hilltop, rebuilt early 16th century. White and blue ceiling. **45 B5**

Cleeve Abbey (EH) *Washford* Rare 13th-century monastic site retaining a complete set of cloister buildings, including the refectory with its magnificent timber roof. 01984 640377 **45 C7**

Glastonbury Abbey *Glastonbury* Story of abbey is mix of fact and legend, some come for ancient Christian links, others to visit legendary burial site of King Arthur. Little remains of monastic buildings. 01458 832267 glastonburyabbey.com **48 D2**

Muchelney Abbey (EH) *Muchelney* Abbot's house is all that remains of former Benedictine monastery. Dating mainly from early 16th century, contains carved woodwork, fragments of wall paintings and stonework excavated from the ruined abbey. 01458 250664 **37 B6**

Oare Church/St Mary's *Oare* Oare Church was the scene of Lorna Doone's wedding in the novel by R D Blackmore. Georgian box pews, pulpit and reading desk. 12th-century font, 15th-century chancel and nave. **44 B3**

St Andrew *Mells* Rebuilt 15th century. Highly decorated church porch. **49 B6**

St Andrew *Stogursey* Norman priory church built c. 1100 and seized by Henry V 1414. Rare Somerset spire. 01278 732884 **46 C4**

St Bartholomew *Crewkerne* Rebuilt at turn of 16th century. Window tracery among most complicated in England. 01460 271188 stbartholomew-crewkerne.org **37 E6**

St Beuno *Culbone nr Porlock Weir* Allegedly the smallest church in England. Walls 12th-century or earlier. 01598 741270 **44 B4**

St Cuthbert *St Cuthbert Street, Wells* Largest parish church in Somerset. Carved 17th-century pulpit. Ornate roof with angels, heralds, rosettes and shields. 01749 673136 stcuthbertwells.co.uk **48 B2**

St George *Dunster* 12th-century priory church, enlarged in the 13th and 15th centuries. Longest screen in England. 01643 821439 **45 C6**

St John *Axbridge* Gothic building with 17th-century fittings. Blue and white nave ceiling. 01934 732824 stjohnthebaptist.axbridge.org.uk **55 F8**

St Mary *Croscombe* Tower with rare Somerset spire. Jacobean woodwork. Two-storey medieval treasury. 01749 890423 **48 C3**

St Mary *Ilminster* Contains 17th-century tombs of founders of Wadham College, Oxford. Memorial brasses. **36 C5**

St Mary *Isle Abbotts* Ham stone and blue lias tower with 10 original statues. Norman font and original furnishings. **36 B5**

St Mary *Stogumber* Chancel decorated in style of William Morris. **46 D1**

St Mary *Westonzoyland* Good tie-beam roof decorated with rosettes and crowned with quatrefoils. **47 D7**

St Mary Magdalene *Hammet Street, Taunton* Tower has sculptures and is highest in Somerset. Oak roof and angels. 01823 272441 stmarymagdalene.org.uk **36 A2**

St Michael *Brent Knoll* Norman with perpendicular additions. Satirical benchends ridiculing church authorities. 17th-century memorial to John Somerset. **47 A6**

St Peter and St Paul *Shepton Mallet* Nave retains original Saxon walls. 14th-century tower. Panelled wagon roof. **48 C4**

Stoke sub Hamdon Priory (NT) *Stoke Sub Hamdon* Complex of buildings including dovecote. **37 C7**

▼ **Gloucester Cathedral**

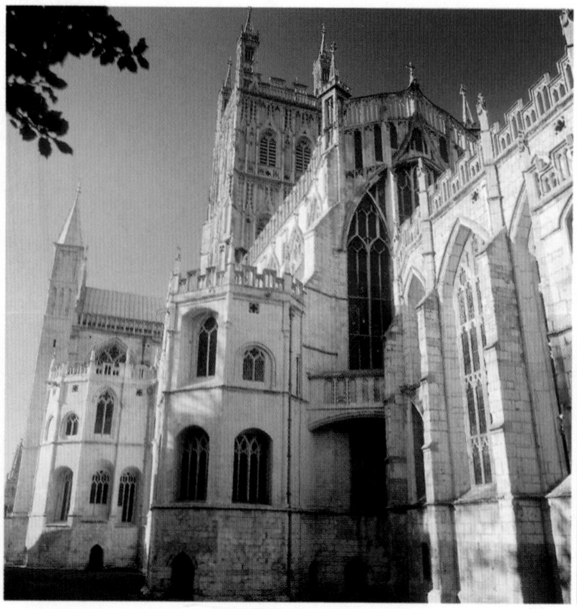

Wells Cathedral *Cathedral Green* Dates from late 12th to early 14th centuries and is renowned for majestic early English west front and great central tower. Noted features of the interior include massive but graceful scissor arches; capitals carved with moral tales, animals and people; 14th-century stained glass of the Lady Chapel; early clock with moving figures; choir stalls with misericords; and deep worn steps to the Chapter House with a spectacular fan-faulted roof. Also Bishops Palace and Vicars Close. 01749 674483 wellscathedral.org.uk **48 B2**

Wiltshire

Malmesbury Abbey *Malmesbury* Abbey founded 7th century, only 12th-century nave survives. Porch with sculptured reliefs depicting scenes from Old Testament, Creation and Life of Christ. Norman stone carvings of apostles on interior walls of porch. Tomb of Saxon King Athelstan (died 939). malmesburyabbey.com **64 E3**

Salisbury Cathedral *The Close, Salisbury* Beautiful Early English building with later Decorated tower and tallest spire in Britain. Notable west front has many niches filled with figures representing the Te Deum. 01722 555118 salisburycathedral.org.uk **51 E8**

St John *Devizes* Mixture of Norman and Gothic styles. **58 D5**

St John the Baptist *Bishopstone* Many decorated features and interesting monuments. **40 A4**

St John the Baptist *Inglesham* Plain exterior 13th-century church saved by William Morris c. 1888-9. Late Saxon relief sculpture. **65 C9**

St Katharine and St Peter *Winterbourne Bassett* Mainly 14th-century Decorated style. Walls mainly of Sarsen stone, the stone from the Marlborough Downs used for Stonehenge. **59 A6**

St Laurence *Bradford on Avon* Built in 10th century, possibly on foundations of 8th-century church. Rediscovered 1871 after serving as barn. Simple interior with carved angels above the chancel. **57 D8**

St Mary *Bishops Cannings* Early Gothic. Vaulted porch with Decorated ballflower. 17th-century pew beneath huge hand intended to warn occupant of sin. **58 D5**

St Mary *Lydiard Tregoze* Mausoleum of Caroleum art. Golden Cavalier monument. **65 F7**

St Mary, St Katherine and All Saints *Edington* Late Gothic completed at time of transition from Decorated to Perpindicular church styles. **50 A3**

St Thomas *High Street, Salisbury* Most complete Doom mural in Britain. 01722 322537 stthomassalisbury.co.uk **51 E8**

Museums and galleries

Arts and crafts

Bath & NE Somerset

American Museum in Britain *Claverton* In Claverton Manor. Development of North American decorative arts. Native American and folk art. See 'Gardens' 01225 460503 www.americanmuseum.org **57 D7**

Holburne Museum of Art *Bath* 17th–18th century fine and decorative art. Old Masters including Gainsborough, Stubbs, Turner. 01225 466669 www.bath.ac.uk/holburne **57 C7**

Museum of East Asian Art *Bath* Five galleries and more than 500 art treasures from East Asia. 01225 464640 www.meaa.org.uk **57 C7**

Victoria Art Gallery *Bath* Paintings, drawings etc. Artists include Gainsborough, Turner, and Sickert. 01225 477233 www.victoriagal.org.uk **57 C7**

Bournemouth

Russell-Cotes Art Gallery and Museum *Bournemouth* Victorian art collection, Japanese art and artefacts, contemporary art. 01202 451858 www.russell-cotes.bournemouth.gov.uk **28 B1**

Bristol

Arnolfini Arts Centre *Bristol* Visual arts centre. 0117 9172300 www.arnolfini.org.uk **56 B4**

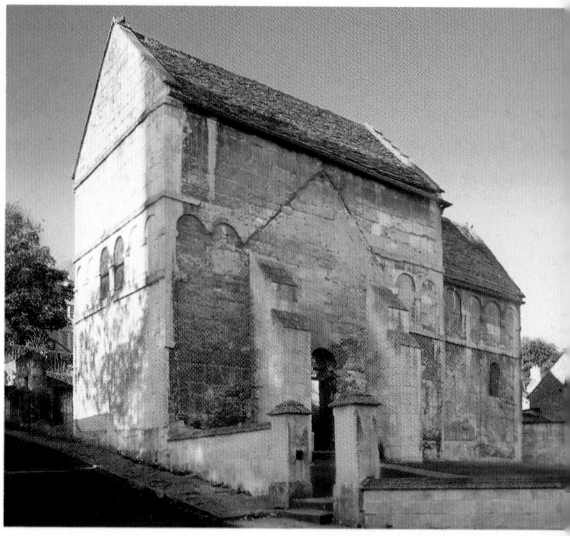

▲ **St Laurence church, Bradford on Avon**

Cornwall

Barbara Hepworth Museum and Sculpture Garden *St Ives* Sculptures in bronze, stone and wood, paintings and drawings. Studio and garden run by Tate Gallery. 01736 796226 www.tate.org.uk/stives/hepworth.htm **3 B6**

Newlyn Art Gallery *Newlyn* Changing exhibitions of contemporary art by leading artists. 01736 363715 www.newlynartgallery.co.uk **2 E5**

Royal Cornwall Museum *Truro* Among the collections are a good number of Newlyn School paintings, some Old Master drawing, Egyptian antiquities including an unwrapped mummy, Greek and Roman objects and a world-famous collection of minerals. 0187 272205 www.royalcornwallmuseum.org.uk **4 B4**

Tate St Ives *St Ives* Over 200 works of modern art as well as special exhibitions from the other Tate galleries. 01736 796226 www.tate.org.uk/stives **3 B6**

Gloucestershire

Nature in Art *Twigworth* Located in Wallsworth Hall. Museum dedicated to art inspired by nature. 0845 450 0233 www.nature-in-art.org.uk **70 C2**

General museums

Bath & NE Somerset

Bath Royal Literary and Scientific Institution *Bath* Geology, natural history, ethnology, archaeology, art and history artefacts. 01225 312084 www.brlsi.org **57 C7**

Museum of Costume *Bath* More than 150 complete outfits on display. 01225 477173 www.museumofcostume.co.uk **57 C7**

Bristol

British Empire and Commonwealth Museum *Bristol* 0117 9254980 www.empiremuseum.co.uk **56 B4**

City Museum and Art Gallery *Bristol* Art and archaeology, geology and natural history, housed in a magnificent early 20th-century building. 0117 9223571 **56 B4**

Fleet Air Arm Museum, Yeovilton

Cornwall

useum of Smuggling *Jamaica Inn* lection of smuggling artefacts ℃01566 250 🖳www.jamaicainn.co.uk/ ugglers_museum **17 E8**

useum of Witchcraft *Boscastle* The rlds largest collection of items related witchcraft. ℃01840 250111 🖳www. seumofwitchcraft.com **57 C7**

ul Corin's Magnificent Music Machines *Keyne* Includes cafe organ, player pianos, herican Wurlitzer theatre pipe organ. 1579 343108 🖳www.paulcorinmusic. m **9 C7**

Devon

l Douglas Centre *Exeter* History of ema. ℃01392 264321 🖳www.billdouglas. **21 B8**

Dorset

valcade of Costume Museum *andford Forum* Historical costumes ering a 250-year period. ℃01258 453006 🖳www.cavalcadeofcostume.com **39 E7**

est's House Museum *Wimborne* *nster* Varied collection including art d archaeology, costume, transport, otography, toys, warfare, medicine and sic ℃01202 882533 **27 A7**

Gloucestershire

eltenham Art Gallery and Museum *eltenham* Nationally important Arts and afts movement collection; furniture, intings, ceramics, jewellery and al history. ℃01242 237431 🖳www. eltenhammuseum.org **71 C5**

olst Birthplace Museum *Cheltenham* iginal piano and manuscripts. ℃01242 4846 🖳www.holstmuseum.org.uk **71 C5**

Plymouth

ty Museum and Art Gallery *Plymouth* intings, ceramics, archaeology, tural history. ℃01752 304774 🖳www. mouthmuseum.gov.uk **10 E5**

Local

Bath & NE Somerset

th Postal Museum *Bath* 4000 years of mmunication, from Sumarian clay tablets the present day. ℃01225 460333 www.bathpostalmuseum.org **57 C7**

ilding of Bath Museum *Bath* History of insformation of Bath, from small provincial a into Georgian splendour. ℃01225 3895 🖳www.bath-preservation-trust. .uk **57 C7**

oman Baths Museum *Bath* Roman temple d bathing complex. ℃01225 477785 www.romanbaths.co.uk **57 C7**

Cornwall

lperro Heritage Museum of Smuggling d Fishing *Polperro* Exhibits and otographs dating from the 18th century 1503 273005 **9 E7**

hipwreck and Heritage Centre *harlestown* Houses largest shipwreck tefact collection in UK. ℃01726 69897 www.shipwreckcharlestown.com **8 E3**

Devon

artmouth Museum *Dartmouth* Historic d maritime museum in former merchant's ouse from 1640. ℃01803 832923 **15 E5**

Dorset

Blandford Museum *Blandford Forum* History of Blandford Forum and neighbouring villages. ℃01258 450388 **39 E7**

Dorset County Museum *Dorchester* Local wildlife, rocks, fossils, archaeology and displays on Dorset writers. ℃01305 262735 🖳www.dorsetcountymuseum. org **25 B8**

The Philpot Museum *Lyme Regis* Winner of Museum of South-west prize and Gulbenkian Prize. ℃01297 443370 🖳www. lymeregismuseum.co.uk **24 B1**

Tolpuddle Martyrs Museum *Tolpuddle* Story of the six workers transported to Australia in 1834 as punishment for forming a trade union. ℃01305 848237 🖳www. tolpuddlemartyrs.org.uk **26 B2**

Gloucestershire

City Museum and Art Gallery *Gloucester* Local history and small collection of British paintings. ℃01452 396131 🖳www. Gloucestershire-city.gov **70 D2**

Corinium Museum *Cirencester* Extensive collection of Romano-British antiquities from Corinium. ℃01285 655611 🖳www.cotswold. gov.uk **65 B5**

Gloucester Folk Museum *Gloucester* Local history exhibits, including stake at which Bishop Hooper was allegedly burned. ℃01452 396868 🖳www.Gloucestershire-city.gov **70 D2**

Scilly Isles

Isles of Scilly Museum *St Mary's* Geology, archaeology, history and natural history. ℃01720 422337 🖳www.iosmuseum.org **6 A3**

Longstone Heritage Centre *St Mary's* History of Isles from prehistoric times. Also 'Papers Past at Longstone' – displays of original newspapers, c. 1793 onwards, including special birthpapers to buy. ℃01720 423770 **6 A3**

Somerset

Somerset Cricket Museum *Taunton* Historic barn containing cricket memorabilia. ℃01823 275893 **36 A2**

Wilts

Alexander Keiller Museum *Avebury* Collection of important local prehistoric material. ℃01672 529203 🖳www.english-heritage.org.uk **59 C7**

Salisbury and South Wiltshire Museum *Salisbury* Includes Stonehenge, settlers from Stone Age to Saxons, Old Sarum and Salisbury, Wedgwood, pre-NHS surgery, costumes. ℃01722 332151 🖳www. salisburymuseum.org.uk **51 E8**

Military history

Cornwall

Duke of Cornwall's Light Infantry Regiment Museum *Bodmin* History of Cornwall's county regiment from 1702–1959. ℃01208 72810 🖳www.armymuseums. org.uk **8 B4**

Devon

Cobbaton Combat Collection *Cobbaton* World War II British and Canadian military equipment. ℃01769 540740 🖳www.cobbatoncombat.co.uk **43 F7**

Dorset

Royal Signals Museum *Blandford Camp* Displays include ENIGMA, Special Operations Executive, SAS. Many displays for children. ℃01258 482248 🖳www.army.mod.uk/royalsignalsmuseum **39 E7**

The Keep Military Museum *Dorchester* History of infantry, cavalry and artillerymen of the counties of Devon and Dorset. ℃01305 264066 🖳www.keepmilitarymuseum. org **25 B8**

The Tank Museum *Bovington* WWI walk-through trench experience. Vehicle collection. ℃01929 405096 🖳www. tankmuseum.org.uk **27 C5**

Gloucestershire

Soldiers of Gloucestershire Museum *Gloucester Docks* ℃01452 522682 🖳www.Gloucestershireters.org.uk **70 D2**

Wellington Aviation Museum *Moreton-in-Marsh* A small museum dedicated to the personnel and trainee pilots of the World War II flight training station ℃01608 650323 🖳www.wellingtonaviation.org **72 A3**

Somerset

Fleet Air Arm Museum *RNAS Yeovilton* More than 90 aircraft and many models and equipment. ℃01935 840565 🖳www.fleetairarm.com **37 B8**

Wiltshire

The Wardrobe *Salisbury* Collections include medals, uniforms, and militaria. ℃01722 419419 🖳www.wardrobe.org.uk **51 E8**

Mills, mines and factories

Bristol

Bristol Industrial Museum *Bristol* Vehicles, shunting engine and Fairbairn steam crane. Bristol Harbour Railway; steam tug *Mayflower* and other boats. New exhibition about the Bristol slave trade. ℃0117 9251470 **56 B4**

Cornwall

Camborne School of Mines *Redruth* Local geological collection of minerals and ores. Art exhibition featuring the works of local artists. ℃01209 714866 🖳www.ex.ac.uk/csm **4 B2**

Cornish Mines and Engine Houses (NT) *Pool* Two great beam engines. ℃01209 315027 🖳www.nationaltrust.org.uk **4 B1**

Geevor Tin Mine Museum *Trewellard* Heritage centre. Tells story of production of tin and of miners. ℃01736 788662 🖳www. geevor.com **2 D3**

Devon

Coldharbour Mill Museum *Uffculme* Displays of Victorian spinning, carding and weaving machines. ℃01884 840960 🖳www.coldharbourmill.org.uk **35 D6**

Dartington Glass Centre *Great Torrington* Tours of the factory, displays of glass-making techniques. Exhibition on history of glass. ℃01805 626262 🖳www.dartington.co,uk **32 C2**

White Mill (NT) *Sturminster Marshall* Rebuilt in 1776. Guided tours only. Open in summer. ℃01258 858051 🖳www.nationaltrust.org. uk **27 A6**

Gloucestershire

Arlington Mill *Bibury* Wool and corn mill, now a museum. ℃01285 740368 **65 A7**

Somerset

Dunster Watermill (NT) *Dunster* 18th century ℃01643 821759 🖳www.nationaltrust.org.uk **45 C6**

Stembridge Tower Mill (NT) *High Ham* Last thatched windmill in England. ℃01458 250818 🖳www.nationaltrust.org.uk **47 E8**

Science and technology

Bath & NE Somerset

Royal Photographic Society *Bath* 18th-century chapel. Gallery and museum. ℃01225 325733 🖳www.rps.org **57 C7**

William Herschel Museum *Bath* Located in the house in which Herschel discovered the planet Uranus. ℃01225 446865 🖳www. bath-preservation-trust.org.uk **57 D6**

Devon

British Photographic Museum, *Bowden House, Totnes* ℃01803 863664 **14 C4**

Dorset

Dinosaur Museum *Dorchester* Fossils, skeletons, reconstructions, interactive computer displays and videos. A World Heritage museum. ℃01305 269741 🖳www. thedinosaurmuseum.com **25 B8**

Gloucestershire

Jenner Museum *Berkeley* Georgian house and gardens. Home of Dr Edward Jenner, smallpox vaccination pioneer. ℃01453 810631 🖳www.jennermuseum.com **63 C5**

Somerset

TV, Radio and Memorabilia Musuem *Montacute* Vintage to modern day radios; film, TV and children's books and toys; televisions, household appliances; advertising signs and packaging. ℃01935 823024 **37 C7**

Wiltshire

Fox-Talbot Museum *Lacock* Commemorates the life and work of the inventor of modern photography ℃01249 730459 🖳www.nationaltrust.org.uk **58 C3**

Transport

Cornwall

Automobilia *St Stephen* Over 50 vehicles dating from 1904 to the 1960s. Automobilia. ℃01726 823092 **8 E1**

British Cycling Museum *Camelford* History of cycles and cycling memorabilia from 1818. ℃01840 212811 🖳www.chycor. co.uk/cycling-museum **17 D7**

National Maritime Museum *Falmouth* National small boat collection, galleries, remote-controlled models and live demonstrations. ℃01326 313388 🖳www.nmmc.co.uk **3 D5**

Devon

Combe Martin Motorcyle Collection *Combe Martin* More than 60 motorcycles, scooters and carriages. ℃01271 882346 **43 B6**

North Devon Maritime Museum *Appledore* North Devon's maritime history illustrated by models, photographs, etc ℃01237 474852 🖳www.devonheritage. com/ndmt/museum.htm **35 D6**

Dorset

Bournemouth Aviation Museum *Christchurch* Comprehensive display of aircraft models. ℃01202 580858 🖳www.aviation-museum.co.uk **28 B3**

Gloucestershire

Cotswold Motoring Museum and Toy Collection *Cheltenham* 30 cars and motorcycles on display with a selection of prams, toy and pedal cars. More than 800 vintage advertising signs. Also toy collection. ℃01451 821255 🖳www.cotswold-motor-museum.com **71 C5**

National Waterways Museum *Gloucester Docks* Located in listed Victorian warehouse. ℃01452 318200 🖳www.nwm.org.uk **70 D2**

North Somerset

The Helicopter Museum *Weston-super-Mare* Examples from around the world with displays. ℃01934 635227 🖳www.helicoptermuseum.co.uk **55 D6**

Plymouth

The Kathleen and May *Plymouth* Last of the west country's wooden trading schooners, now a museum. 🖳www. kathleen-and-may.co.uk **10 E5**

Somerset

Haynes Motor Museum *Yeovil* Britain's largest collection of automobilia. ℃01963 440804 🖳www.haynesmotormuseum. com **37 C9**

Wiltshire

Atwell-Wilson Motor Museum Trust *Calne* Vintage and classic cars. Classic motorbikes. ℃01249 813119 🖳www.atwellwilso.org.uk/ **58 B5**

Steam *Swindon* Museum of the Great Western Railway. ℃01793 466646 🖳www.steam-museum.org.uk **65 E8**

The Kennet and Avon Canal Museum *Devizes* ℃01380 729489 🖳www.katrust.org.uk **58 D5**

Camborne Tin Mines, Cornwall

Sports

Activity centres

Cornwall

Hotrocks *Newquay* This centre offers abseiling, climbing, coasteering, hill-walking, navigating, scrambling and surfing. 07952 317159 www.hotrockclimbs.com/home.htm **7 C6**

Penhale Adventure Centre *Newquay* A wide range of activities, including abseiling, archery, ballooning, buggying, climbing, flying, gliding, hang gliding, helicopter flights, karting, kayaking, kite surfing, landboarding, land yachting, microlighting, mountain biking, mountain boarding, off-road motor biking, orienteering, paintballing, parachuting, paragliding, powerkiting, rib rides, quad biking, rock climbing, sailing, scuba diving, shooting, surfing, survival training, tank driving, wakeboarding, waterskiing and 4 x 4 driving 0800 781 6861 www.itsadventuresouthwest.co.uk **7 C6**

Devon

Ashcombe Adventure Centre *Ashcombe, nr Dawlish* Among the activities are archery, clay pigeon shooting, fishing, karting, paint-balling and quad biking. 01626 866766 www.ashcombeadventure.co.uk **21 E8**

Mountain Water Experience *Kingsbridge* Activities include abseiling, assault course, body boarding, canyoning, caving, coasteering, gorge walking, high-wire walking, kayak training, open boat instruction, rock climbing and white water kayaking. 01548 550 675 www.mountainwaterexperience.com **13 D5**

Skern Lodge Outdoor Centre *Appledore* Activities on offer include abseiling, archery, assault course, canoeing, climbing, high ropes, orienteering, rafting, surf skiing and a zipwire. 01237 475992 www.skernlodge.co.uk **42 E4**

North Somerset

The Action Centre *Churchill* Centre offering abseiling, archery, clay pigeon shooting, climbing, mountain boarding, power kiting, quad biking, shooting, skateboarding, skiing, snowblading, snowboarding, tobogganing and 4 x 4 driving. 01934 852 335 www.highaction.co.uk **55 D8**

Somerset

Aardvark Endeavours *Cheddar* Aardvark Endeavours offer abseiling, archery, caving, climbing, kayaking, raft building, rifle shooting and a 100-m zip-wire. 01934 744878 www.aardvarkendeavours.com **56 F1**

Cycling

Bath & NE Somerset

Avon Valley Cyclery *Bath* 01225 442442 **57 C7**

Bournemouth

Bournemouth Mountain Bikes Centre *Bournemouth* 01202 514344 **28 B1**

Bristol

Sustrans *Bristol* Cycle hire and specially designed cycle routes. 0117 9628893 www.sustrans.org.uk **56 B4**

Cornwall

Aldridge Cycles *Camborne* 01209 714970 **3 B9**

Bike Services *Helston* Bike sales, repair, and hire. 01326 564654 www.bikeservices.co.uk **4 E1**

Bissoe Tramway Cycle Hire *Truro* Sales, servicing, hire. 01872 870341 www.cornwallcyclehire.com **4 B4**

Bridge Bike Hire *Wadebridge* 01208 813050 www.cornwall-online.co.uk/bridgebikehire **8 A2**

Bridge Cycle Hire *Wadebridge* 01208 814545 www.cyclehirecornwall.com **8 A2**

Brinhams Cycle and Tool Hire *Padstow* 01841 532594 **16 E3**

Cycle Nucleus *St Austell* 01726 68569 **8 E3**

Elm Farm Cycle Hire *Redruth* 01209 891498 www.elm-farm.co.uk **4 B2**

Glynn Valley Cycle Hire *Bodmin* 01208 74244 **8 B4**

Hayle Cycles *Hayle* 01736 753825 **3 C7**

Newquay Cycle Hire *Newquay* 01637 874040 **7 C7**

Family attractions

Cornwall

Bens Play World *St Austell* Adventure centre. 01726 815553 www.bensplayworld.co.uk **8 E4**

Bodmin and Wenford Railway *Bodmin* Restored steam engines and rides. 01208 73666 www.bodminandwenfordrailway.co.uk **8 B4**

Bodmin Jail *Bodmin* Former county prison dating back to 1776. Dungeons, plus displays. 01208 76292 **8 B4**

Brocklands Adventure Park *Kilkhampton* Adventure park and wildlife centre. Two-seater super-carts, 'Supa Bouncer' for all ages, bumper-boats, train rides, pony rides, paddle boats, ride-on racing cars, crazy golf, trampolines, mini assault course. 01288 321920 www.brocklands.com **31 D5**

Crealy Great Adventure Park *Wadebridge* Outdoor adventures, aerial walkways, slides, log flume, horses, farm animals and parkland 0870 1163333 www.crealy.co.uk **8 B1**

Dobwalls Family Adventure Park *Dobwalls* Miniature train rides, adventure park, art exhibition. 01579 320325 www.dobwalls.com **9 B7**

Goonhilly Earth Station *Helston* Largest satellite Earth station in the world. Guided tours, interactive displays and film shows. 0800 679593 www.goonhilly.bt.com **4 E1**

Hidden Valley *Launceston* Treasure hunt centre. Also 9-hole golf course, nature reserve, farm animals, miniature railway and play area. 01566 86463 www.hidden-valley.co.uk **18 D2**

Holywell Bay Fun Park *Newquay* Pitch and putt, kid's go-karting, rides, bumper boats, maze, indoor adventure area. 01637 830095 www.holywellbay.co.uk **7 D6**

Killarney Springs *Bude* Adventure playground, boating lake, BMX track, basketball. Fishing lake, white-water rapids, etc. 01288 331475 **31 C5**

Land of Legend and Model Village *Polperro* Internationally famous model village. 01503 272378 **9 E7**

Lappa Valley Steam Railway *Newquay* 01872 510317 www.lappavalley.co.uk **7 C7**

Launceston Steam Railway *Launceston* 01566 775665 www.launcetonsr.co.uk **18 D3**

Poldark Mine *Wendron* Underground workings with guided tour. Children's play area. 01326 573173 www.poldark-mine.co.uk **4 D1**

Spirit of the West *St Columb Major* American themed park, American town recreations. 01637 881160 www.wildwestthemepark.co.uk **7 C7**

Tamarisk Miniature Railway *Nr Padstow* 01841 540829 **16 E3**

The Flambards Experience *Helston* Recreation of Victorian and war-time street. Cornwall Aero Park and Exploratorium. Rides include log flume and rollercoasters. 0845 6018684 www.flambards.co.uk **4 E1**

World in Miniature *Goonhavern* Miniature versions of the world's landmarks 01872 572828, 0870 4584433 www.worldinminiature.co.uk **7 E6**

Devon

Beer Quarry Caves *Beer* Caverns dating from Roman times. Tours and exhibits. 01297 680282 www.beerquarrycaves.fsnet.co.uk **23 A6**

Bicton Woodland Railways *East Budleigh* 01395 658465 www.bictongardens.co.uk **22 D3**

Bideford and Instow Railway Group *Bideford* Brake van rides. www.bidefordrail.co.uk **42 F3**

Crealy Adventure Park *Clyst St Mary* Rides including log flume and rollercoaster, go-karts, indoor adventure play centre, farm animals and parkland 01395 233200 www.crealy.co.uk **22 B2**

Dartmoor Railway *Crediton* Operates on the route of the old Southern Railway line from Crediton to Okehampton and Meldon Quarry. 01837 55637 www.dartmoorrailway.co.uk **34 F1**

Devon Railway Centre *Bickleigh* Operating 2-ft narrow-gauge railway, as well as short section of standard-gauge. 01884 855671. www.devonrailwaycentre.co.uk **11 C7**

Diggerland *Verbeer Manor, Cullompton* Adventure park with JCBs and dumper trucks. 08700 344437 www.diggerland.com **35 E5**

Finch Foundry (NT) *Sticklepath* 19th-century water-powered forge. 01837 840046 www.nationaltrust.org.uk **20 B2**

Lynton and Barnstaple Railway *Martinhoe Cross* 01598 763487 www.lynton-rail.co.uk **43 B8**

Lynton Cliff Railway *Lynton* Oldest working water operated cliff railway. 01598 753908 www.cliffrailwaylynton.co.uk **44 B1**

Morwellham Quay *Tavistock* Underground train-ride, horse drawn carriage rides and costumes. 01822 832766 www.morwellham-quay.co.uk **19 F6**

Norman Lockyer Observatory *Sidmouth* Victorian telescopes, planetarium and displays. Visits by arrangement. 01395 579941 www.ex.ac.uk/nlo **22 C4**

Once Upon a Time *Woolacombe* Children's adventure playground, ages 3–11. 01271 870900 www.watermouthcastle.com **42 C4**

Pecorama Pleasure Gardens *Beer* Miniature train. Aviary, crazy golf, children's activity area. 01297 21542 www.peco-uk.com/pecorama.htm **23 C6**

Prehistoric Hilltop Settlement *Capton* Reconstruction of a prehistoric hill settlement. Produce for sale. 01803 712452 **14 E4**

Seaton and District Electric Tramway *Seaton* Miniature tramway system. 01297 20375 www.tram.co.uk **10 E2**

South Devon Railway *Totnes* Historic line follows the scenic River Dart. 08453 451420 www.southdevonrailway.org **14 C4**

The Gnomes Reserve and Pixie Kiln *Princetown* 0870 8459012 www.gnomereserve.co.uk **20 F1**

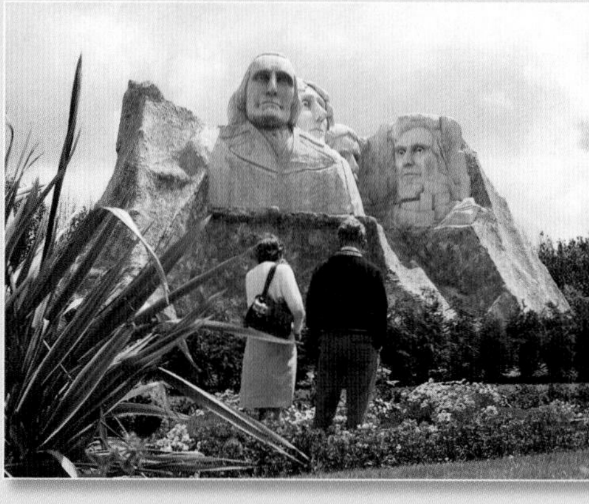

▲ **World in Miniature, Goonhavern, Cornwall**

The Milky Way Adventure Park *Clovelly* Rides, adventure play area, archery, golf driving, railway, bird and sheep dog displays, etc. 01237 431255 www.themilkyway.co.uk **31 B6**

Underground passages *Exeter* Vaulted medieval passageways built to house the lead water pipes that supplied the city. Closed until 2007 01392 265206 www.exeter.gov.uk **21 B8**

Watermouth Castle and Family Theme Park *nr Ilfracombe* Rides, adventure playground, mini golf, mazes, model railway, tube slides, crazy snooker, Gnomeland and swing boats. 01271 867474 www.watermouthcastle.com **43 B6**

Dorset

Adventure Wonderland *Hurn* 2.8 ha (7 acres) of landscaped park with variety of activities. 01202 483444 www.adventurewonderland.co.uk **28 A2**

Charmouth Heritage Coast Centre *Charmouth* Discover fossils with guided walks, theatre and displays. 01297 560772 www.charmouth.org **24 B2**

K's *Swanage Bay* Children's play area and soft play area. www.ks-entertainment-centres.co.uk **27 D7**

Moors Valley Railway *Ashley Heath* 01425 471415 www.moorsvalleyrailway.co.uk **41 E6**

Swanage Railway *Swanage* Line currently operates between Swanage and Norden. 01929 425800 www.swanagerailway.co.uk **27 E7**

Weymouth Bay Miniature Railway, *Lodmoor Country Park, Weymouth* 01305 785747 **25 E8**

Gloucestershire

Bourton Model Railway *Bourton-on-the-Water* 01451 820686 www.bourtonmodelrailway.co.uk **72 C2**

Cattle Country Adventure Park *Berkeley* Large outdoor park and indoor slides. 01453 810510 www.cattlecountry.co.uk **63 C5**

Dean Forest Railway *Lydney* Steam railway running between Lydney and Parkend. 01594 845840 www.deanforestrailway.co.uk **62 B4**

Fundays *Bourton-on-the-Water* Large indoor children's adventure playground. Special evenings for teenagers and adults. 01451 822999 www.fundaysplaybarn.com **72 C2**

Gloucestershire Warwickshire Steam Railway *Toddington* 01242 621405 www.gwsr.com **71 A6**

Model Village *Bourton-on-the-Water* Copy of village. 01451 820467 **72 C2**

Perrygrove Railway *Coleford* 01594 834991 www.perrygrove.co.uk **69 E5**

The Merchant's House *Tewkesbury* One of row of restored cottages built around 1450. Restored to show medieval merchant's shop and house. 01684 297174 **70 A3**

North Somerset

Weston Miniature Railway *Weston-super-Mare* 01934 643510 **55 D6**

Plymouth

Plym Valley Railway *Plympton* Steam and diesel locomotives. www.plymrail.co.uk **11 D6**

Plymouth Dome *Plymouth* Interactive displays covering 400 years of Plymouth history. 01752 603300 www.plymouthdome.info **10 E5**

Plymouth Miniature Steam Locomotive Society *Southway* **11 C5**

Poole

Gus Gorilla's Jungle Playground *Poole* Adventure playground for children up to 12 years. Spiral slides, aerial walkways, tube slides, tarzan ropes, roller challenge, ball pool. 01202 717197 www.gusgorillas.co.uk **27 B7**

Tower Park *Poole* Indoor playworld. UCI cinema, Megabow Quasar and amusement arcade. 01202 723671 **27 B7**

South Gloucestershire

Avon Valley Railway *Bitton* Along former branch of old Midland Railway. Wide variety of main-line industrial steam and diesel locomotives. 0117 932 5538 www.avonvalleyrailway.co.uk **57 C5**

Somerset

Brean Leisure Park *Brean* Pool complex with four water shutes. Funfair. 01278 751595 www.brean.com **55 F5**

Cheddar Caves and Gorge *Cheddar* Cave carved out by rivers over a million years. The show caves have massive stalactites and stalacmites, the Cheddar cannibal and a Crystal Quest adventure. 01934 742343 www.cheddarcaves.co.uk **56 F1**

East Somerset Railway *Cranmore* Strawberry Line through the Mendip Hills. Loco shed, museum, art gallery, and play area. 01749 880417 www.eastsomersetrailway.com **49 C5**

Jungle Jungle *Yeovil* Jungle playground. 01935 433833 **37 C8**

K's *Minehead* Children's play area and soft play area. www.ks-entertainment-centres.co.uk **45 B6**

Peat Moors Centre *Glastonbury* Reconstruction of Iron Age roundhouses. 01458 860697 www.somerset.gov.uk/somerset/cultureheritage/heritage/pmc **48 D2**

Rug Ratz *Yeovil* Children's play centre 01935 476989 www.rug-ratz.co.uk **37 C8**

West Somerset Railway *Minehead* Britain's longest steam railway. 01643 704996 www.west-somerset-railway.co.uk **45 B6**

Wookey Hole *Wookey* Spectacular caves and legendary home of Witch of Wookey. 01749 672243 www.wookey.co.uk **48 B2**

Swindon

The Jolly Roger Adventure *Swindon* Children's indoor pla area. 01793 522044 www.jollyrogerplay.com **65 E8**

Torbay

Babbacombe Model Village *Torquay* 01803 315315 www.babbacombemodelvillage.co.uk **15 C6**

Bygones *Torquay* Victorian street, giant model railway, World War I trench, Anderson Shelter. 01803 326108 www.bygones.co.uk **15 C6**

Fun Factory *Torquay* Indoor adventure centre. 01803 201606 **15 C6**

K's *Torquay* Children's play area and soft play area. www.ks-entertainment-centres.co.uk **15 C6**

Kents Cavern *Torquay* Prehistoric remains and the life of the Caveclan. Guided tours. 01803 215136 www.kents-cavern.co.uk **15 C6**

Paignton and Dartmouth Steam Railway *Paignton* 01803 555872 www.paignton-steamrailway.co.uk **15 C5**

Rainbow Fun House *Torquay* 01803 296926 www.rainbowfunhouse.co.uk **15 C6**

Wiltshire

Swindon and Cricklade Railway *Near Swindon* 01793 771615 www.swindon-cricklade-railway.org **65 E7**

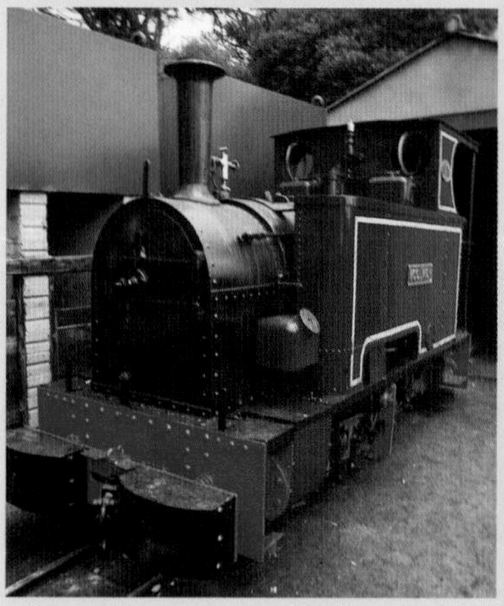

► **Bicton Woodland Railway, Devon**

orth Coast Cycles *Bude* ☎01288 352974 **) E4**

adstow Cycle Hire *Padstow* ☎01841 3533 🖥www.cornwall-online.co.uk/ dstow-cycle-hire **16 E3**

edals Bike Hire *Penzance* ☎01736 360600 **D5**

entewan Valley Cycle Hire *St Austell*)1726 844242 🖥www. ntewanvalleycyclehire.co.uk **8 E3**

e Cycle Centre *Penzance* ☎01736 351671 www.cornwallcyclecentre.co.uk **3 D5**

ail and Trek *Truro* ☎01872 561124 **4 B4**

uro Cycles *Truro* ☎01872 271703 **4 B4**

evon

ycle *Honiton* ☎01404 47211 www.cycle1.co.uk **35 F7**

artmoor Cycles *Tavistock* ☎01822 618178 www.dartmoorcycles.co.uk **19 F6**

xmoor Biketrail Cycle Hire *Barnstaple*)1598 763263 🖥www.biketrail.co.uk **3 E6**

iffords Cycles *Holsworthy* ☎01409 54020 **31 F6**

ot Pursuit *Totnes* ☎01803 865174 www.hotpursuit-cycles.co.uk **14 C4**

nobblies *Exmouth* ☎01395 270182 **22 D2**

kehampton Cycles *Okehampton* ☎01837 3248 🖥www.bostocks.co.uk **20 B1**

nabike *Newton Abbot* ☎01626 334664 **5 A5**

tter Cycle Hire *Braunton* ☎01271 813339 **2 D4**

addles and Paddles *Exeter* Canoe and ke hire. ☎01392 424241 **21 B8**

arka Trail Cycle Hire *Barnstaple* ☎01271 24202 **43 E6**

avistock Cycles *Tavistock* ☎01822 617630 **9 F6**

orset

ikeabout *Swanage* ☎01929 425050 **27 E7**

orchester Cycles *Dorchester* ☎01305 76977 **25 B8**

orset Cycles *Sturminster Newton* ☎01963 52476 **39 D5**

Vestham Cycles *Weymouth* ☎01305 76977 **25 E8**

loucestershire

ompass Holidays *Cheltenham* ☎01242 50642 🖥www.compass-holidays.com **1 C5**

otswold Country Cycles *Chipping ampden* ☎01386 438706 🖥www. otswoldcountrycycles.co.uk **77 E6**

otswold Water Park & Keynes Country ark *Cirencester* See under Country Parks **5 B5**

ountry Lanes Cycle Centre *Moreton- -Marsh* ☎01608 650065 🖥www. ountrylanes.co.uk **72 A3**

ycle Clinic *Stroud* ☎01453 835200 **64 A2**

orest Adventure *Coleford* ☎01594 834661 **9 E5**

lymouth

lltrax *nr Plymouth* ☎01752 863553 www.alltraxcycles.co.uk **10 E5**

oole

ool Cats Leisure *Poole* ☎01202 701100 **7 B7**

omerset

lue Bell Cycle Hire *Bridgwater* ☎01278 22123 **47 D5**

ow Bridge Cycles *Langport* Cycle hire and ails. ☎01458 250350 **47 F8**

H Cycle Centre *Burnham on Sea* ☎01278 82350 **47 B6**

an's Cycle Centre *Taunton* ☎01823 365917 www.ianscyclecentre.co.uk **36 A2**

ing's Cycles *Wellington* ☎01823 662260 www.kingscycles.co.uk **35 B7**

ing's Cycles *Taunton* ☎01823 352272 www.kingscycles.co.uk **36 A2**

oger Joseph Cycles *Bridgwater* ☎01278 63545 **47 D5**

he Bicycle Chain *Taunton* ☎01823 252499 www.bicyclechain.co.uk **36 A2**

orbay

ycleh ire *Torbay* ☎01803 521068 **15 C5**

Viltshire

ayball Cycle Centre *Salisbury* ☎01722 11378 🖥www.hayball.co.uk **51 E8**

owpath Trail *Bradford on Avon* ☎01225 67187 **57 D8**

Football

Bristol

Bristol City FC *Bristol* ☎0117 9630630 🖥www.bcfc.co.uk **56 B3**

Bristol Rovers FC *Horfield* ☎0117 909648 🖥www.bristolrovers.co.uk **56 A3**

Devon

Exeter City FC *Exeter* ☎01392 411243 🖥www.exetercityfc.co.uk **21 B8**

Gloucestershire

Cheltenham Town FC *Cheltenham* ☎01242 573558 🖥www.cheltenhamtownfc.co.uk **71 C5**

Plymouth

Plymouth Argyll FC *Plymouth* ☎01752 562561 🖥www.pafc.co.uk **10 D5**

Swindon

Swindon Town FC *Swindon* ☎01793 513626 🖥www.swindontownfc.co.uk **65 E8**

Torbay

Torquay United FC *Torquay* ☎01803 388666 🖥www.torquayunited.com **15 B6**

Golf

The following is a selection of courses that welcome visitors at most times. Those marked * may have restricted times for visitors, recommend advance booking or require a valid handicap certificate. It is advisable always to telephone in advance before visiting.

Cornwall

Bude & North Cornwall GC *Bude* An 18-hole, par-71 course in the centre of the coastal resort. ☎01288 352006 🖥www.budegolf.co.uk **30 E4**

Cape Cornwall G&CC *St Just* An 18-hole course overlooking the rugged west Cornish coast. ☎01736 788611 🖥www.capecornwall.com **2 D3**

Carlyon Bay GC *Carlyon Bay* An 18-hole course overlooking St Austell Bay. ☎01726 814250 🖥www.carlyonbay.co.uk **8 E4**

China Fleet CC *Saltash* 18-hole course overlooking the Tamar. ☎01752 848668 🖥www.china-fleet.co.uk **10 D4**

Falmouth GC *Falmouth* 18-hole course near Swanpool Beach. ☎01326 311262/314296 🖥www.falmouthgolfclub.com **4 D3**

Killiow Golf Park *Kea* An 18-hole course south of Truro. ☎01872 70246 **4 B4**

Lanhydrock GC *Bodmin* An 18-hole course on the high ground south of Bodmin. ☎01208 73600 🖥www.lanhydrock-golf.co.uk **8 C4**

Looe GC *Looe* An 18-hole course on the higher ground lookinger Whitesands Bay. ☎01503 240239 **9 E8**

Lostwithiel G&CC *Polscoe* An 18-hole course just outside Lostwithiel. ☎01208 873550 🖥www.golf-hotel.co.uk **9 C5**

Merlin GC *Mawgan Porth, Newquay* An 18-hole course inland from Cornwall's west coast and overlooking the Vale of Mawgan. ☎01841 540222 🖥www.merlingolfcourse.co.uk **7 B8**

Newquay GC *Newquay* An 18-hole course, right next to the surfer paradise of Fistral Beach. ☎01637 872091 **7 C7**

Perranporth GC *Perranporth* An 18-hole links course right next to the south-west coast of Cornwall. ☎01872 572454 🖥www.perranporthgolfclub.com **7 E6**

Porthpean GC *St Austell* An 18-hole course overlooking St Austell Bay. ☎01726 64613 **8 E3**

St Mellion Hotel G&CC *St Mellion* Two 18-hole courses, the Nicklaus Course and the Old Course set in East Cornish woodland ☎01579 351351 🖥www.st-mellion.co.uk **10 B3**

Tregenna Castle Hotel *St Ives* An 18-hole course overlooking St Ives Bay. ☎01736 795254 **3 C6**

Whitsand Bay Hotel *Portwrinkle* 18-hole course on with views over Whitesand Bay. ☎01503 230470 **10 E3**

Devon

Ashbury GC *Okehampton* Four 18-hole courses set in woodland: Pines, Beeches, Oakwood and Willows (par 3) ☎01837 55453 🖥www.ashburygolfhotel.com **19 B8**

Bigbury GC *Bigbury-on-Sea* 18-hole course overlooking the River Avon. ☎01548 810055 🖥www.bigburygolfclub.com **12 C4**

Dainton Park GC *Ipplepen* An 18-hole parkland course in East Devon. ☎01803 815000 🖥www.daintonparkgolf.co.uk **14 B4**

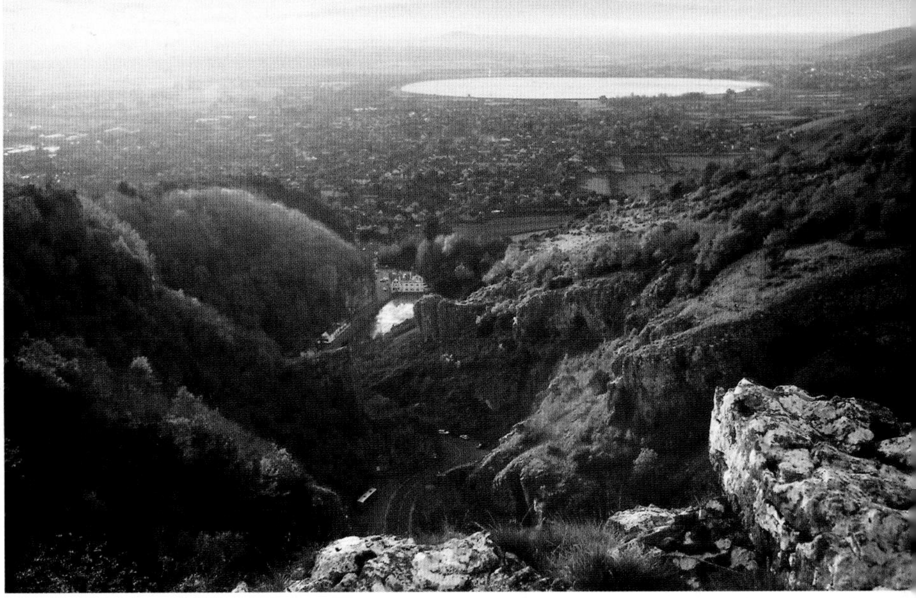

▲ **Cheddar Gorge, Somerset**

East Devon GC *Budleigh Salterton* 18-hole links course over looking the English Channel. ☎01395 443370 🖥www.edgc.co.uk **22 D2**

Exminster Golf Centre *Exminster* A 9-hole course and floodlit driving range overlooking the River Exe. ☎01392 833838 🖥www.exminstergolf.com **21 C8**

Fingle Glen GC* *Tedburn St Mary* An 18-hole course near the northern edge of Dartmoor. ☎01647 61817 🖥www.fingleglen.com **21 B6**

High Bullen GC* *Chittlehamholt* 18-hole course in wooded parkland ☎01769 540561, 🖥www.highbullen.co.uk **33 B6**

Holsworthy GC* *Killatree, Holsworthy* An 18-hole course in northwest Devon. ☎01409 253177 **31 F6**

Honiton GC* *Honiton* An 18-hole course in the East Devon hills ☎01404 44422 **23 A5**

Hurdwick GC *Tavistock* An 18-hole course near the western edge of Dartmoor. ☎01822 612746 **19 F6**

Ilfracombe GC* *Ilfracombe* An 18-hole course in moorland above high cliffs overlooking the Bristol Channel. ☎01271 862176 🖥www.ilfracombegolfclub.com **43 B5**

Newton Abbot (Stover) GC* *Stover* An 18-hole woodland course near the edge of Dartmoor. ☎01626 352460 🖥www.stovergolfclub.co.uk **14 A4**

Okehampton GC* *Okehampton* An 18-hole course near the northern edge of Dartmoor. ☎01837 52113 🖥www.okehamptongc.co.uk **19 B8**

Royal North Devon GC* *Westward Ho!* An 18-hole links course in a popular resort. ☎01237 473824 🖥www.royalnorthdevongolfclub.co.uk **42 F3**

Saunton GC* *Saunton* Two 18-hole links courses (East and West) by the sands of Braunton Burrows. ☎01271 812436 🖥www.sauntongolf.co.uk **42 D4**

Sidmouth GC* *Sidmouth* An 18-hole course on the edge of a popular resort. ☎01395 513023 🖥www.sidmouthgolfclub.co.uk **22 C4**

Tavistock GC *Tavistock* An 18-hole course on the edge of Dartmoor. ☎01822 612344 **19 F6**

Teignmouth GC* *Teignmouth* An 18-hole course overlooking the Teign. ☎01626 777070 🖥www.teignmouthgolfclubltd.co.uk **21 E8**

Thurlestone GC* *Thurlestone* An 18-hole course next to Warren Point. ☎01548 560405 🖥www.thurlestonegc.co.uk **12 D4**

Tiverton GC* *Tiverton* An 18-hole lowland course. ☎01884 252114 **34 D4**

Warren GC* *Dawlish Warren* An 18-hole links course on the promontary of Dawlish Warren ☎01626 862255 🖥www.dwgc.co.uk **22 E1**

Waterbridge GC *Down St Mary* A 9-hole course in the heart of Devon. ☎01363 85111 **33 F8**

Woodbury Park GC* *Woodbury* Two courses: the 18-hole Oaks and the 9-hole Acorn. ☎01395 233500 **22 C2**

Wrangaton GC *Wrangaton* An 18-hole course on the southern edge of Dartmoor. ☎01364 73229 🖥www.wrangatongolfclub.co.uk **14 D1**

Yelverton GC* *Yelverton* An 18-hole course on the heights of Roboough Down. ☎01822 852824 **11 B6**

Dorset

Bridport & West Dorset GC* *Bridport* An 18-hole course with a 9-hole pitch and put. ☎01308 421095/422597 🖥www.bridportgolfclub.org.uk **24 B4**

Broadstone GC* *Broadstone* An 18-hole course on the on the hills behind Poole Harbour. ☎01202 692595 🖥www.broadstonegolfclub.com **27 A7**

Bulbury Woods GC *Lytchett Matravers* 18-hole course on the edge of Wareham Forest. ☎01929 459574 🖥www.bulbury-woods.co.uk **27 B5**

Canford Magna GC *Canford Magna* Three courses: the 18-hole Parkland and Riverside and the 9-hole Knighton. ☎01202 592552 🖥www.canfordmagnagc.co.uk **27 A7**

Chedington Court GC* *South Perrott* An 18-hole course in the north Dorset hills. ☎01935 891413 **37 E7**

Christchurch GC *Bournemouth* Two courses, one 18-hole and the other a 9-hole short course. ☎01202 436436 **28 B3**

Crane Valley GC* *Verwood* Two courses: the 18-hole Valley and the 9-hole Woodland. ☎01202 814088 **40 E4**

Dudsbury GC* *Ferndown* Tel 01202 593499 🖥www.thedudsbury.co.uk **27 A8**

Ferndown Forest GC *Ferndown* An 18-hole links course on the edge of Ferndown Forest. ☎01202 876096 🖥www.ferndownforestgolf.co.uk **40 F4**

Ferndown GC* *Ferndown* A heathland links with the 18-hole Championship course and the 9-hole Presidents course. ☎01202 874602 🖥www.ferndown-golf-club.co.uk **27 A8**

Halstock GC* *Halstock* An 18-hole woodland course in the hills of north Dorset. ☎01935 891689 **37 E8**

Highcliffe Castle GC* *Highcliffe-on-Sea* An 18-hole course overlooking Christchurch Bay. ☎01425 272210/272953 **28 B3**

Isle of Purbeck* *Studland* Two courses: the 18-hole Purbeck course and the 9-hole Dene course. ☎01929 450361 🖥www.purbeckgolf.co.uk **27 D7**

Lyme Regis GC* *Lyme Regis* An 18-hole course at one end of Lyme Bay. ☎01297 442963 🖥www.lymeregisgolfclub.co.uk **23 B8**

Sherborne GC* *Sherborne* An 18-hole course on the hills north of Sherborne. ☎01935 812274 **38 C2**

The Ashley Wood GC* *Blandford Forum* An 18-hole course set on the Dorset Downs. ☎01258 452253 🖥www.ashleywoodgolfclub.com **39 E8**

Wareham GC* *Wareham* An 18-hole heathland course. ☎01929 554147 🖥www.warehamgolfclub.com **27 C5**

Weymouth GC* *Weymouth* An 18-hole links course in the hills between Weymouth and Dorchester. ☎01305 773981 🖥www.weymouthgolfclub.co.uk **25 E8**

Gloucestershire

Cleeve Hill GC *Cheltenham* An 18-hole course on the edge of the Cotswolds. ☎01242 672025 🖥www.cleevehill.com **71 B5**

Cotswold Edge GC* *Wotton-under-Edge* 18- hole course in the Cotwolds. ☎01453 844167 🖥www.cotswoldedgegolfclub.org.uk **63 D7**

Cotswold Hills GC* *Ullenwood* An 18-hole woodland course. ☎01242 515264 🖥www.cotswoldhills-golfclub.com **70 D4**

Forest Hills GC* *Coleford* An 18-hole parkland course. ☎01594 810620 🖥www.foresthillsgolfclub.co.uk **69 E5**

Forest of Dean GC* *Coleford* An 18-hole course on the edge of the Forest of Dean. ☎01594 832583 **69 E5**

Lilley Brook GC* *Cheltenham* An 18-hole course on the edge of the Cotswolds overlooking Cheltenham. ☎01242 526785 **71 D5**

Minchinhampton GC* *Minchinhampton* Three courses: the Old, the Avening and the Cherington (all 18 holes) ☎01453 833840 **64 B2**

Painswick GC* *Painswick* An 18-hole course at the foot of Painswick Hill. ☎01452 812180 🖥www.painswickgolf.com **70 E3**

Rodway Hill GC* *Highnam* 18-hole Championship-length course set between woodland and the Vale of Gloucester. ☎01452 384222 🖥www.rodway-hill-golf-course.co.uk **70 C1**

Shirehampton Park GC* *Shirehampton* An 18-hole parkland course. ☎0117 982 2083 🖥www.shirehamptonparkgolfclub.co.uk **56 A2**

Stinchcombe Hill GC* *Dursley* An 18-hole course on the edge of the Cotswolds ☎01453 542015 **63 C6**

The Gloucestershire GC* *Tracy Park Estate, Wick* Two courses: the Crown and the Cromwell (both 18 holes) ☎0117 937 2251 🖥www.thegloucestershire.com **57 B6**

Thornbury Golf Centre* *Thornbury* Two courses: High and Low (both 18 holes), and a driving range. ☎01454 281144 **62 E4**

Woodlands G&CC *Almondsbury* An 18-hole woodland course. ☎01454 619319 🖥www.woodlands-golf.com **62 F4**

Plymouth

Staddon Heights GC* *Plymstock* An 18-hole course on high ground overlooking Plymouth Sound. ☎01752 402475 **11 E5**

Somerset

Bath GC* *Bath* 18-hole downland course on hills east of the city. ☎01225 425182 🖥www.bathgolfclub.org.uk **57 C7**

Burnham & Berrow GC* *Burnham-on-Sea* Two courses: 18-hole Championship course and 9-hole Channel course ☎01278 783137 **47 A5**

Clevedon GC* *Clevedon* 18-hole course overlooking the Severn Estuary. ☎01275 874057 **55 B8**

Enmore Park GC* *Enmore* 18-hole course on the edge of the Quantock Hills. ☎01278 672100 **46 D4**

Frome GC *Frome* 18-hole course in rolling countryside. ☎01373 453410 🖥www.fromegolfclub.fsnet.co.uk **48 B7**

Isle of Wedmore GC* *Wedmore* 18-hole course set in the Somerset levels with panoramic views of the levels and the surrounding hills. ☎01934 712452 ⌨www.wedmoregolfclub.com **47 B8**

Lansdown GC* *Bath* An 18-hole course on the heights above Bath. ☎01225 422138 ⌨www.lansdowngolfclub.co.uk **57 B6**

Long Ashton GC* *Long Ashton* An 18-hole course in open, hilly country. ☎01275 392229 ⌨www.longashtongolfclub.co.uk **56 B2**

Long Sutton GC* *Long Load* An 18-hole parkland course set in rolling countryside. ☎01458 241017 ⌨www.longsuttongolf.com **37 B7**

Mendip Spring GC* *Congresbury* Two courses: the 18-hole Brinsea and the 9-hole Lakeside. ☎01934 853337 **55 D8**

Minehead & West Somerset GC* *Minehead* An 18-hole course close to the seafront and town centre. ☎01643 702057 ⌨www.mineheadgolf.co.uk **45 B6**

Orchardleigh GC* *Frome* An 18-hole parkland course. ☎01373 454200 **49 A7**

Stockwood Vale GC* *Keynsham* An 18-hole undulating parkland course. ☎0117 986 6505 **56 C4**

Taunton Vale GC* *Creech Heathfield* Two courses: the 18-hole Charlton course and the 9-hole Durston course. ☎01823 412220 ⌨www.tauntonvalegolf.co.uk **?? ??**

Vivary GC *Taunton* 18-hole course in Vivary Park. ☎01823 289274 **47 F5**

Wells GC* *Wells* 18-hole course on the eastern edge of the town, overlooking the Somerset Levels. ☎01749 675005 **48 B3**

Wheathill GC *Wheathill* 18-hole course on the edge of the Somerset Levels. ☎01963 240667 **48 E3**

Windwhistle GC* *Cricket St Thomas* An 18-hole course on a ridge with amazing panoramic views. ☎01460 30231 ⌨www.windwhistlegolf.co.uk **36 E5**

Yeovil GC* *Yeovil* Two courses: the 18-hole Old course and the 9-hole Newton course. ☎01935 475949 **38 C1**

Torbay

Torquay GC* *St Marychurch* An 18-hole course on the northern edge of Torbay with views over Babbacombe Bay. ☎01803 327471 ⌨www.torquaygolfclub.org.uk **15 B6**

Wiltshire

Bowood G&CC* *Derry Hill* An 18-hole course set in undulating parkland. ☎01249 822228 ⌨www.bowood.org **58 B4**

Brinkworth GC *Brinkworth* A welcoming 18-hole course below the Marlborough Downs. ☎01666 510277 **64 E5**

Erlestoke GC* *Erlestoke* 18-hole course set in a blend of lakes and woodland ☎01380 831069 ⌨www.erlestokegolfclub.co.uk **58 F4**

High Post GC* *Salisbury* An 18-hole course in the downland north of Salisbury. ☎01722

782356 ⌨www.highpostgolfclub.co.uk **51 F7**

Marlborough GC* *Marlborough* An 18-hole club set in the rolling countryside of the Marlborough Downs. ☎01672 512147 ⌨www.marlboroughgolfclub.com **59 B8**

North Wilts GC *Bishops Cannings* An 18-hole course set on the western edge of the Wessex Downs. ☎01380 860257 ⌨www.northwiltsgolf.com **58 C5**

Ogbourne Downs GC* *Ogbourne St George* An 18-hole course in the Wessex Downs. ☎01672 841327 **59 B8**

Rushmore Golf Club GC *Tollard Royal* An 18-hole Championship course set in parkland surrounded by Cranborne Chase. ☎01725 516326 ⌨www.rushmoregolfclub.co.uk **40 C2**

Salisbury & South Wilts GC* *Netherhampton* Two courses: the 18-hole main and the 9-hole Bibury. ☎01722 742645 **51 F7**

Upavon GC* *Upavon* An 18-hole course on the south edge of the Wiltshire downs. ☎01980 630787 ⌨www.upavongolfclub.co.uk **59 F7**

West Wilts GC* *Warminster* An 18-hole course on the edge of Salisbury Plain. ☎01985 213133 ⌨www.westwiltsgolfclub.co.uk **50 B2**

Wrag Barn G&CC* *Highworth* An 18-hole downland course overlooking the Thames Valley. ☎01793 861327 ⌨www.wragbarn.com **65 D8**

Horse Racing

Bath & NE Somerset

Bath Racecourse *Bath* Several flat meetings during spring, summer and autumn ☎01225 424609 ⌨www.bath-racecourse.co.uk **57 C6**

Devon

Exeter Racecourse *Exeter* National Hunt racing takes place throughout the autumn, winter, spring and early summer. ☎01392 832999 ⌨www.exeter-racecourse.co.uk **21 D8**

Newton Abbot Racecourse *Newton Abbot* National Hunt racing throughout the year. ☎01626 353235 ⌨www.newtonabbotracing.com **15 A5**

Gloucestershire

Cheltenham Racecourse *Cheltenham* There are 16 National Hunt meetings throughout the year, including the world-famous Festival in spring. ☎01242 513014 ⌨www.cheltenham.co.uk **71 C5**

Somerset

Taunton Racecourse *Taunton* National Hunt meetings are held here during autumn, winter and spring. ☎01823 325035 ⌨www.tauntonracecourse.co.uk **36 B2**

▲ Canoeing, Plymouth

Wiltshire

Salisbury Racecourse *Netherhampton* Flat meetings take place during spring, summer and autumn. ☎01722 326461 ⌨www.salisburyracecourse.co.uk **51 F7**

Motor Sports

Bristol

The Raceway *Bristol* A 450-m (1475-ft) indoor karting circuit. ☎0800 376 6111 ⌨www.theraceway.co.uk **56 A2**

Cornwall

Menheniot Supertrack *Menheniot* An outdoor circuit. ☎01579 347229 **9 C8**

St Eval Kart Circuit *St Eval* A 1-km (½ mile) outdoor circuit. ☎01637 860160 **6 B2**

Devon

Raceworld *Woodbury Salterton* A 280-m (918-ft) indoor circuit. ☎01395 233397 ⌨www.raceworld-karting.co.uk **22 C2**

Dorset

Circuit Chevron *Pidletrenthide* An outdoor circuit, 250 m (820 ft) in length. ☎01300 348499 **38 F8**

Indoor Karting Centre *Christchurch* A 200-m (656-ft) indoor circuit. ☎01202 570022 **28 A2**

Gloucestershire

JDR Karting *Gloucester* An indoor circuit, 280 m (918 ft) in length. ☎01452 311211 ⌨www.jdrkarting.co.uk **70 D2**

West Country Karting *Bradley Stoke* An outdoor circuit, 350 m (1148 ft) in length. ☎01454 202666 ⌨www.westcountrykarting.co.uk **62 F8**

Somerset

Somerset Pro Karting *Westonzoyland* A 700-m outdoor circuit. ☎01278 691953 **47 E7**

Wiltshire

Wessex Raceway Indoor Karting *Coombe Bisset* An indoor circuit, 750 m (2297 ft) in length. ☎01725 519 599 ⌨www.wessexraceway.co.uk **40 A5**

Riding

There are numerous stables and riding schools located throughout the southwest. Consult local directories or information centres.

Rugby clubs

Bath & NE Somerset

Bath Rugby *Bath* ☎01225 325200 ⌨www.bathrugby.co.uk **57 C7**

Bristol

Bristol Rugby *Horfield* ☎0117 952 0500 ⌨www.bristolrugby.co.uk **56 A3**

Gloucester

Gloucester Rugby *Gloucester* ☎0871 871 87 81 ⌨www.gloucesterrugby.co.uk **70 D2**

Water sports

Bath & NE Somerset

Bath and Dundas Canal Co. *Bath* Day boat hire, canoe hire, bike hire. ☎01225 722292 ⌨www.bathcanal.com **57 C7**

Bath Boating Station *Bath* Hire a rowing boat, punt or canoe. ☎01225 466407 ⌨www.bathboating.co.uk **57 C7**

Bath Narrowboats *Bath* Narrowboat hire ☎01225 447276 ⌨www.bath-narrowboats.co.uk **57 C7**

Bristol

West Country Waterpark *Bristol* Windsurfing, jet and water skiing, shooting and canoeing. ☎01454 773599 ⌨www.westcoastsurfari.com **56 B4**

Cornwall

Adventure Sports *Redruth* BSA-approved surfing school ☎01209 218962 **4 B2**

BSA National Surfing Center *Newquay* BSA surfing school ☎01637 850737 ⌨www.nationalsurfingcentre.co.uk **7 C6**

Cornish Cruising *Falmouth* Yachts available. ☎01386 211800 ⌨www.cornishcruising.com **4 D4**

Coverack Windsurfing Centre *Coverack* Holidays and windsurfing courses to all standards. ☎01326 280939 ⌨www.coverack.co.uk **5 G3**

Dolphin Surf School *Newquay* BSA-approved surfing school ☎01637 873707 ⌨www.surfschool.co.uk **7 C7**

ESF Surf School *Newquay* BSA-approved surfing school ☎01637 879571 ⌨www.englishsurfschool.com **7 E6**

Eves of St Mawes & Bluebell Classic Sailing Ltd *Portscatho* Traditional sailing boats. ☎01872 58 00 22 **5 C5**

Falmouth School of Sailing *Falmouth* ☎01326 211311 **4 D4**

Fowey Cruising and Sailing School *Fowey* Skippered holidays. ☎01840 770990 **9 E5**

Harlyn Bay Surf School *Padstow* BSA-approved surfing school ☎01841 533076 ⌨www.harlynsurf.co.uk **16 E3**

Killarney Springs *Bude* See 'Activity Centres' **30 E4**

Red River Surf School *Hayle* BSA-approved surfing school ☎01209 713687 **3 C7**

Reef Surf School *Newquay* BSA-approved surfing school ☎01637 879058 ⌨www.reefsurfschool.com **7 C7**

Roadford Lakes Angling & Watersports Centre *Nr Launceston* Canoeing, sailing, windsurfing and archery. Rowing boats to hire. Visitor centre. ☎01409 211507 **18 D3**

Seven Bays Surf School *Newquay* BSA-approved surfing school ☎01841 521314 **7 C7**

Shore Surf School *St Ives Bay* BSA-approved surfing school ☎01736 755556 ⌨www.shoresurf.com **3 B6**

Siblyback Watersports *Nr Liskeard* Play area, sailing, trout fishing, wind surfing, sailing, canoeing, rowing boats for hire. ☎01579 346522 **9 C8**

Stithians Lake *Redruth* Windsurfing, canoeing, trout fishing, boat hire, sailing. ☎01209 860301 **4 B2**

Surf's up *Polzeath* BSA-approved surfing school ☎01208 862003 ⌨www.surfsupsurfschool.com **16 E3**

Tamar Watersports Centre *Kilkhampton* Sailing, windsurfing and canoeing. ☎01288 321712 **31 D5**

Trysail *Falmouth* ☎01326 212320 ⌨www.trysail.net **4 D4**

West Coast Surfari *Newquay* BSA-approved surfing school ☎01637 876083 **7 C7**

Devon

Beam House PGL Adventure *Nr Bideford* BSA-approved surfing school ☎01805 622992 ⌨www.pgl.co.uk **42 F3**

Big Blue Surf School *Bideford* BSA-approved surfing school ☎01288 331764 ⌨www.bigbluesurfschool.co.uk **42 F3**

Canoe Adventures *Totnes* ☎01803 36530 **14 C4**

River Maid Motor Launch Service *Kingsbridge* ☎01548 853525 **13 D5**

Saddles and Paddles *Exeter* Canoeing. See 'Cycling'. **21 B8**

Salcombe Boat Hire *Salcombe* ☎01548 844475 **13 E5**

Salcombe Powerboat School *Salcombe* Sailing, powerboating and canoeing. ☎015-42 ⌨www.salcombepowerboats.co.uk **13 E5**

Start Point Sailing *Ringmore* ☎01548 810917 ⌨www.sail-west.co.uk **12 C4**

Surf Seekers *Woolacombe* BSA-approved surfing school ☎07977 924588 **42 C4**

Surf South West *Croyde Bay* BSA-approved surfing school ☎01271 890400 ⌨www.surfsouthwest.com **42 D3**

Surfrider Action Holidays *Woolacombe* BSA-approved surfing school ☎01271 870365 **42 C4**

Whitestrand Boat Hire *Salcombe* ☎01548 843818 **13 E5**

Gloucestershire

Cotswold Water Park, Keynes Country Park *Cirencester* See Country Parks **65 B5**

Dartmouth Yacht Cruise School *Bussage* Yacht hire. ☎01803 863162 ⌨www.dycs.net **64 B2**

Glevum Boat Hire *Slimbridge* Self-drive narrowboat hire ☎01453 899190 ⌨www.glevum-boat-hire.co.uk **63 B6**

Plymouth

Carter Boat hire *Plymouth* Boat hire ☎01752 872189 **10 E5**

Dittisham Sailing School *Totnes* Sailing tuition. Daily and weekly hire of boats and dingies. ☎01803 722365 **14 C4**

Mount Batten Centre *Plymouth* Sailing and watersports ☎01752 404567 ⌨www.mbc.eclipse.co.uk **10 E5**

Plymouth Boat Cruises Ltd *Plymouth* ☎01752 822797 **10 E5**

Plymouth Sailing School *Plymouth* ☎01752 493377 ⌨www.plymsail.demon.co.uk **10 E5**

Portway Yacht Charters *Plymouth* ☎01752 606999 ⌨www.portwayyachtcharters.co.uk **10 E5**

Southdown Yacht Club, Sea School & Charter Co. Ltd *Plymouth* ☎01752 822925 **10 E5**

Tamar Cruising *Plymouth* ☎01752 822105 ⌨www.tamarcruising.com **10 E5**

Somerset

Wimbleball Lake *Dulverton* Sailing, fishing, camping. ☎01398 371460 **45 F5**

Torbay

Plain Sailing *Brixham* Channel crossings, weekend breaks. ☎01803 853843 ⌨www.plainsailing.co.uk **15 D6**

Windsurfing off the Dorset coast

Orkney Islands

Lewis

Outer Hebrides

Harris

North Uist

Skye

South Uist

Inner Hebrides

Durness · Thurso · Wick
Ledmore
Ullapool
Kincardine
Achnasheen
Invergordon · Elgin · Fraserburgh · Peterhead
Inverness
Gairloch
Uig
Kyle of Lochalsh
Mallaig
Newtonmore
Aberdeen
Fort William
Braemar
Montrose
S C O T L A N D
Oban · Crianlarich · Perth · Forfar · Arbroath
Dundee
St. Andrews
Glenrothes
Stirling · Kirkcaldy · Dunfermline
Greenock · Clydebank · Falkirk · Cumbernauld
Edinburgh
Glasgow · Coatbridge · Airdrie · Livingston
Paisley · East Kilbride · Motherwell · Peebles · Berwick-upon-Tweed
Largs · Irvine · Kilmarnock · Coldstream · Galashiels
Arran · Ayr · Sanquhar · Hawick · Jedburgh · Alnwick
Campbeltown · Girvan · Moffat · Morpeth · Ashington
Islay · Jura · Mull · Newton Stewart · Dumfries · Ashington
Stranraer · Cairnryan · Castle Douglas · Gretna · **Newcastle-upon-Tyne** · Tynemouth · South Shields
Carlisle · Hexham · Gateshead · **Sunderland** · Washington
Workington · Keswick · Penrith · Durham · Hartlepool
Whitehaven · Ambleside · Windermere · Kendal · **Stockton-on-Tees** · Redcar
Barrow-in-Furness · Brough · **Middlesbrough** · Whitby
E N G L A N D · Northallerton · Scarborough
Morecambe · Ripon · Bridlington
Lancaster · Skipton · Harrogate · York
Fleetwood · Clitheroe · Keighley · Selby · **Kingston upon Hull**
Blackpool · **Bradford** · **Leeds** · Goole · Grimsby
Preston · Blackburn · Halifax · Dewsbury · Wakefield · Scunthorpe
Southport · Burnley · Rochdale · **Huddersfield** · Barnsley · Doncaster
Crosby · **Bolton** · Bury · Oldham · Rotherham · Gainsborough
St. Helens · Salford · **Manchester** · **Sheffield** · Lincoln
Wallasey · **Liverpool** · **Stockport** · Worksop · Skegness
Holyhead · **Birkenhead** · **Warrington** · Macclesfield · Chesterfield · Mansfield
Llandudno · Runcorn · Northwich · Buxton · Newark-on-Trent · Boston
Anglesey · Conwy · Chester · Congleton · Matlock · Sleaford
Bangor · Ellesmere Port · **Stoke-on-Trent** · **Derby** · Grantham · Spalding · King's Lynn
Caernarfon · Betws-y-Coed · Whitchurch · Newcastle-under-Lyme · **Nottingham** · Melton Mowbray · Cromer
Queensferry · Wrexham · Stafford · Loughborough · Stamford · Wisbech · Great Yarmouth
Porthmadog · Bala · Llangollen · Burton-upon-Trent · **Leicester** · Oakham · Peterborough · **Norwich**
Oswestry · Shrewsbury · Lichfield · Corby · Diss · Lowestoft
Dolgellau · **Telford** · **Walsall** · Market Harborough · Thetford · Beccles
Welshpool · **Wolverhampton** · **West Bromwich** · **Coventry** · Kettering · Ely · Bury St. Edmunds · **Ipswich**
Machynlleth · Newtown · **Dudley** · Solihull · **Northampton** · Wellingborough · Newmarket · Harwich
Aberystwyth · Llanidloes · W A L E S · **Birmingham** · Warwick · St. Neots · Cambridge · Sudbury · Felixstowe
Rhayader · Kidderminster · Redditch · Stratford-upon-Avon · Bedford · Colchester
Llandrindod Wells · Worcester · Evesham · Banbury · **Milton Keynes** · **Luton** · Stevenage · Clacton-on-Sea
Builth Wells · Ledbury · **Milton Keynes** · Dunstable · Hemel Hempstead · Bishop's Stortford
Cardigan · Llandovery · Hereford · Cheltenham · Aylesbury · St. Albans · Chelmsford · Brentwood
Fishguard · Brecon · Ross-on-Wye · Gloucester · Oxford · High Wycombe · Watford · Harlow · **Basildon**
Haverfordwest · Carmarthen · Llandeilo · Abergavenny · Monmouth · Cirencester · Slough · **LONDON** · Tilbury · **Southend-on-Sea**
Milford Haven · St. Clears · Cwmbran · Chepstow · Stroud · Swindon · **Reading** · Croydon · Sheerness · Margate
Pembroke · Tenby · Llanelli · Neath · **Newport** · Bath · Newbury · Woking · Sevenoaks · **Maidstone** · Ramsgate
Swansea · Port Talbot · **Cardiff** · **Bristol** · Chippenham · Basingstoke · Guildford · Royal Tunbridge Wells · Canterbury
Bridgend · Weston-super-Mare · Trowbridge · Andover · Farnham · East Grinstead · Ashford · Dover · Folkestone
Minehead · Shepton Mallet · Frome · Warminster · Winchester · Alton · Crawley · Hawkhurst
Barnstaple · Glastonbury · Salisbury · Petersfield · Horsham · Lewes · Hastings
Bideford · Taunton · Yeovil · **Southampton** · Midhurst · **Brighton** · Eastbourne
Bude · Blandford Forum · Ringwood · Fareham · Chichester · Bognor Regis · Newhaven · Worthing
Launceston · Okehampton · Dorchester · **Portsmouth** · Gosport · Isle of Wight
Wadebridge · Tavistock · **Exeter** · **Poole** · **Bournemouth** · Weymouth
Newquay · Bodmin · Liskeard · Torquay · Paignton
Redruth · St. Austell · **Plymouth**
Penzance · Truro · Falmouth

Isles of Scilly

Isle of Man

N O R T H E R N I R E L A N D
Londonderry · Limavady · Coleraine · Ballymoney
Letterkenny · Strabane · Ballymena · Larne
Cookstown · Antrim · Carrickfergus
Belfast · Lisburn · Bangor · Newtownards
Armagh · Lurgan · Portadown · Saintfield · Ardglass
Newry · Newcastle
Warrenpoint

R E P U B L I C O F I R E L A N D
Dunfanaghy · Donegal · Ballina · Manorhamilton · Enniskillen · Monaghan · Carrickmacross · Dundalk
Sligo · Longford · Cavan · Drogheda · Balbriggan · Swords
Westport · Mullingar · Navan · Dunshaughlin · **Dublin**
Athlone · Lucan · Dun Laoghaire
Roscrea · Naas · Bray
Nenagh · Johnstone · Carlow · Wicklow
Cashel · Portlaoise · Kilkenny · Arklow
Clonmel · Carrick-on-Suir · New Ross · Enniscorthy · Gorey
Caher · Waterford · Wexford · Rosslare
Mitchelstown · Youghal

0   25   50   75   100 Miles
0   50   100   150 Kms

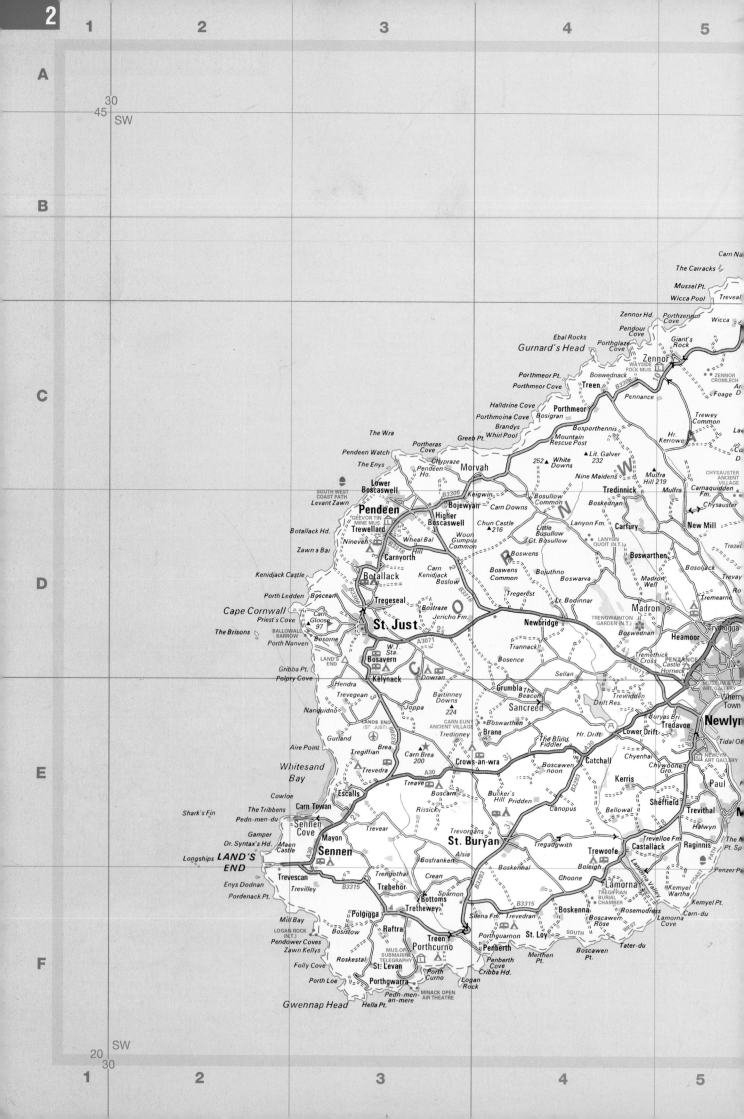

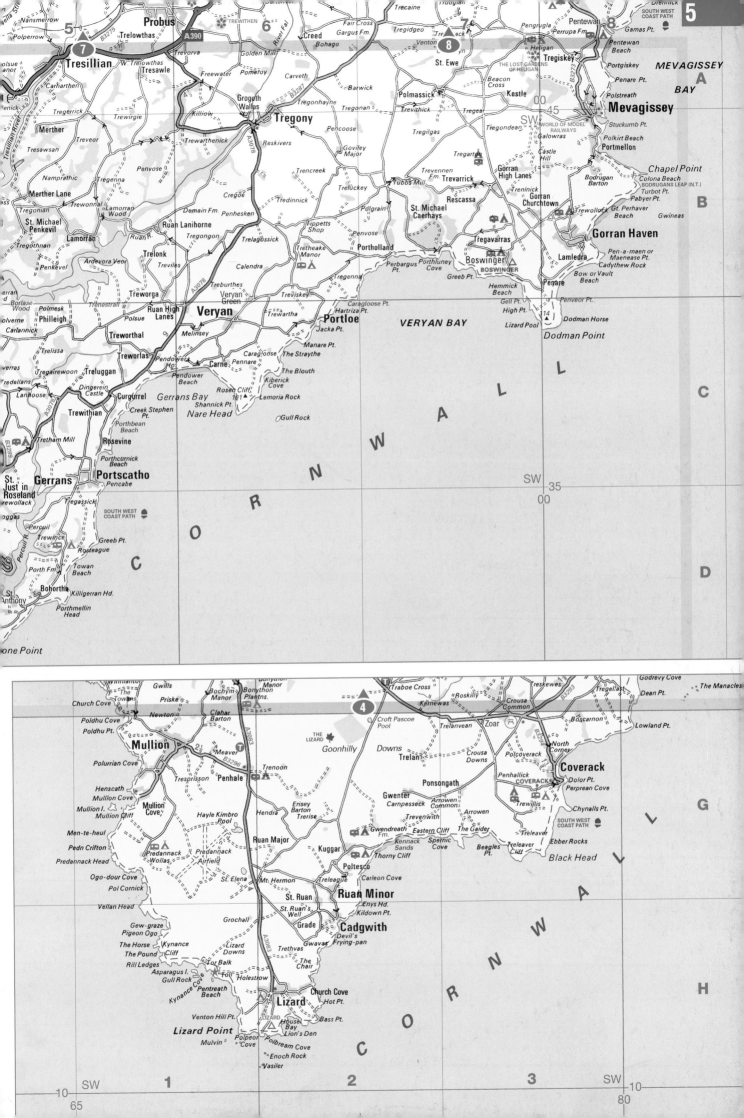

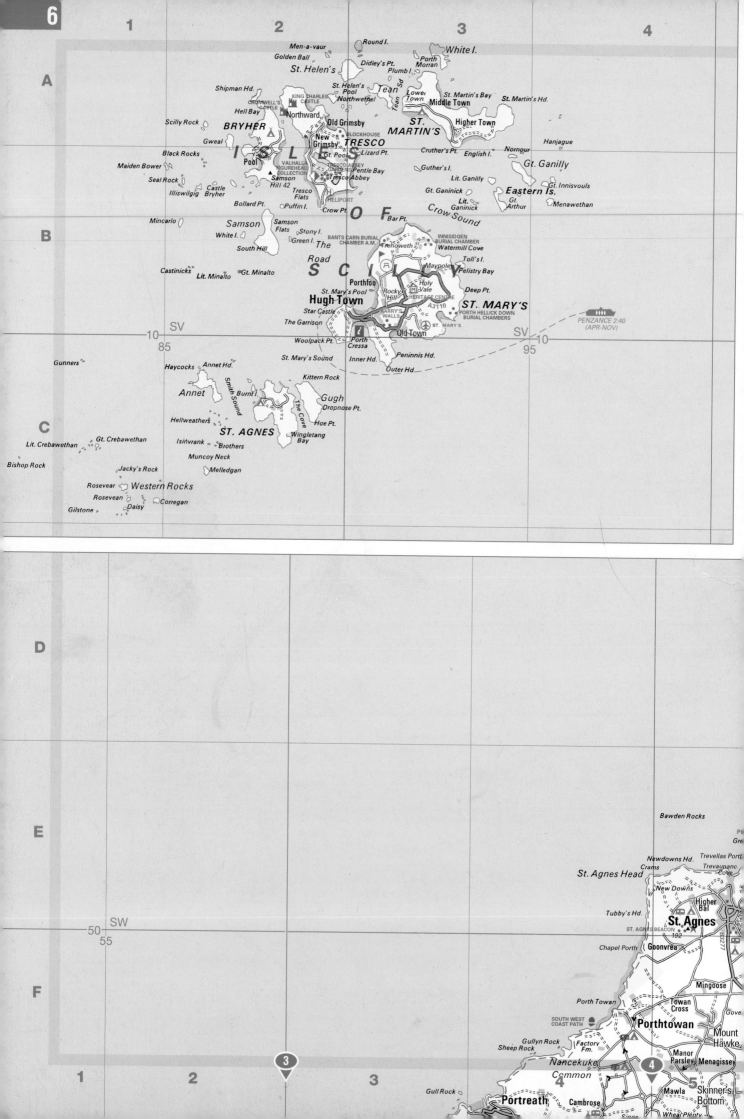

Isles of Scilly

A

Men-a-vaur
Round I.
White I.
Golden Ball
Didley's Pt.
Porth Morran
St. Helen's
Plumb I.
Shipman Hd.
St. Helen's Pool
Northwethel
Lower Town
St. Martin's Bay
St. Martin's Hd.
Hell Bay
KING CHARLES CASTLE
Middle Town
CROMWELL'S CASTLE
Scilly Rock
Northward
BRYHER
Old Grimsby
Higher Town
Gweal
New Grimsby
TRESCO
BLOCKHOUSE
ST. MARTIN'S
Black Rocks
I S L E S
Gt. Pool
Lizard Pt.
Maiden Bower
Pool
Cruther's Pt.
English I.
Hanjague
VALHALLA FIGUREHEAD COLLECTION
Pentle Bay
Norngur
Seal Rock
Samson
TRESCO ABBEY GARDENS
Guther's I.
Gt. Ganilly
Illiswilgig
Castle Bryher
Hill 42
Tresco Abbey
Gt. Ganinick
Gt. Innisvouls
Bollard Pt.
Tresco Flats
O F
Lit. Ganilly
Eastern Is.
Puffin I.
HELIPORT
Bar Pt.
Lit. Ganinick
Gt. Arthur
Menawethan
Crow Pt.
Crow Sound

B

Mincarlo
Samson Flats
Stony I.
BANTS CARN BURIAL CHAMBER A.M.
INNISIDGEN BURIAL CHAMBER
White I.
Green I.
S C I L L Y
Trehoweth
Watermill Cove
Samson Flats
The
Maypole
Toll's I.
Castinicks
Lit. Minalto
Gt. Minalto
South Hill
Road
Porthloo
Holy Vale
Pelistry Bay
St. Mary's Pool
Rocky Hill
Deep Pt.
Hugh Town
HERITAGE CENTRE
A3110
Star Castle
HARRY'S WALLS
ST. MARY'S
The Garrison
PORTH HELLICK DOWN BURIAL CHAMBERS
Woolpack Pt.
Old Town
ST. MARY'S
PENZANCE 2:40 (APR-NOV)
Porth Cressa
SV
SV
10
95
85

C

Gunners
Haycocks
Annet Hd.
Kittern Rock
St. Mary's Sound
Inner Hd.
Peninnis Hd.
Outer Hd.
Burnt I.
Annet
Smith Sound
Gugh
Dropnose Pt.
Hellweathers
The Cove
Hoe Pt.
ST. AGNES
Wingletang Bay
Lit. Crebawethan
Gt. Crebawethan
Isinvrank
Brothers
Bishop Rock
Muncoy Neck
Melledgan
Jacky's Rock
Rosevear
Western Rocks
Rosevean
Daisy
Corregan
Gilstone

D

E

Bawden Rocks
Newdowns Hd.
Trevellas Porth
Crams
Trevaunance Cove
St. Agnes Head
New Downs
Higher Bal
Tubby's Hd.
St. Agnes
ST. AGNES BEACON 192
SW
Chapel Porth
Goonvrea
50
55

F

Mingoose
Towan Cross
Porth Towan
SOUTH WEST COAST PATH
Porthtowan
Mount Hawke
Gullyn Rock
Factory Fm.
Sheep Rock
Nancekuke
Manor Parsley
Menagissey
Common
Gove
Gull Rock
Mawla
Skinner's Bottom
Portreath
Cambrose
③

1   2   3   4   5

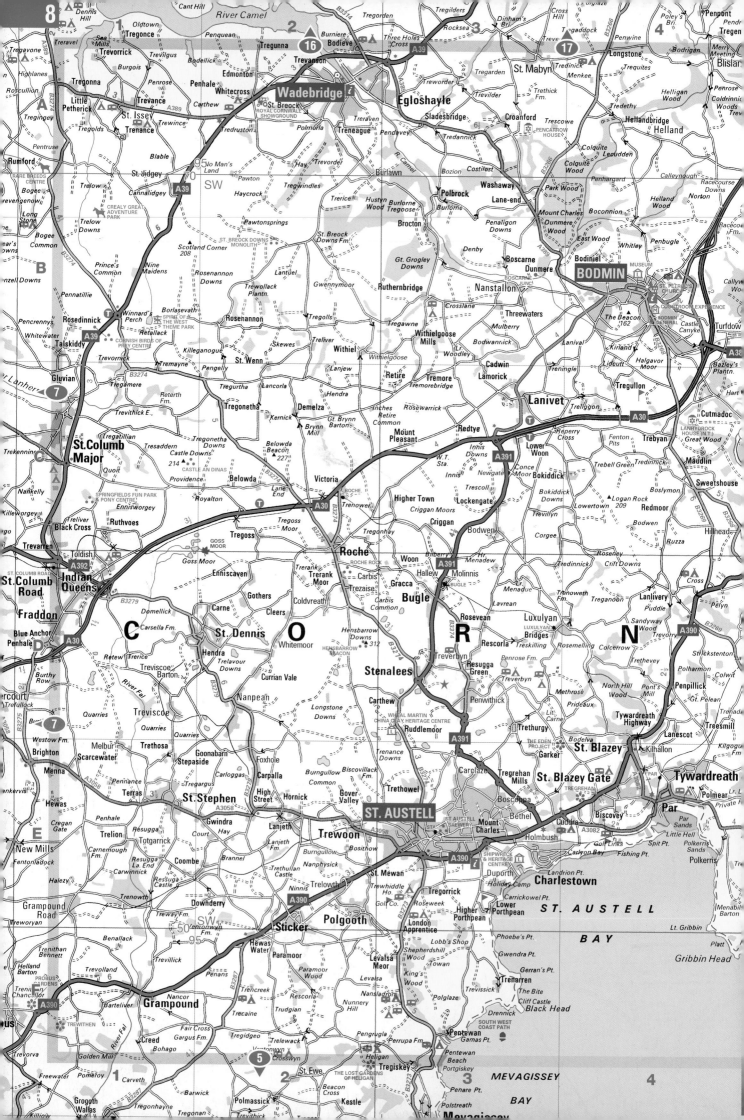

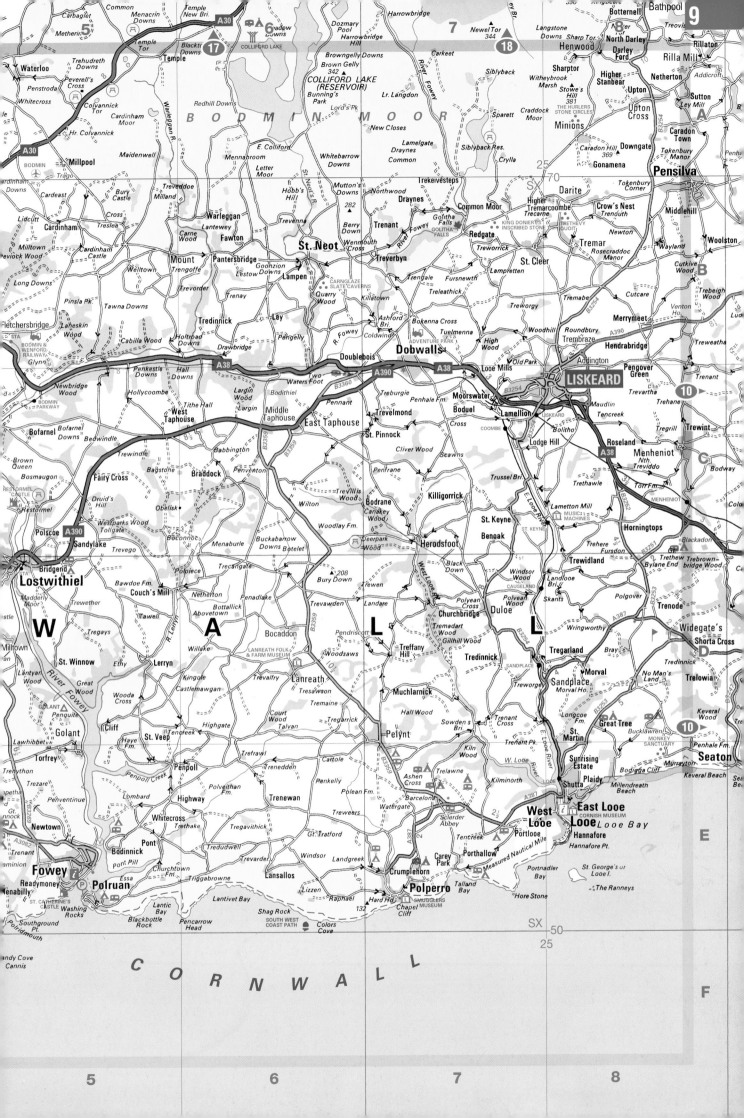

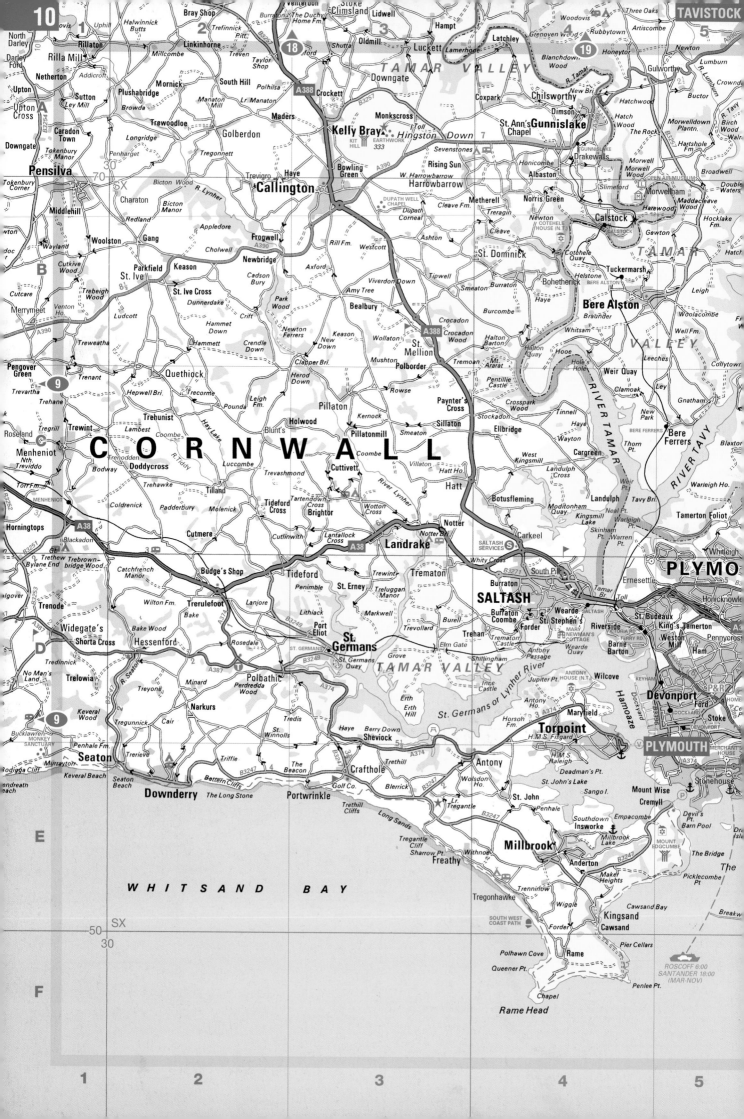

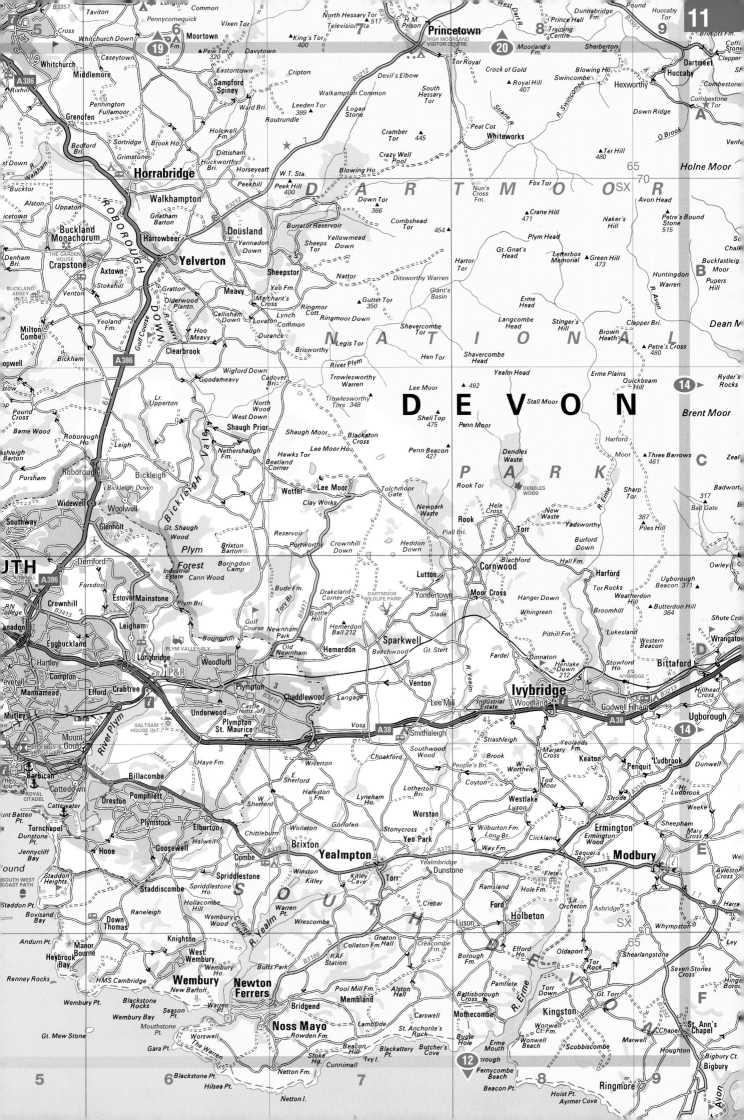

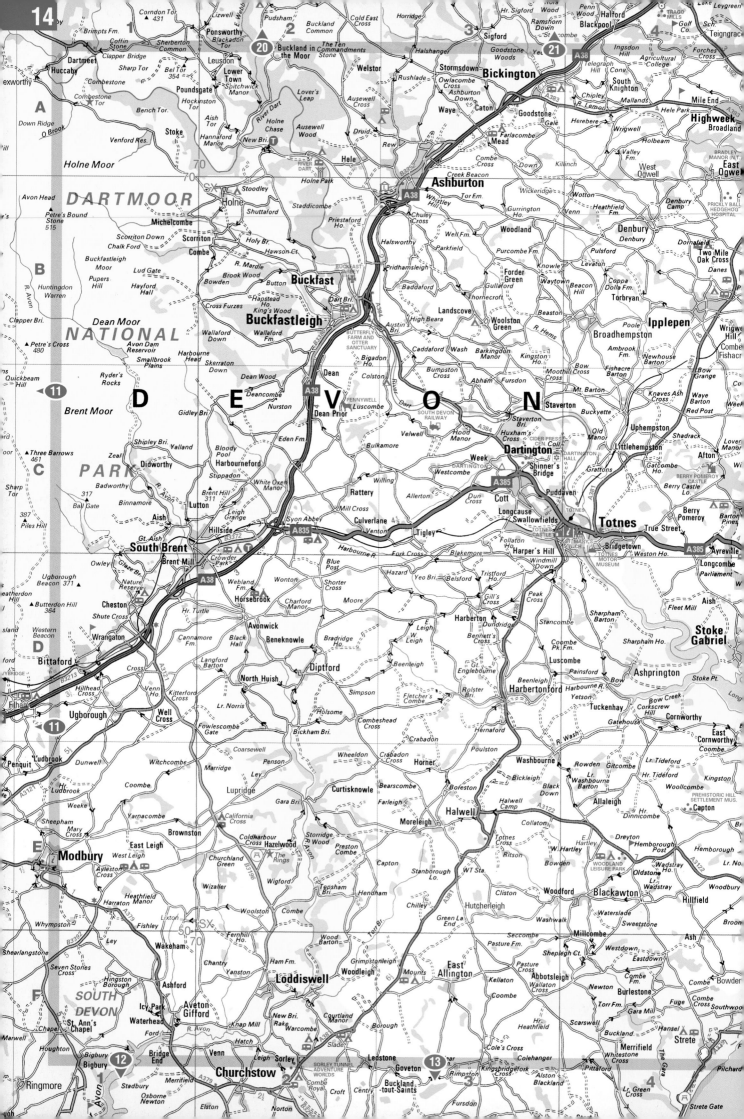

1　　　2　　　3　　　4　　　5

85
00
SW

A

B

C

D

Port Isaac Bay
Delabo
Barrett's Za
Ranie Pt

The Mouls
Varley Hd.
Tresungers Pt.

Newland
Rumps Pt.
Kellan Hd.
Scarnor Pt.
Pine Lobber
Haven Pt.

Pentire Point
83
Port Quin Bay
Doyden Pt.
Portquin
Port Isaac
Portgaverne

Com Head
Carnweather Pt.
Trevan Pt.
Castle
Roscarrock
LONG CROSS
VICTORIAN GDNS.
Trefreock
Trewetha
Treore

Pentire Fm.
Pentireglaze
Porteath
Scarrabine
B3267

Pentireglaze
Haven
Hayle Bay
New Polzeath
Trelights
Tresungers

Padstow Bay
The
Carruan
Mesmear
Plain
Street
B3314
St. Endellion
B3314
Treharrc

Gulland Rock
Stepper Pt.
Polzeath
Shilla Mill
Treglines
Convena Fm.
Treswarrow
Trevinnick

Pepper Hole
Butter Hole
Trebetherick
Rosewin
Trevathan
Tregellist

E

SOUTH WEST
COAST PATH
Gunver Hd.
Lellizzick
Hawker's Cove
Daymer Bay
St. Enodoc Ch.
Trewint
Trevanger
Tredrizzick
St. Minver
Trevine
Trevose Head
Cat's Cove
Merope Rocks
Crugmeer
Harbour Cove
Gun Pt.
Pityme
Tregwarmond
Treglyn
Rooke
Trewethern
St. Kew

Stinking Cove
Polventon or
Mother Ivey's Bay
Porthmissen
Bridge
Tregirls
Rock
Splatt
Penmayne
Blakes
Keiro
Gutt Bri.
Chapel Amble
Pellengarrow
Carclaze

Quies
Dinas Hd.
Cataclews Pt.
Trevone Bay
Porthmissen
PRIDEAUX PLACE
Golf Co.
Stoptide
Carlyon
Tregena
Lr. Amble
Hendra

Toll
Trevose
Harlyn Bay
Trethillick
Treator
B3276
Porthilly
Porthilly Cove
Cant Cove
B3314
Tregorden
Tregilders

Booby's Bay
Harlyn
Golf Co.
Trevone
Windmill
Padstow
THE NATIONAL
LOBSTER HATCHERY
Cant Hill
River Camel
Tregonna
Rocksea

F

Constantine Bay
Constantine
Bay
Trelowsa
Dinas
Dennis Hill
Oldtown
Penquean
Burniere
Bodieve
Three Holes
Cross
A39

Treyarnon Pt.
TREYARNON
Trethias I. BAY
Treyarnon
Towan
St. Merryn
Tregella
Sea Mills
Trevorrick
Trevilgus
Trevanson
Treworder

Pepper Cove
Fox Cove
Trethias
Shop
Trehemborne
7
Tregavone
Tregolds
Highlanes
Tregonna
Penhale
8
Edmonton
Whitecross
Wadebridge
Egloshayle

Minnows Is.
Carnevas
Rosken
Roscullion
Bodellick
Porthcothan Beach
Trescore Is.
Porth Mear
Porthcothan
Tregonna
Little
Trevance
Carthew
St. Breock
A39

1　　　2　　　3　　　4　　　5

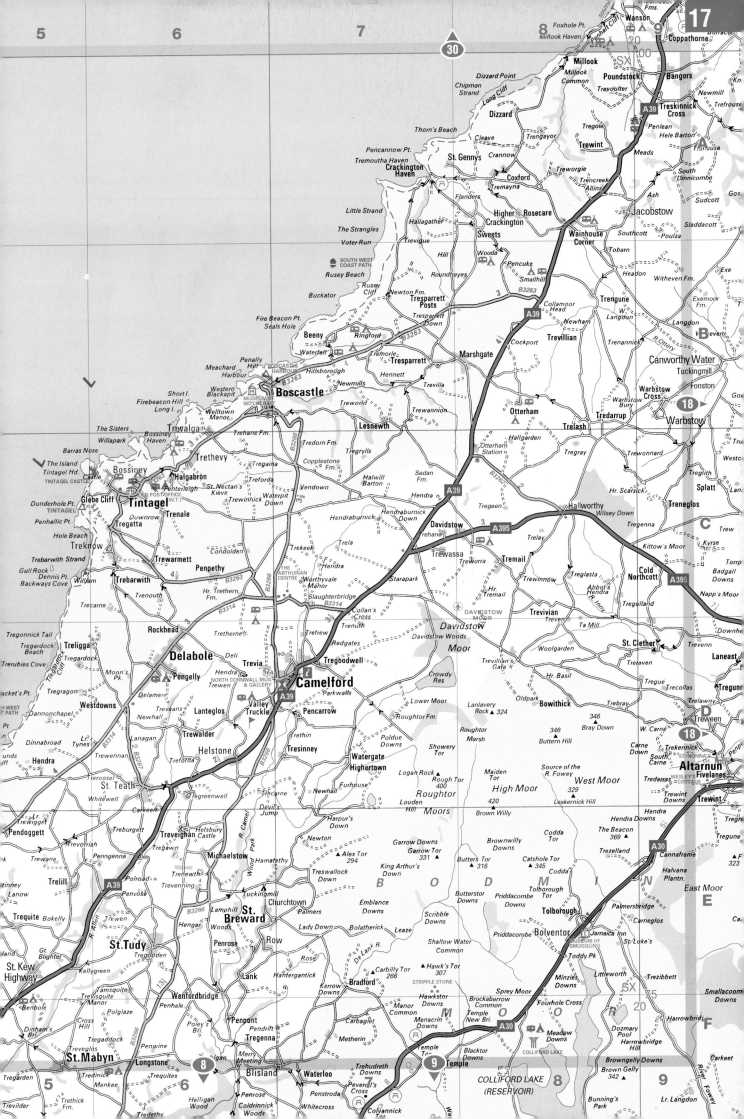

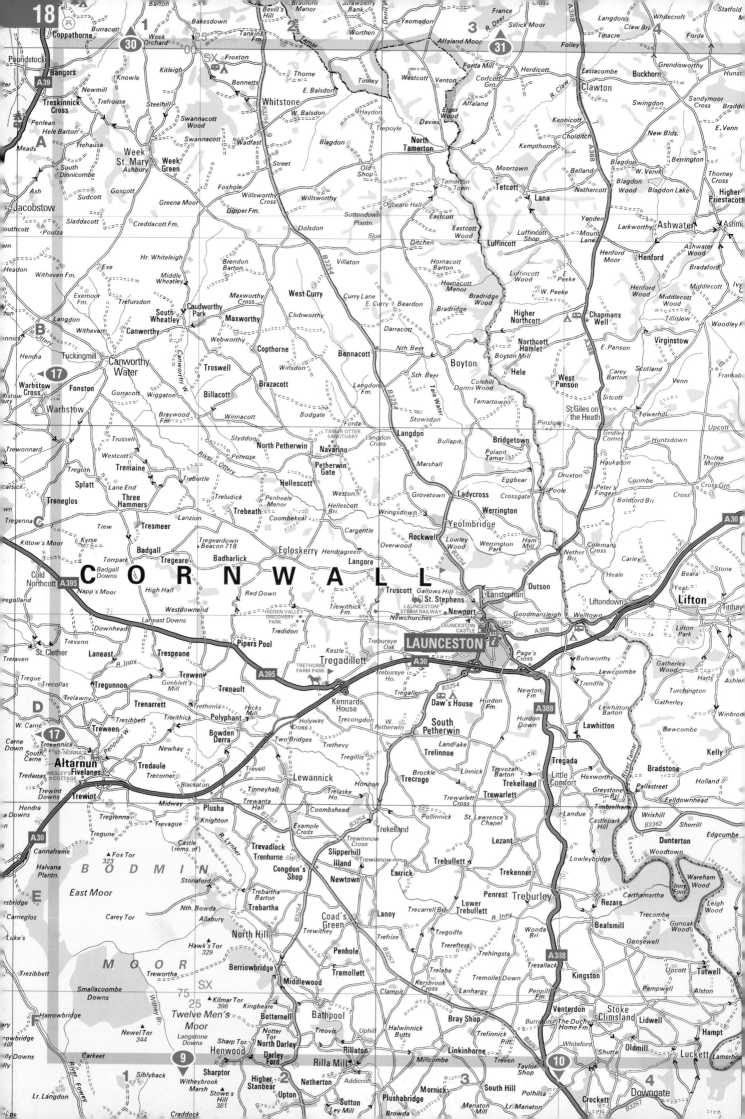

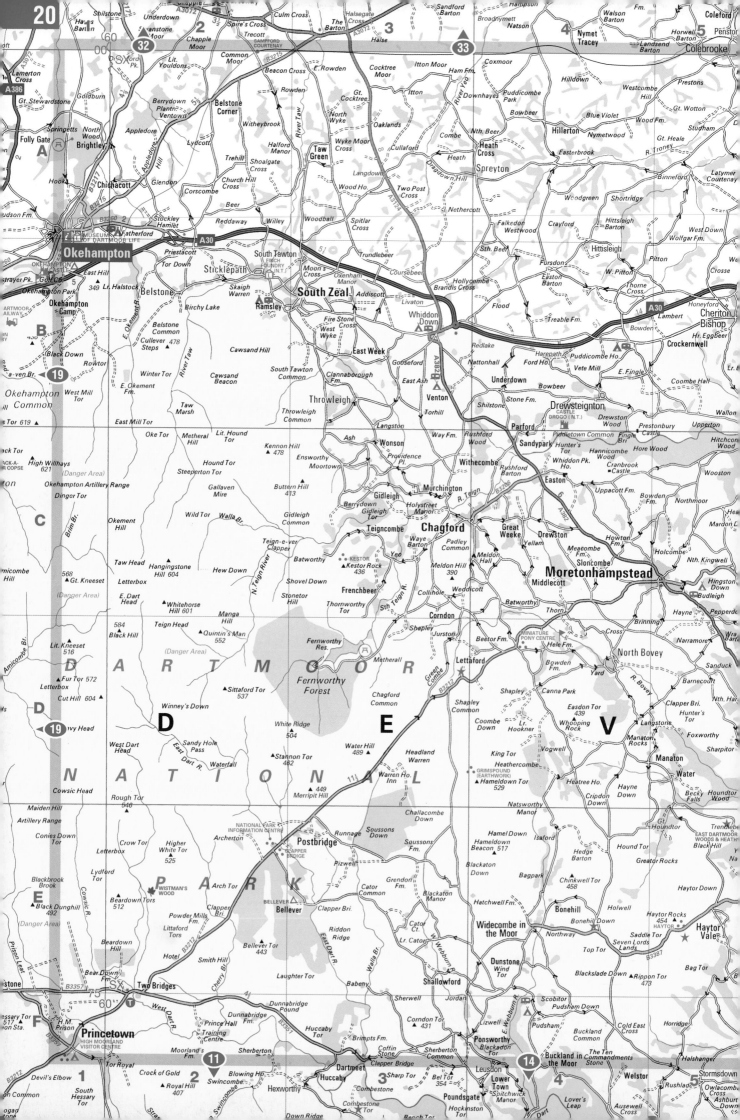

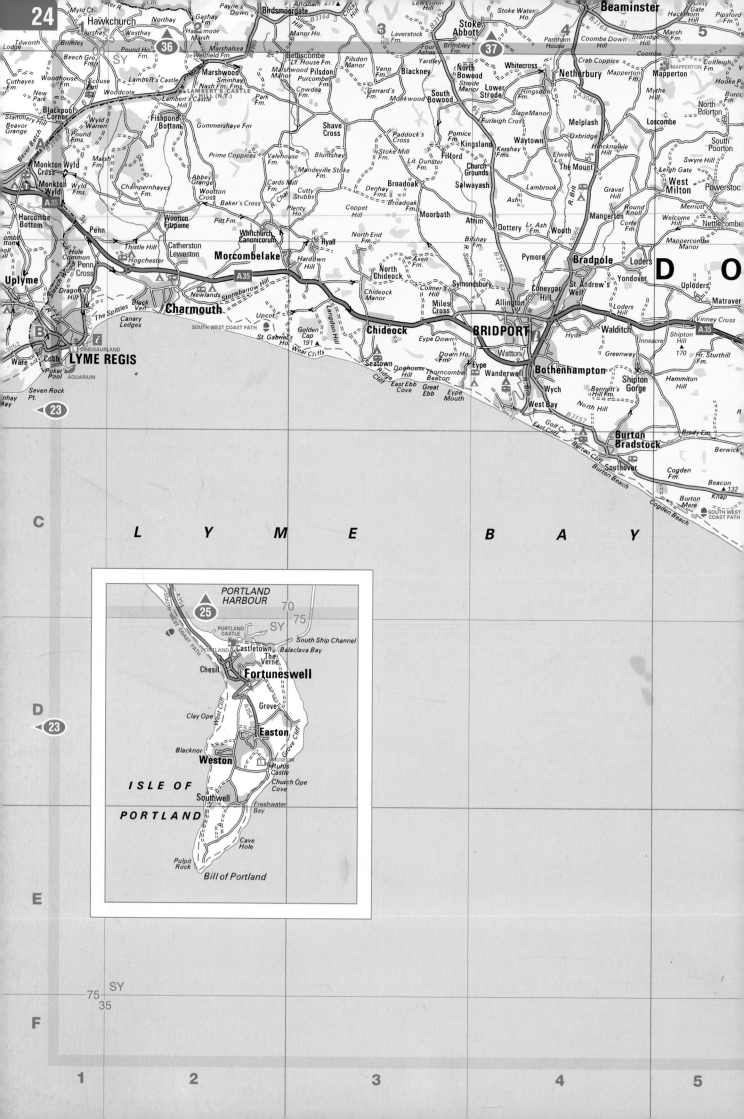

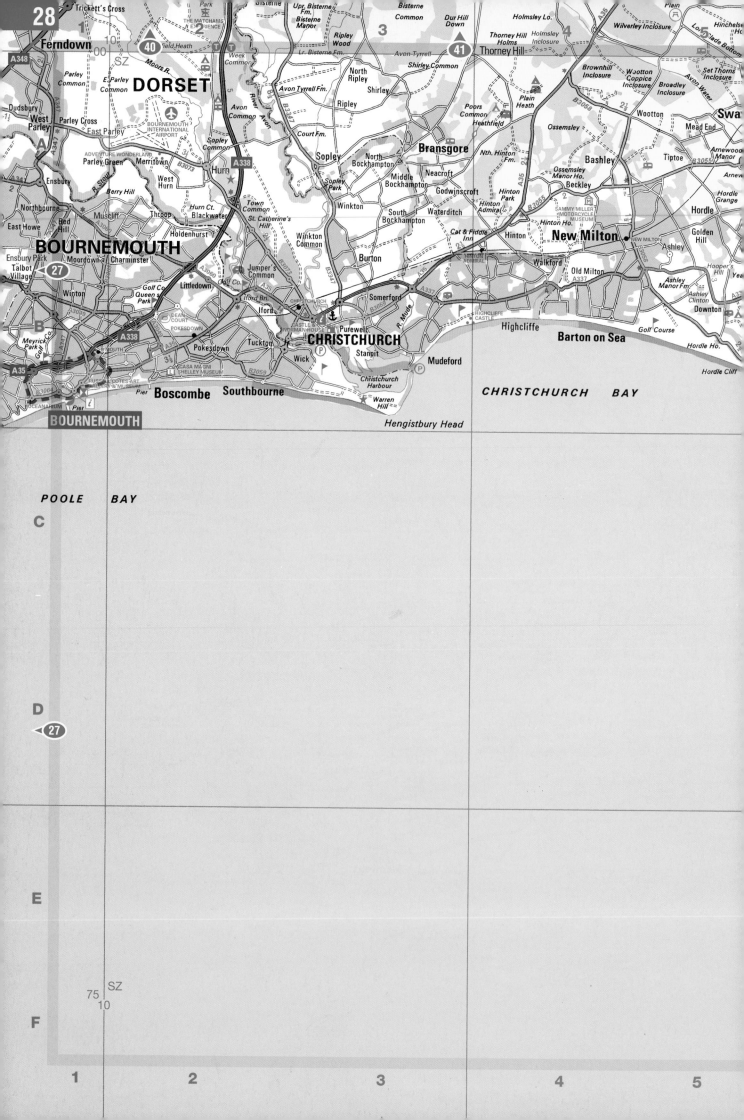

1   2   3   4

A

10
25
SS

B

Hartland
Point
Bailey
Bay
Shiplo
Ba
Blagdon Fm.   Titch
Cow & Calf   Toll
Upright
Cliff
Damehole Pt.
Blegberry
Broad Beach   Downe Fm.
The   Berry
Warren
Toll
HARTLAND
QUAY MUS.   Hartland   Stoke   HARTLAN
Quay   ABBEY
Speke's Mill
Mouth   Kernstone   Wargery
Longpeak
Lymebridge
SOUTH WEST
COAST PATH   Milford
Mansley   ELMSCOTT
Cliff   Elmscott   Edisto
Docton

C

Nabor   Hardisworthy
Pt. South Hole
E
Wembsworth
Embury Beach   Embury
Beacon   Putshole
157
Cranham
Knaps
Longpeak   Knap
head   Welcombe   D
Tredown
Welcombe Mouth   Darracott
Mead
Marsland Mouth
Gull Rock
Gooseham
Mill
Marsland   Hackr
Yeol Mouth   Cornakey   Gooseham
▲ 143
Henna Cliff   Bryaton   Lopthon
Lucky Hole   Morwenstow   Rule Cross
Hr.   ST. JOHN THE BAPTIST
Sharpnose Pt. CHURCH   Shop   Milte
Crosstown
Woodford
Stanbury   Cross
Darzle
Hippa Rock   Eastaway Woodford   Stu
Stanbury Mouth   Holla
Lr. Sharpnose Pt.
Lee   Herda

D

N
O
R
K

Lee
BRC
ADV
PAF
Steeple Pt.   Coombe   Burridge
Duckpool   Coombe Valley
Penstowe
Houndapit   Stanbury
Stowe   Stibb
Cliffs   Scadghill
Sandy Mouth   CORNWALL   Killock
4
Coll
Dunsmouth   Tiscott
Menachurch Pt.   Ivyleaf
Northcott Mouth   Northcott   Fm.
Crockwood   A39
Maer Cliff
Poughill
Maer   Bush

E

Wrangle Pt. Flexbury   Colebrook
Crooklets Beach   Burn 1643
Golf Co.   Stratton
Bude Haven
BUDE   Diddies   Cro
Compass Pt.
Efford   Launcells
Beacon i   Howard
A3072
Lynstone
A3073   West
Upton   Thorne Grove   Thu
Rodd's Br.
Phillip's Pt.
Phillips   Combepark
Hele   Bra.

F

Hr. Longbeak
Marhamchurch
Helebridge
Lr. Longbeak
Salthouse   Woodknowle
Helscott   Rattenbury
Widemouth   Hackthorne
Sand   Widemouth   Woolstone
Bay   7½
Wanson Mouth   Box's Shop
Widemouth   Langford
Fms.   Barton   Titson
Wanson   A39
Foxhole Pt.   Burracott
Millook Haven   Penhall Cliff   Coppathorne   Week
Orchard

00
SS
10

1   2   3   4
17   18

Dizzard Point   Millook   Poundstock   Bangors   Knowle   Kitleigh
Chipman   Common   Newmill
Strand   Trevoulter
Long Cliff   Treskinnick Cross   Trefrouse
Steelhi

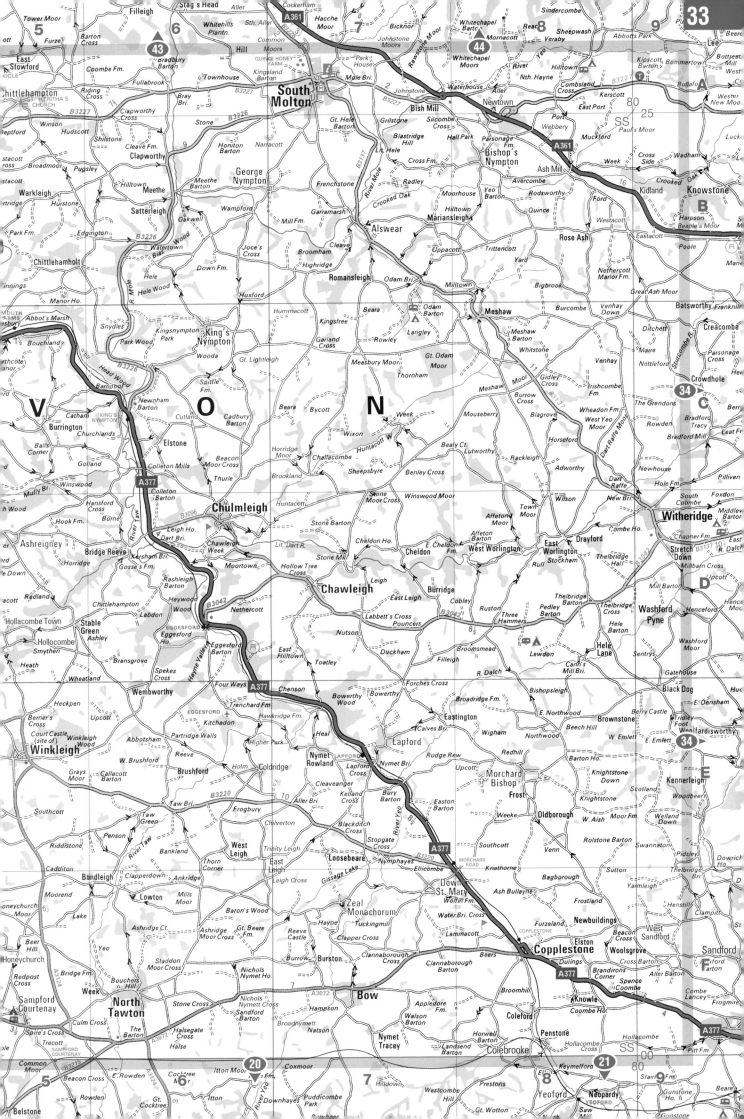

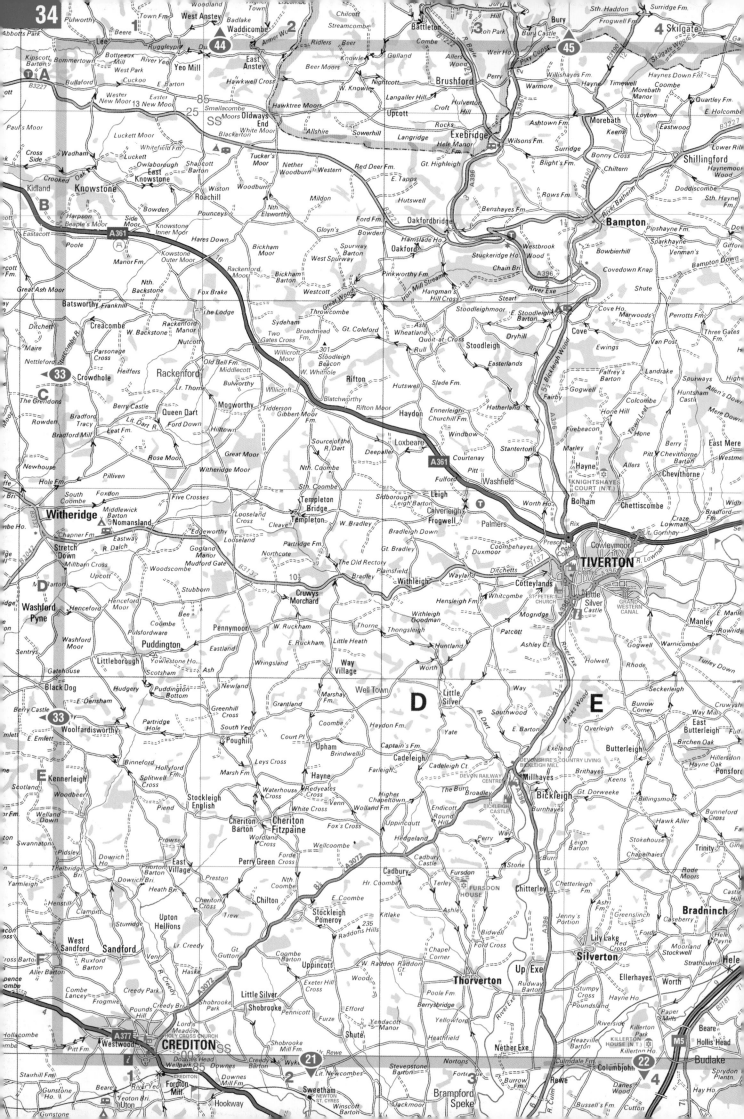

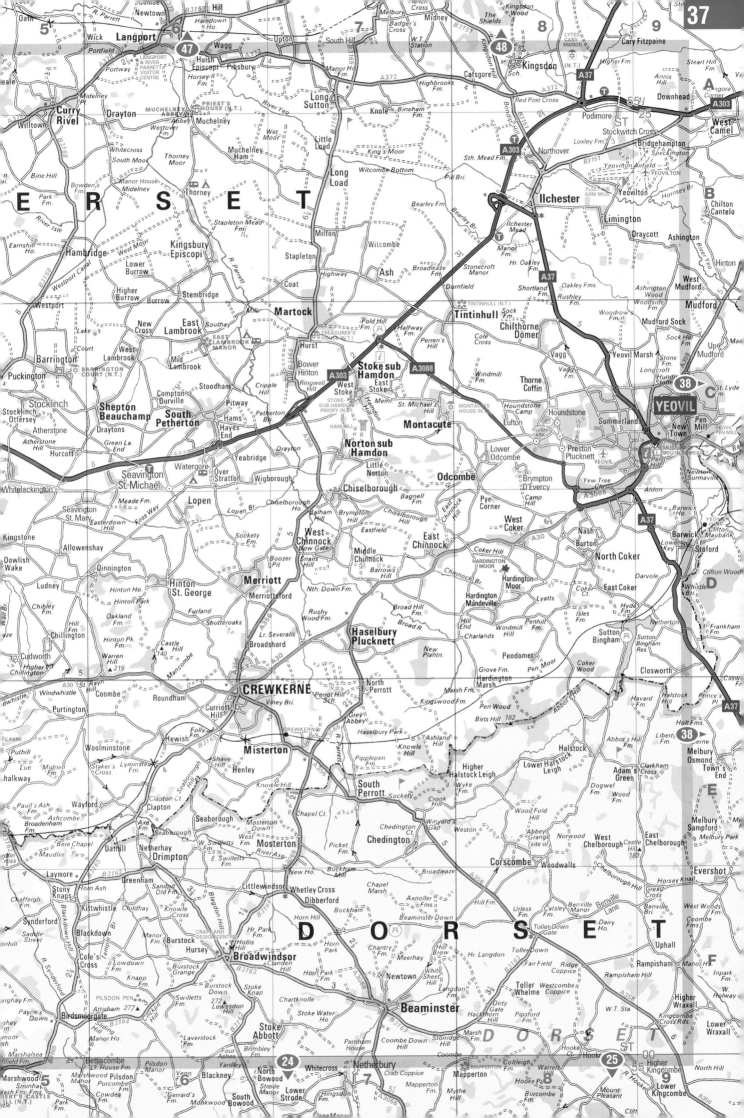

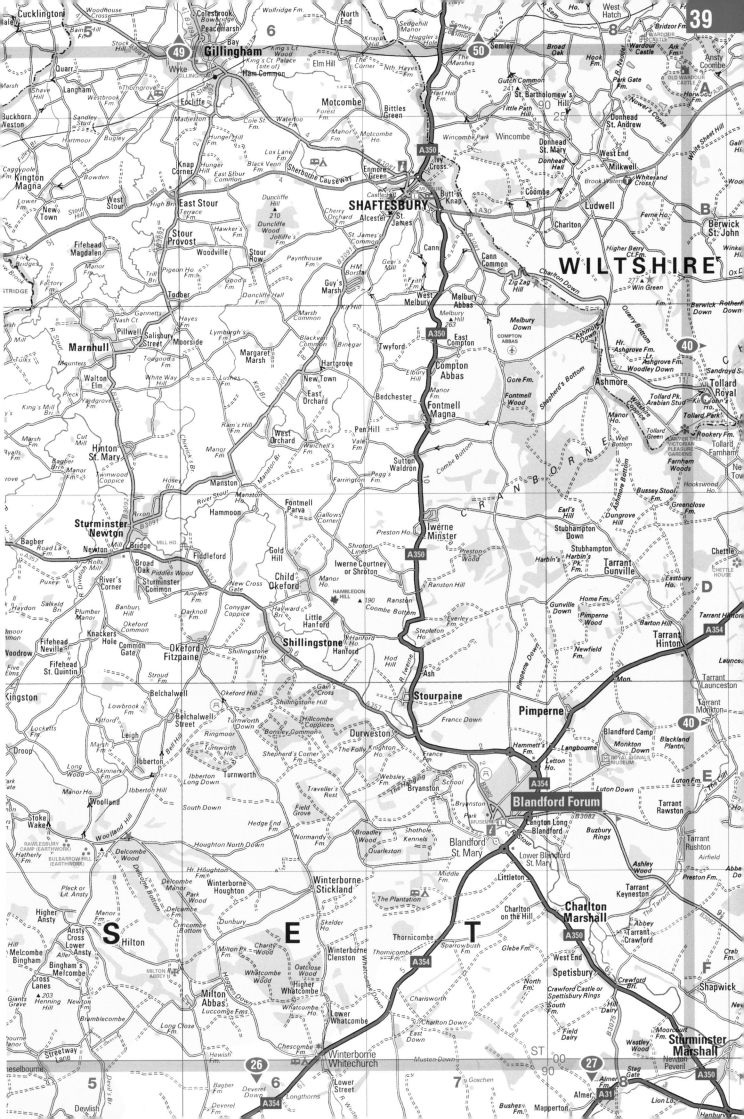

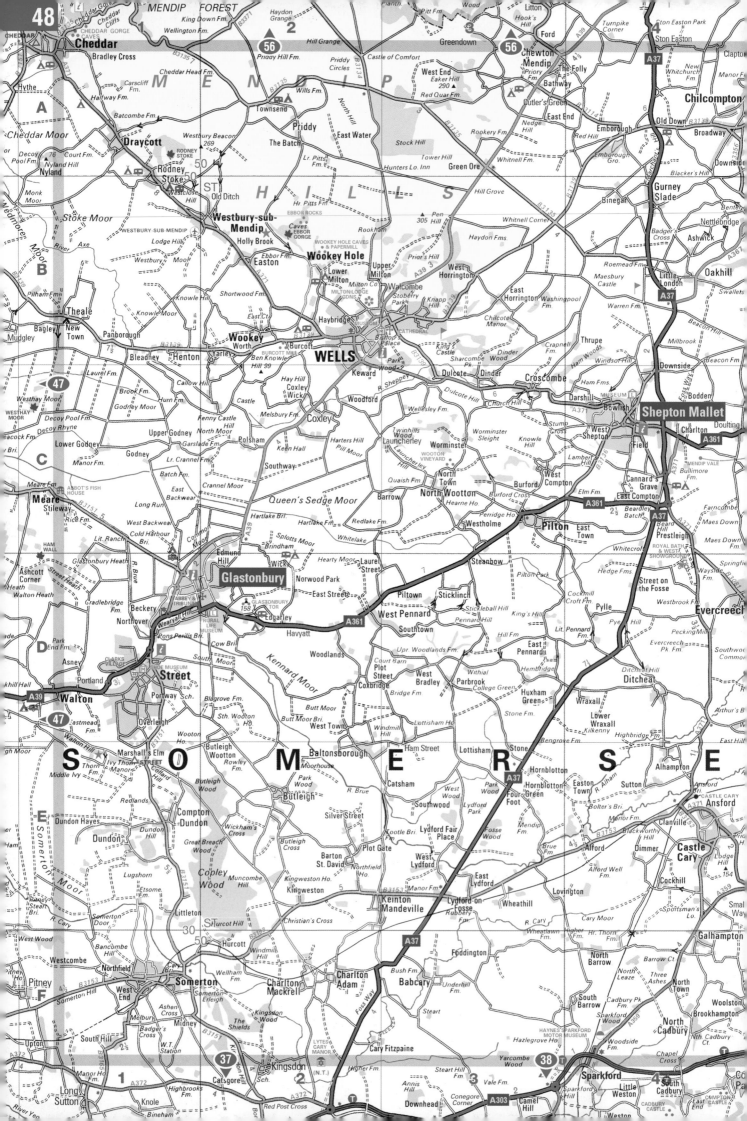

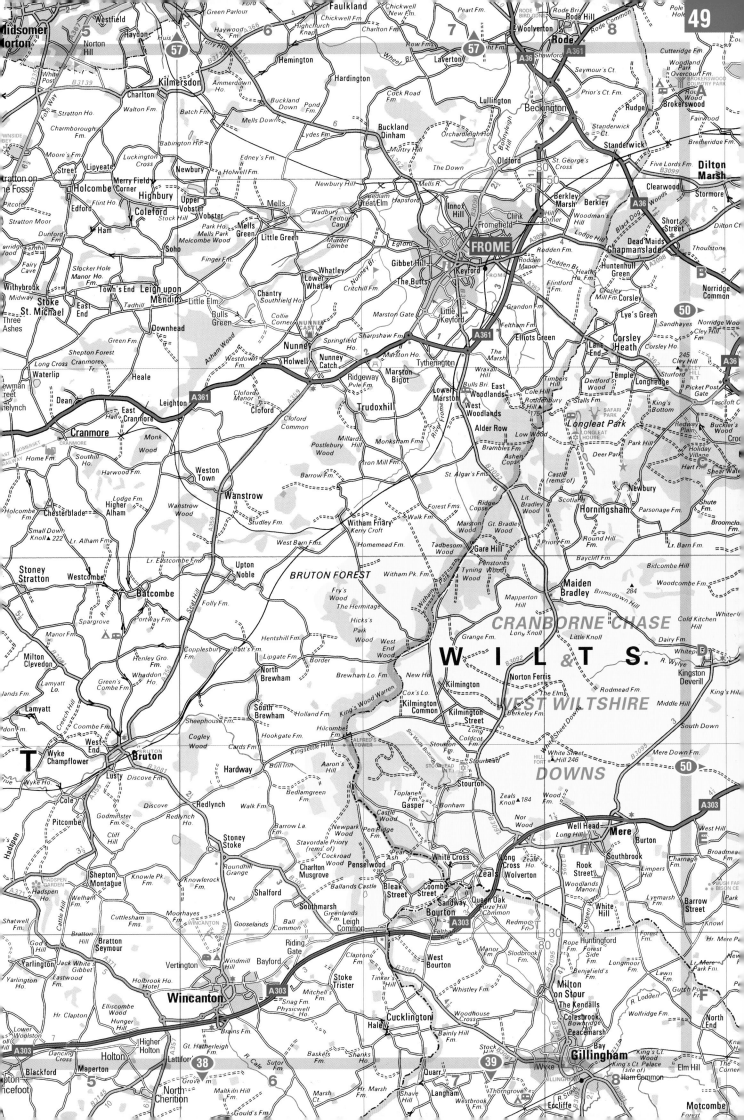

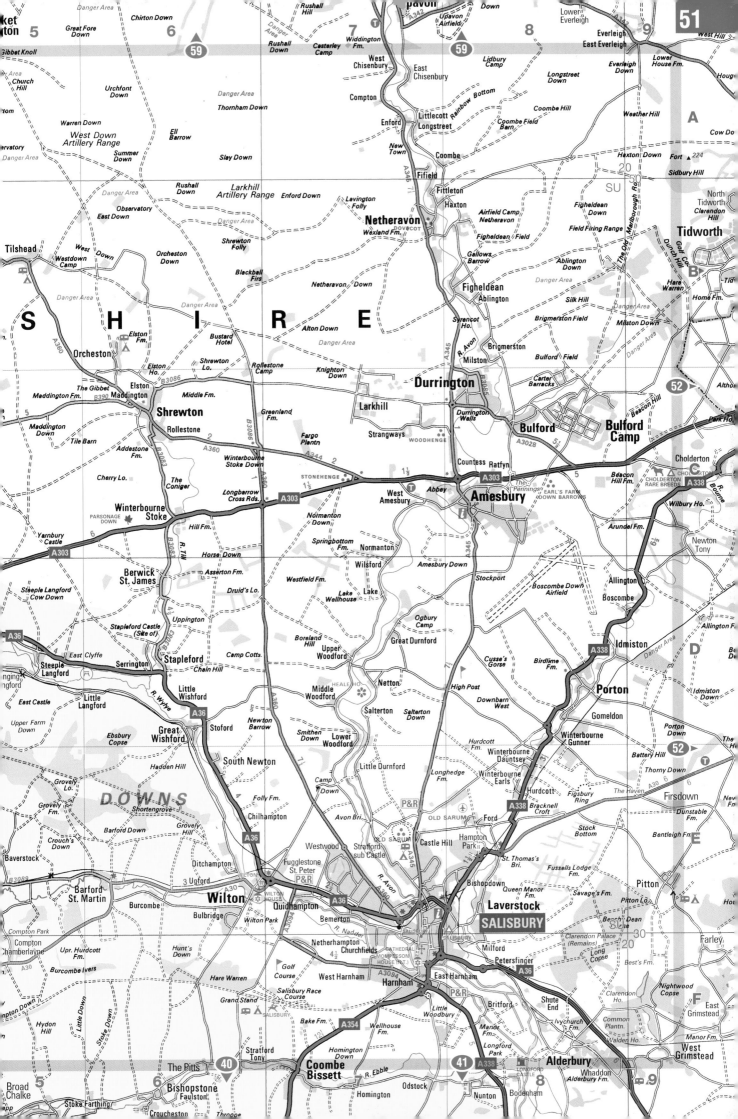

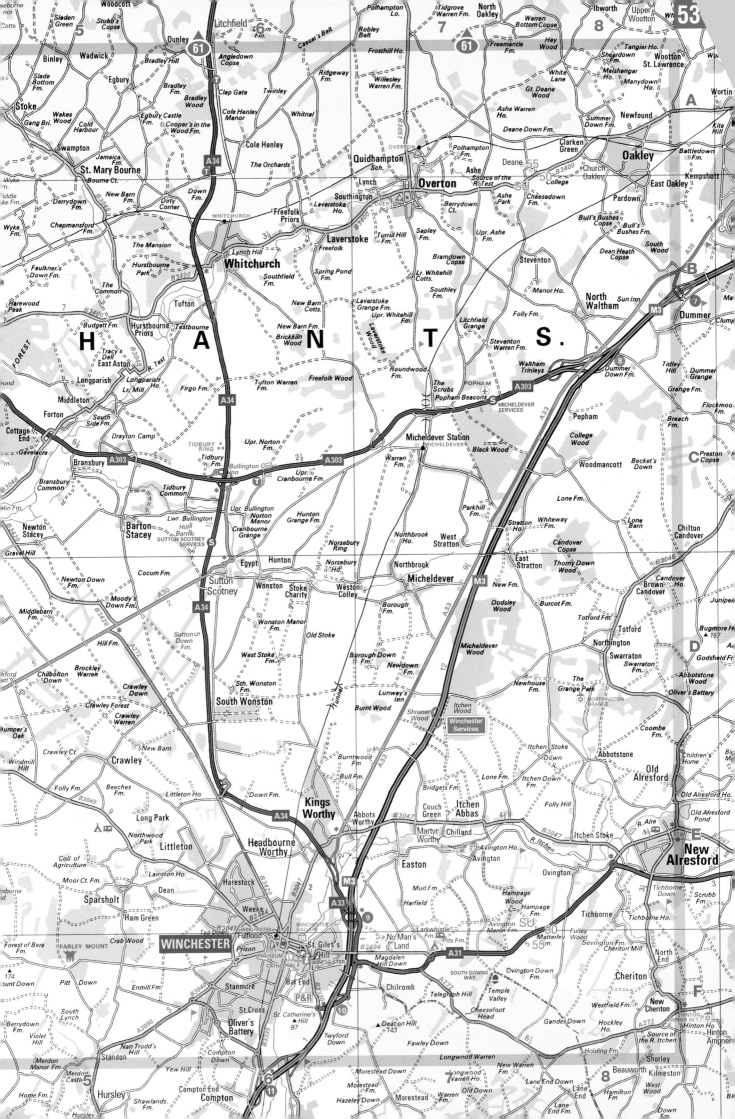

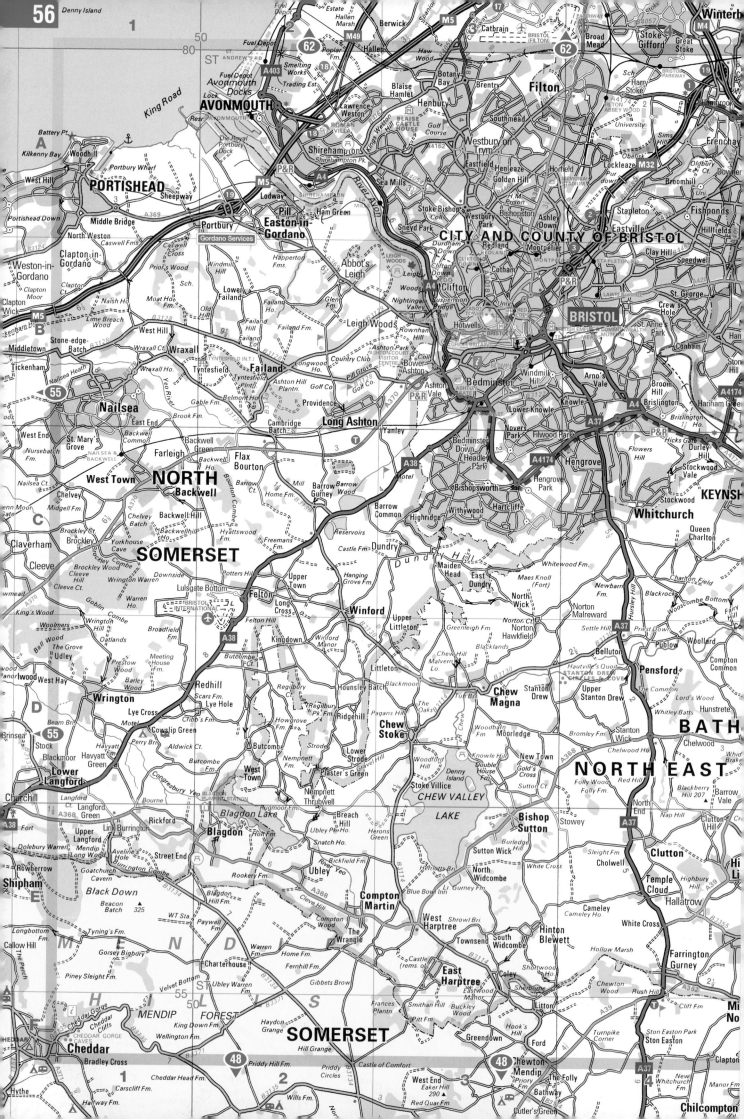

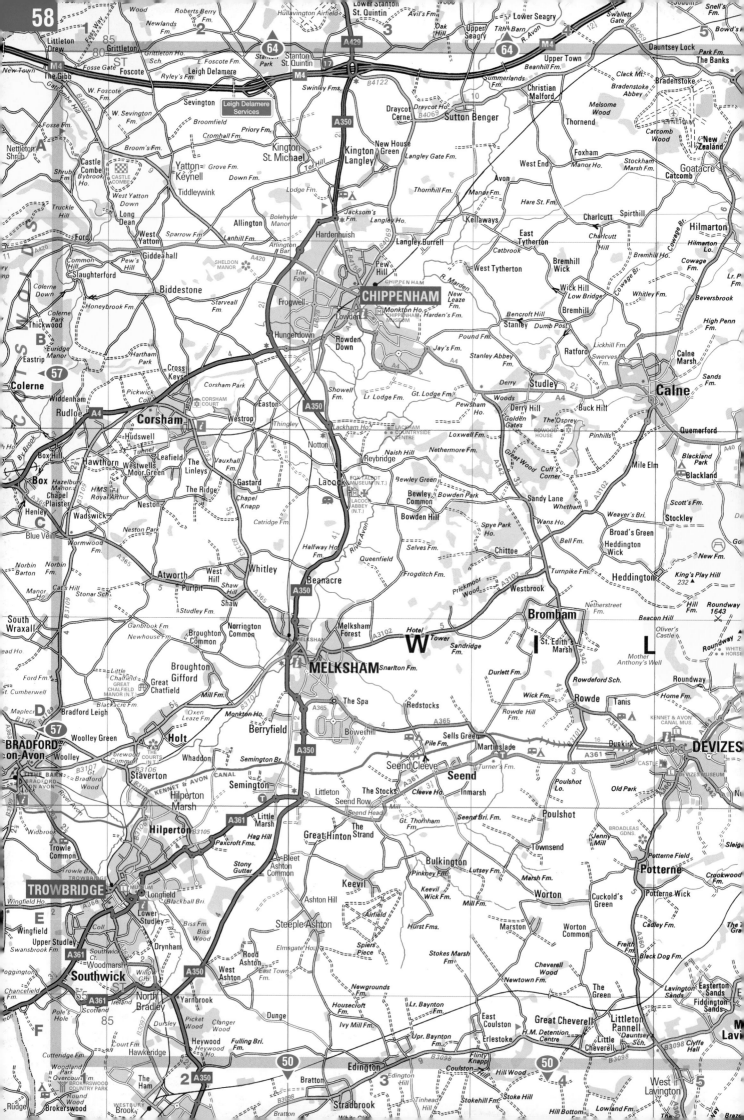

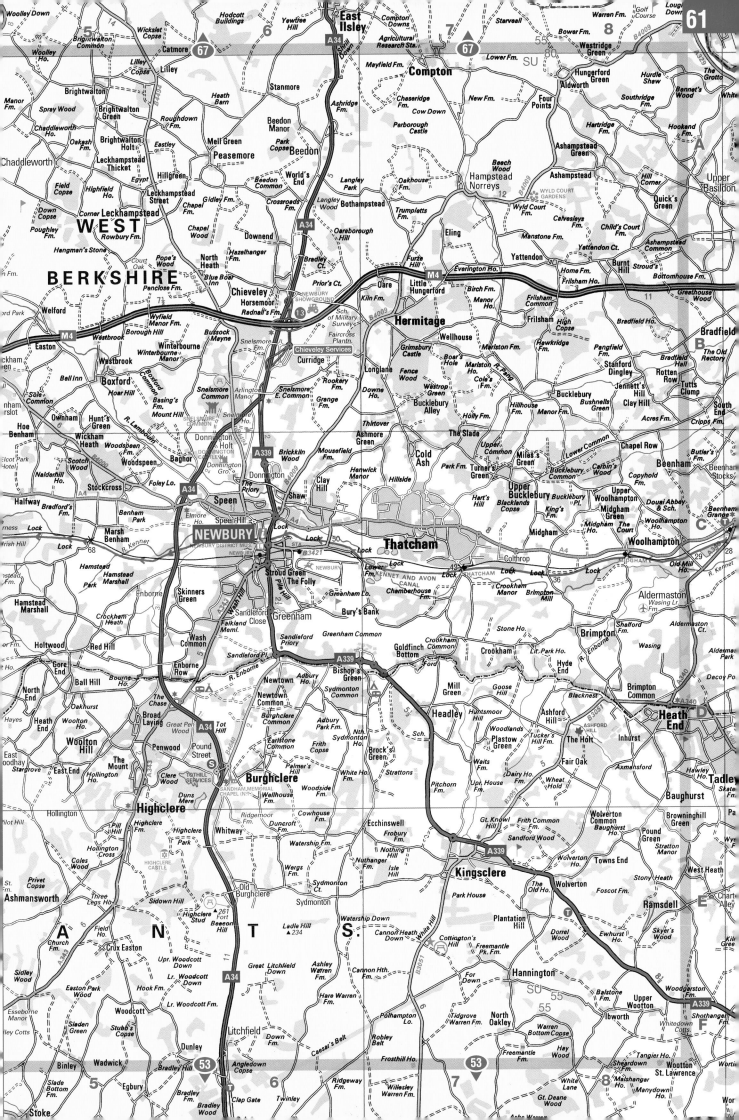

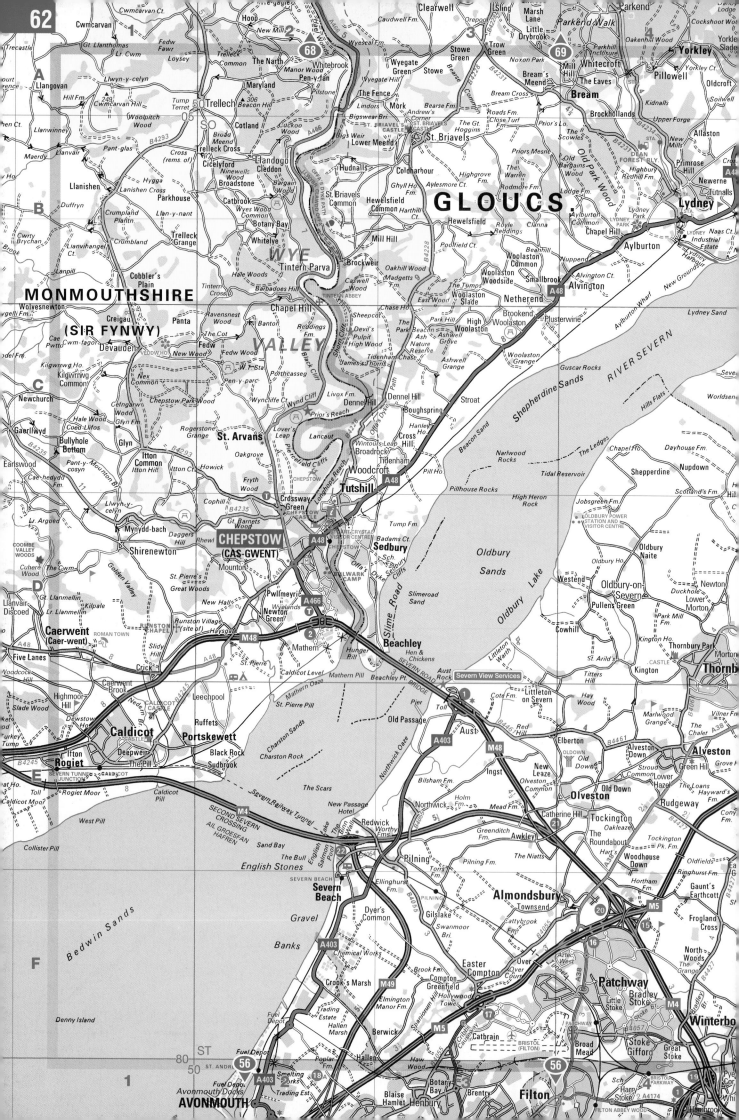

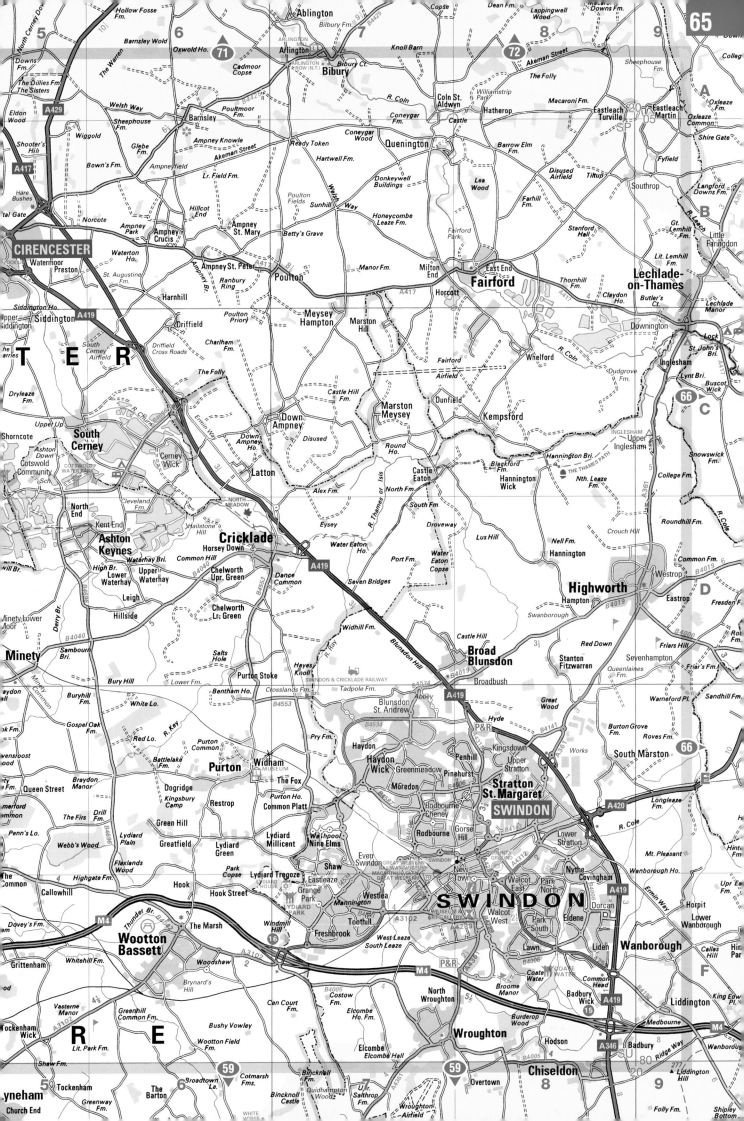

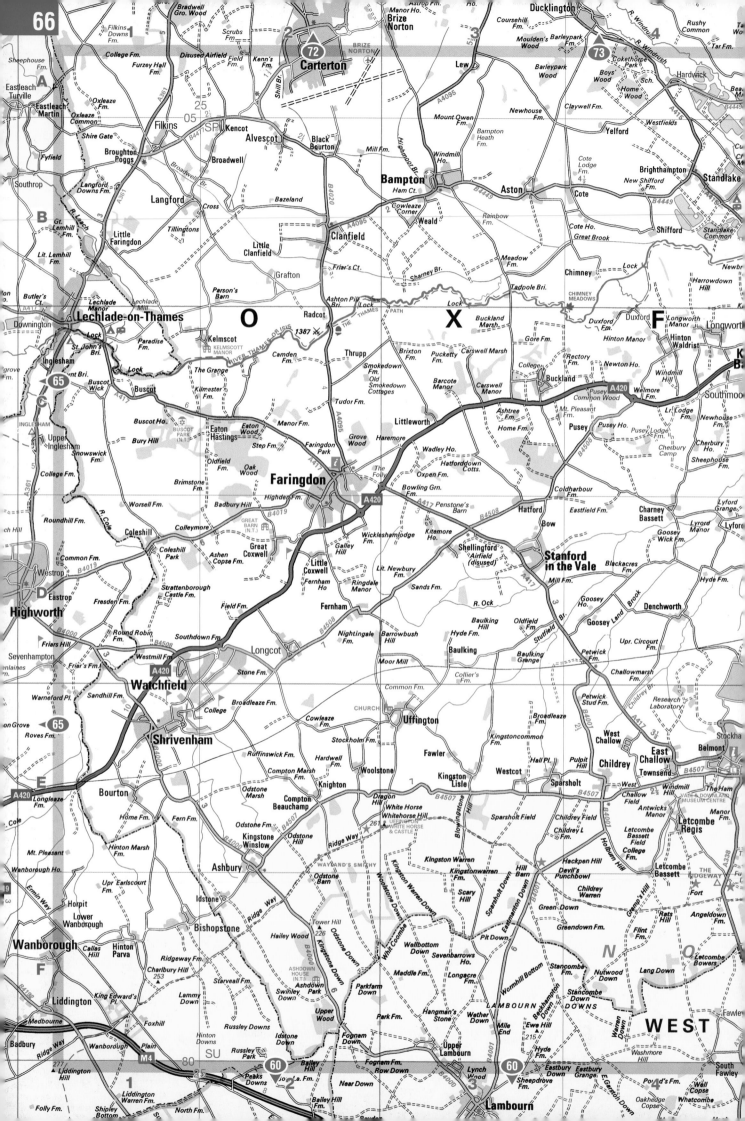

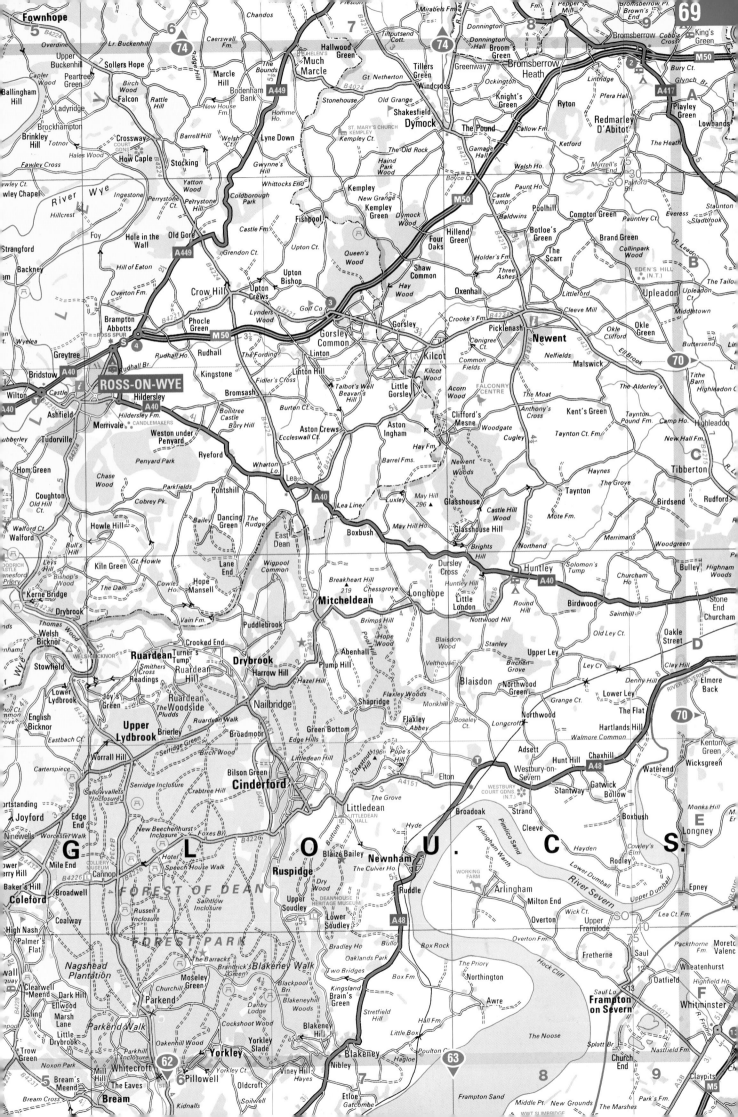

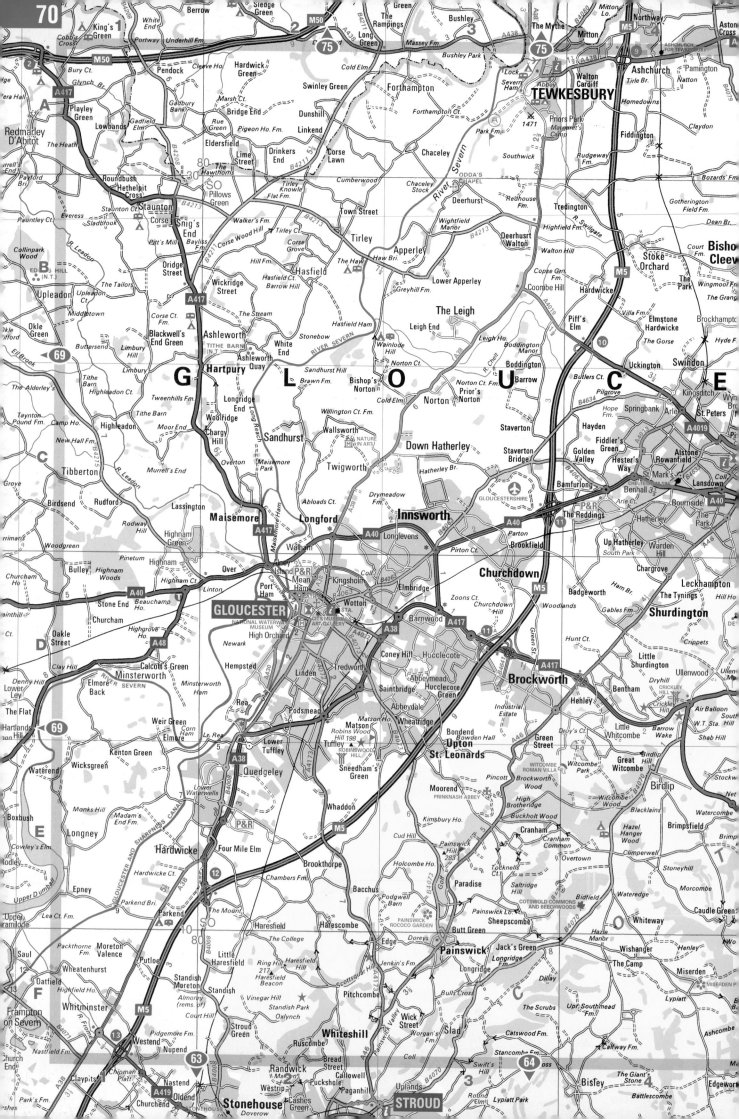

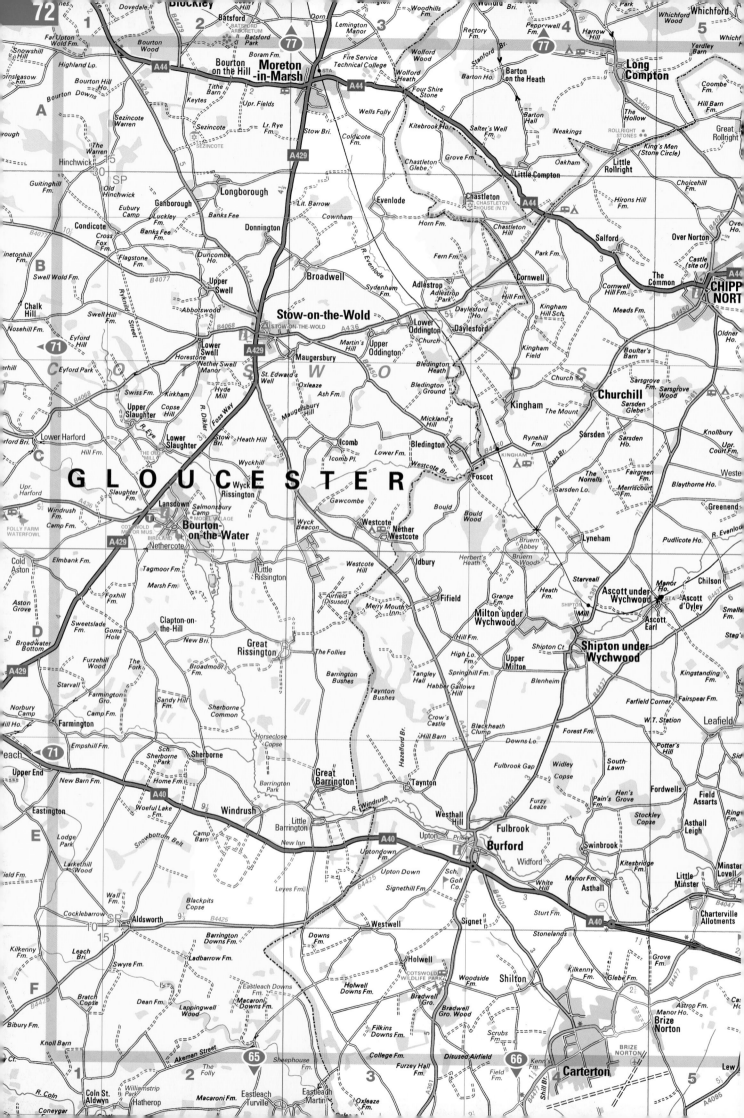

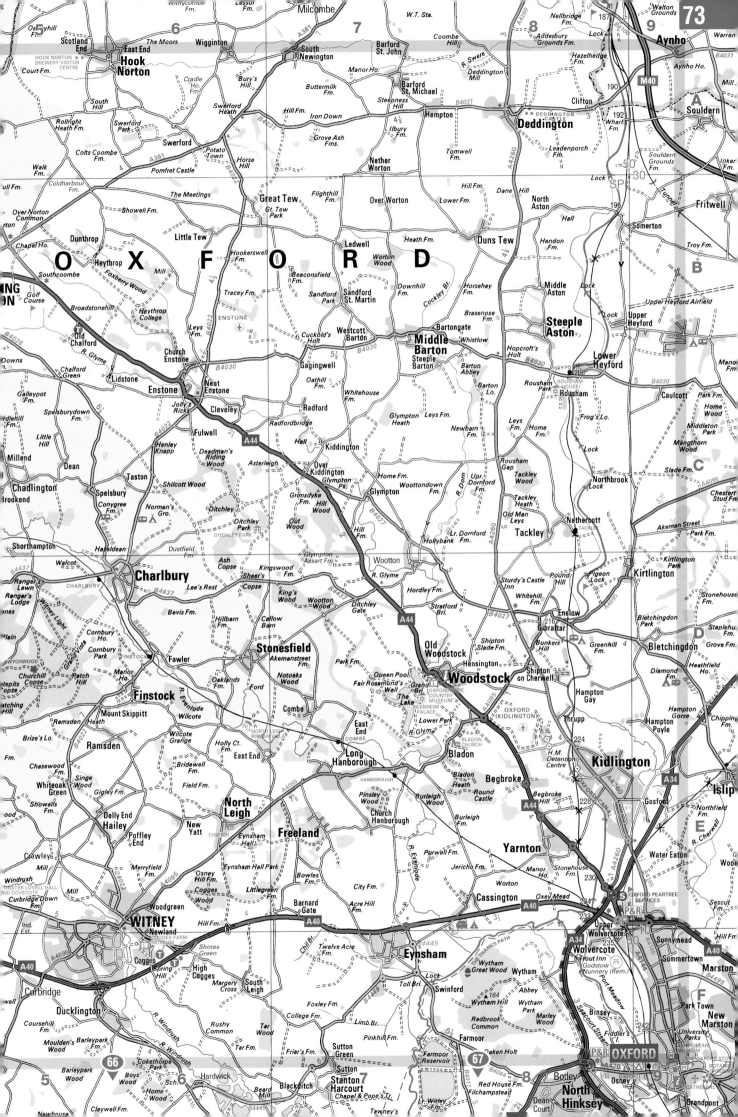

Key to Town Plan Symbols

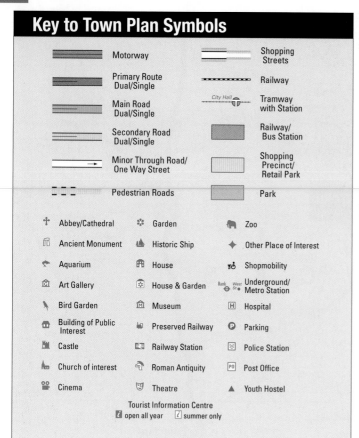

Motorway		Shopping Streets
Primary Route Dual/Single		Railway
Main Road Dual/Single	City Hall	Tramway with Station
Secondary Road Dual/Single		Railway/ Bus Station
Minor Through Road/ One Way Street		Shopping Precinct/ Retail Park
Pedestrian Roads		Park

† Abbey/Cathedral — ✤ Garden — 🐘 Zoo
🏛 Ancient Monument — ⚓ Historic Ship — ◆ Other Place of Interest
⚓ Aquarium — 🏠 House — ♿ Shopmobility
📷 Art Gallery — 🏠 House & Garden — Bank West St Underground/ Metro Station
🐦 Bird Garden — 🏛 Museum — H Hospital
🏛 Building of Public Interest — 🚂 Preserved Railway — P Parking
🏰 Castle — 🚉 Railway Station — Police Station
⛪ Church of interest — Roman Antiquity — PO Post Office
🎬 Cinema — Theatre — ▲ Youth Hostel

Tourist Information Centre
🄵 open all year   🄸 summer only

Bath

0   Miles   ¼

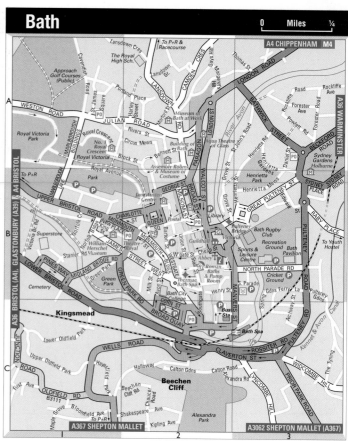

Bath

Bristol

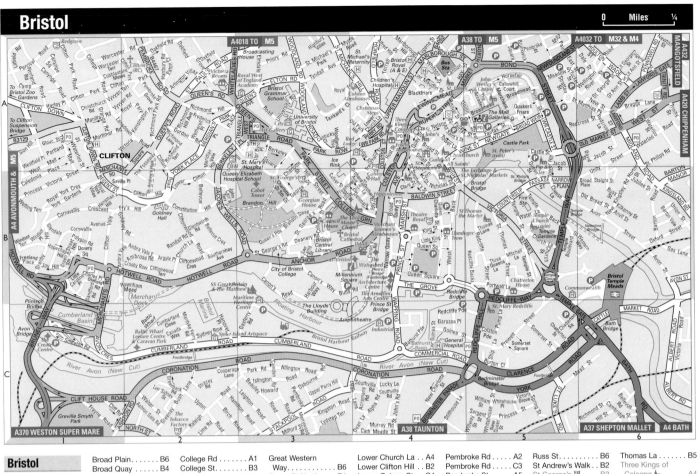

0 — Miles — ¼

Bournemouth

0   Miles   ¼

Cheltenham

0   Miles   ¼

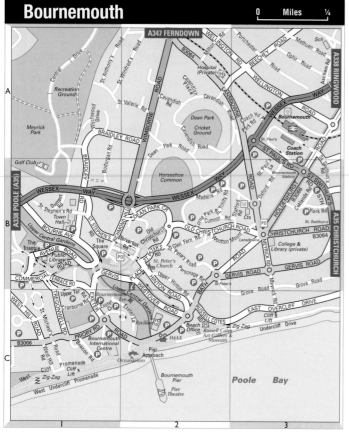

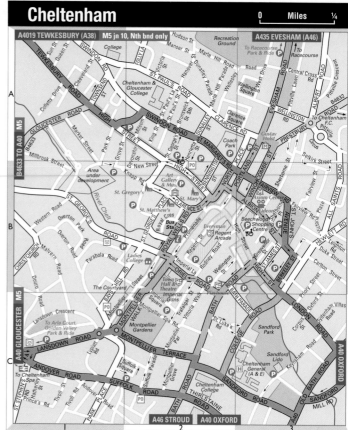

Exeter

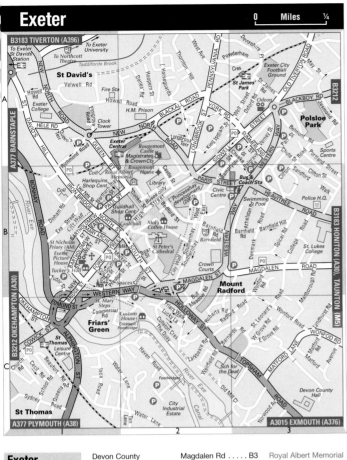

Gloucester

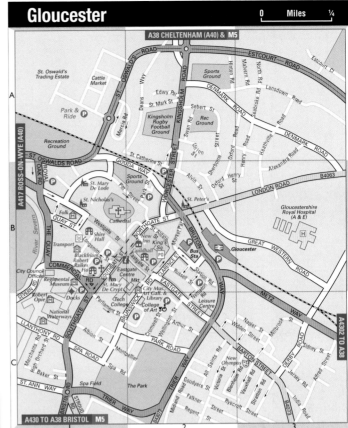

Exeter

Alphington St C1
Athelstan Rd B3
Bampfylde St B2
Barnardo Rd C3
Barnfield Hill B3
Barnfield Rd B2/B3
Barnfield
  Theatre 🎭 B2
Bartholomew
  St East B1
Bartholomew
  St West B1
Bear St B2
Beaufort Rd C1
Bedford St B2
Belgrave Rd A3
Belmont Rd B3
Blackall Rd A2
Blackboy Rd A3
Bonhay Rd B1
Bull Meadow Rd. . . C2
Bus & Coach
  Station B3
Castle St. B2
Cecil Rd C1
Cheeke St. A3
Church Rd C1
Chute St A3
City Industrial
  Estate C2
City Wall B1/B2
Civic Centre B2
Clifton Rd B3
Clifton St B3
Clock Tower A1
College Rd B3
Colleton Cr C2
Commercial Rd . . . C1
Coombe St. B2
Cowick St. C1
Crown Courts B2
Custom House 🏛 . . C2
Danes' Rd. A2
Denmark Rd B3

Devon County
  Hall C3
Devonshire Pl A3
Dinham Rd B1
East Grove Rd C3
Edmund St C1
Elmgrove Rd. A1
Exe St B1
Exeter Central
  Station ≥ A1
Exeter City
  Football Ground . . A3
Exeter College A1
Exeter Picture
  House 🎦 B1
Fire Station A1
Fore St B1
Friars Walk C2
Guildhall 🏛 B2
Guildhall Shopping
  Centre. B2
Harlequin's Shopping
  Centre. B1
Haven Rd C2
Heavitree Rd. B3
Hele Rd. A1
High St B2
HM Prison A2
Holloway St C2
Hoopern St. A2
Horseguards A2
Howell Rd. A1
Information Ctr 🅹 . . B3
Iron Bridge B1
Isca Rd C1
Jesmond Rd A3
King William St. . . . A2
King St B1
Larkbeare Rd C2
Leisure Centre C1
Library B2
Longbrook St A2
Longbrook Terr. . . . A2
Lucky La. C2
Lower North St. . . . B1
Lyndhurst Rd C3

Magdalen Rd B3
Magdalen St. B2
Magistrates &
  Crown Courts. . . . A2
Market B2
Market St B2
Marlborough Rd . . . C3
Mary Arches St. . . . B1
Matford Rd C3
Matford Ave C3
Matford La C3
May St A3
Mol's Coffee
  House 🏛 B2
New Bridge St B1
New North Rd . . A1/A2
North St B1
Northernhay St. . . . B1
Norwood Ave C3
Odeon 🎦 A3
Okehampton St . . . C1
Old Mill Cl. C2
Old Tiverton Rd . . . A3
Oxford Rd. A3
Paris St B2
Parr St A3
Paul St B1
Pennsylvania Rd. . . A2
Police H.Q. 🚔 B3
Portland Street . . . A3
Post Office 🅿
  . . . . A3/B1/B3/C1
Powderham Cr A3
Preston St B1
Princesshay
  development. B2
Queen St A1
Queen's Rd. C1
Queen's Terr A1
Radford Rd C2
Richmond Rd A1
Roberts Rd C2
Rougemont
  Castle 🏰 A2
Rougemont
  House ✦ B2

Royal Albert Memorial
  Museum 🏛 B2
St David's Hill A1
St James' Park
  Station A3
St James' Rd A3
St Leonard's Rd . . . C3
St Lukes College . . B3
St Mary Steps 🏛 . . C1
St Mary's
  Priory (AM) ✝ B1
St Peter's
  Cathedral ✝ B2
St Thomas
  Station ≥ C1
Sandford Walk B3
School for the Deaf C2
School Rd. C1
Sidwell St A2
Smythen St. B1
South St B2
Southernhay East. . B2
Southernhay West . B2
Spacex Gallery 🏛 . B1
Spicer Rd B3
Sports Centre. A3
Summerland St . . . A3
Swimming Pool . . . B3
Sydney Rd C1
Tan La. C2
The Quay C2
Thornton Hill. A2
Topsham Rd C3
Tucker's Hall 🏛 . . . B1
Tudor St B1
Velwell Rd. A1
Verney St A3
Water La C1/C2
Weirfield Rd C2
Well St A3
West Ave A2
West Grove Rd C3
Western
  Way A3/B1/B2
Wonford Rd . . . B3/C3
York Rd. A2

Gloucester

Albion St C1
Alexandra Rd B3
Alfred St C2
All Saints Rd C2
Alvin St B2
Arthur St C2
Baker St C1
Barton St C2
Blackfriars ✝ B1
Blenheim Rd. C2
Bristol Rd C1
Brunswick Rd C2
Bruton Way. B2
Bus Station B2
Cattle Market A1
City Council
  Offices B1
City Mus., Art Gall.
  & Library 🏛 B2
Clarence St. B2
College of Art C2
Commercial Rd . . . B1
Cromwell St C2
Deans Way A2
Denmark Rd A3
Derby Rd C3
Docks ⚓ C1
Eastgate Centre . . . B1
Eastgate St. B2
Edwy Pde A2
Estcourt Cl A3
Estcourt Rd A3
Falkner St C2

Folk Museum 🏛 . . . B1
Gloucester
  Cathedral ✝ B1
Gloucester
  Station ≥ B2
Gloucestershire
  Royal Hospital
  (A & E) 🏥 B3
Goodyere St C2
Gouda Way. A2
Great Western Rd. . B3
Guildhall 🏛 B2
Heathville Rd A3
Henry Rd B3
Henry St B2
High Orchard St . . . C1
Hinton Rd A2
India Rd C3
Information Ctr 🅹 . . B1
Jersey Rd C3
King's Sq B2
Kingsholm Rd. A2
Kingsholm Rugby
  Football Ground . . A2
Lansdown Rd A3
Leisure Centre C2
Llanthony Rd C1
London Rd B3
Longsmith St B1
Malvern Rd A3
Market Pde B2
Merchants Rd C1
Mercia Rd A1
Metz Way C3
Midland Rd C2

Millbrook St C3
Market B2
Montpellier C1
Napier St C3
National
  Waterways 🏛 . . . C1
Nettleton Rd C2
New Inn 🏛 B2
New Olympus 🎭 . . C3
North Rd. A3
Northgate St. B2
Oxford Rd A2
Oxford St B2
Park & Ride
  Gloucester A1
Park Rd C2
Park St B2
Parliament St C1
Pitt St B1
Police Station 🚔 . . B1
Post Office 🅿 B2
Quay St B1
Recreation Gd . A1/A2
Regent St C2
Regimental 🏛 B1
Robert Opie 🏛 . . . C1
Robert Raikes
  House 🏛 B1
Royal Oak Rd B1
Russell St B2
Ryecroft St C2
St Aldate St B2
St Ann Way. C1
St Catherine St. . . . A2
St Mark St A2

St Mary De
  Crypt 🏛 B1
St Mary De
  Lode 🏛 B1
St Nicholas's 🏛 . . . B1
St Oswald's Rd . . . A1
St Oswald's Trading
  Estate A1
St Peter's 🏛 B2
Seabroke Rd A3
Sebert St A2
Severn Rd C1
Sherborne St B1
Shire Hall 🏛 B1
Sidney St C3
Southgate St . . B1/C1
Spa Field C1
Spa Rd C1
Sports Ground . A2/B2
Station Rd B2
Stratton Rd C3
Stroud Rd C1
Swan Rd A2
Technical College . . C1
The Park C2
The Quay B1
Transport 🏛 . . . C1/C2
Trier Way. C1/C2
Union St A1
Vauxhall Rd C3
Victoria St C2
Wellington St C2
Westgate St B1
Widden St C3
Worcester St. B2

Oxford

0   Miles   ¼

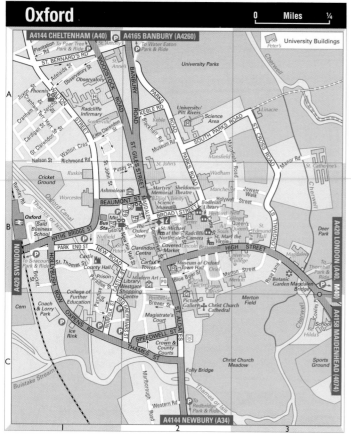

Plymouth

0   Miles   ¼

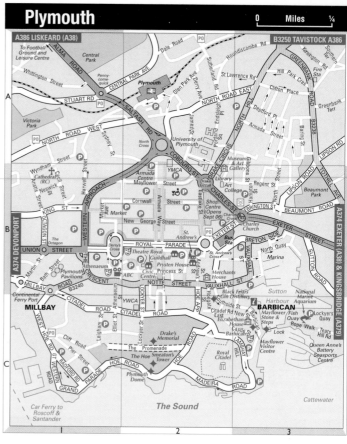

Oxford

Plymouth

Salisbury

0 Miles ¼

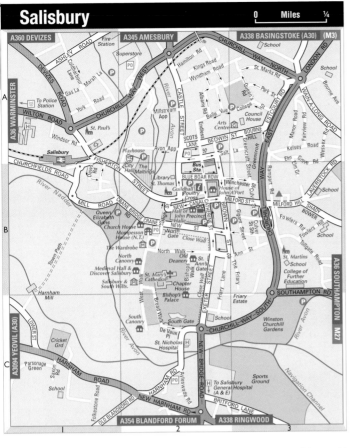

Stratford-upon-Avon

0 Miles ¼

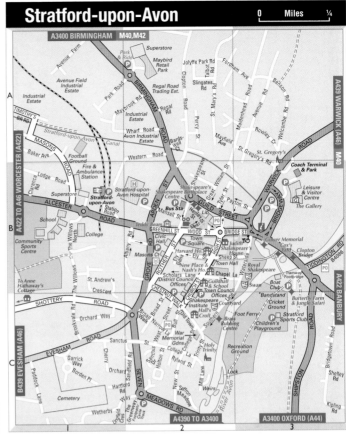

Swindon

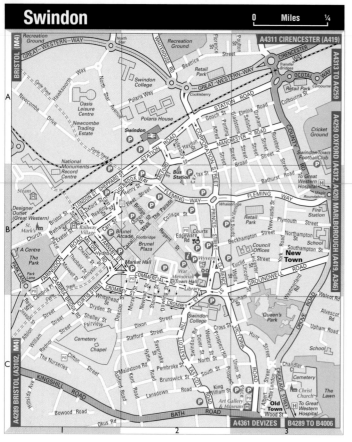

0　Miles　¼

Taunton

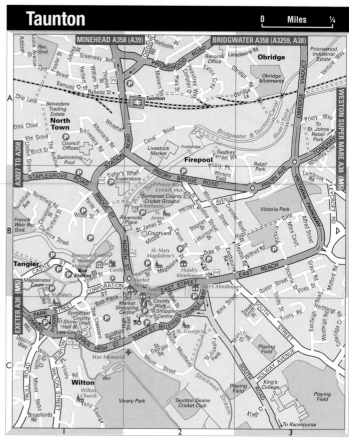

0　Miles　¼

Torquay

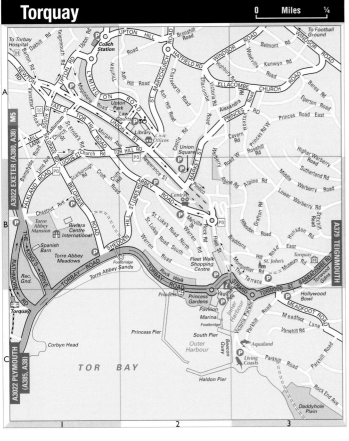

0 Miles ¼

Worcester

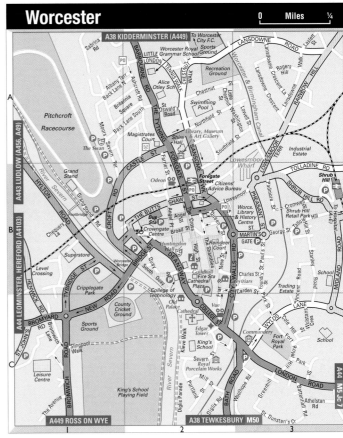

0 Miles ¼

Torquay

Abbey Rd B2	
Alexandra Rd A2	
Alpine Rd B3	
Aqualand ⚓ C3	
Ash Hill Rd A2	
Babbacombe Rd . . B3	
Bampfylde Rd B1	
Barton Rd A1	
Beacon Quay C2	
Belgrave Rd . . A1/B1	
Belmont Rd A3	
Berea Rd A3	
Braddons Hill	
Rd East B3	
Bronshill Rd A2	
Castle Rd A2	
Cavern Rd A2	
Central ☕ B2	
Chatsworth Rd A2	
Chestnut Ave B1	
Church St A1	
Civic Offices 🏛 . . A2	
Coach Station A1	
Corbyn Head C1	
Croft Hill B1	
Croft Rd B1	
Daddyhole Plain . . . C3	
East St A1	
Egerton Rd A3	
Ellacombe	
Church Rd A3	
Ellacombe Rd A2	
Falkland Rd B1	
Fleet St B2	
Fleet Walk	
Shopping Centre . B2	

Grafton Rd B3	
Haldon Pier C2	
Hatfield Rd A2	
Highbury Rd A2	
Higher	
Warberry Rd A3	
Hillesdon Rd B3	
Hollywood Bowl . . . C3	
Hoxton Rd A3	
Hunsdon Rd B3	
Information Ctr 🅕 . B2	
Inner Harbour C3	
Kenwyn Rd A3	
Laburnum St. A1	
Law Courts. A2	
Library A2	
Lime Ave. A2	
Living Coasts C3	
Lower	
Warberry Rd B3	
Lucius St B1	
Lymington Rd A1	
Magdalene Rd B2	
Marina. C2	
Market St B2	
Meadfoot Lane C3	
Meadfoot Rd C3	
Melville St. B2	
Middle	
Warberry Rd B3	
Mill Lane. A1	
Montpellier Rd B3	
Morgan Ave A1	
Museum Rd B3	
Newton Rd A1	
Oakhill Rd. A1	
Outer Harbour C2	
Parkhill Rd C3	

Pavilion. C2	
Pimlico B2	
Police Station 🛈 . . A1	
Post Office 🅟	
. . . . A2/B1/B2	
Princes Rd A3	
Princes Rd East . . . A3	
Princes Rd West. . . A3	
Princess	
Theatre 🎭. C2	
Princess Gdns C2	
Princess Pier C2	
Rathmore Rd B1	
Recreation Grd B1	
Riviera Centre	
International B1	
Rock End Ave. C3	
Rock Rd B2	
Rock Walk B2	
Rosehill Rd A3	
St Efride's Rd A1	
St John's 🅐 B3	
St Luke's Rd. B2	
St Luke's	
Rd North B2	
St Luke's	
Rd South B2	
St Marychurch Rd . A2	
Scarborough Rd. . . . B1	
Shedden Hill. B2	
South Pier. C2	
South St A1	
Spanish Barn B1	
Stitchill Rd B3	
Strand. B2	
Sutherland Rd B3	
Teignmouth Rd A1	
Temperance's St . . . B2	

The King's Drive . . . B1	
The Terrace. B3	
Thurlow Rd. A1	
Tor Bay B1	
Tor Church Rd A1	
Tor Hill Rd. A1	
Torbay Rd. B2	
Torquay	
Museum 🏛. B3	
Torquay	
Station ≠ C1	
Torre Abbey	
Mansion 🏛 B1	
Torre Abbey	
Meadows B1	
Torre Abbey	
Sands B1	
Torwood Gdns B3	
Torwood St B3	
Union Square A2	
Union St A1	
Upton Hill A1	
Upton Park A1	
Upton Rd A1	
Vanehill Rd C3	
Vansittart Rd. A1	
Vaughan Parade. . . C2	
Victoria Parade. . . . C3	
Victoria Rd A2	
Warberry Rd West . B2	
Warren Rd B2	
Windsor Rd . . . A2/A3	
Woodville Rd A3	

Worcester

Albany Terr A1	
Alice Otley School . A2	
Angel Pl B2	
Angel St B2	
Ashcroft Rd A2	
Athelstan Rd. C3	
Back Lane North . . A1	
Back Lane South . . A1	
Barbourne Rd A1	
Bath Rd C2	
Battenhall Rd C3	
Bridge St B2	
Britannia Sq A1	
Broad St B2	
Bromich La C1	
Bromich Rd C1	
Bromyard Rd C1	
Bus Station B2	
Carden St B3	
Castle St. A2	
Cathedral † C2	
Cathedral Plaza . . . B2	
Charles St. B3	
Chequers La. B1	
Chestnut St A2	
Chestnut Walk A2	
Citizens' Advice	
Bureau B2	
City Walls Rd B2	
Cole Hill C3	
College of	
Technology B2	
College St. B2	
Commandery 🏛 . . C3	
County Cricket	
Ground C1	

Cripplegate Park . . B1	
Croft Rd B1	
Cromwell St B3	
Crowngate	
Centre. B2	
Deansway. B2	
Diglis Pde C2	
Diglis Rd. C2	
Edgar Tower ✦. . . . C2	
Farrier St. A2	
Fire Station B2	
Foregate St. B2	
Foregate St ≠. B2	
Fort Royal Hill. C3	
Fort Royal Park . . . C3	
Foundry St B3	
Friar St C2	
George St. B3	
Grand Stand Rd. . . B1	
Greenhill C3	
Greyfriars 🏛. B2	
Guildhall 🏛 B2	
Henwick Rd B1	
High St B2	
Hill St B3	
Huntingdon	
Hall 🏛. B2	
Hylton Rd B1	
Information Ctr 🅕. . B2	
King's School C2	
King's School	
Playing Field. . . . C2	
Kleve Walk C2	
Lansdowne Cr A3	
Lansdowne Rd A3	
Lansdowne Walk . . A3	
Laslett St A3	
Leisure Centre A3	

Library, Museum	
& Art Gallery 🏛 . . A2	
Little Chestnut St . . A2	
Little London A2	
London Rd C3	
Lowell St. A3	
Lowesmoor. B2	
Lowesmoor Terr . . . A3	
Lowesmoor Wharf . A3	
Magistrates Court. . A2	
Midland Rd. B3	
Mill St C2	
Moors Severn Terr . A1	
New Rd C1	
New St B2	
Northfield St A2	
Odeon 🎦 B2	
Old Palace 🏛. B2	
Oswald's Rd A2	
Padmore St B3	
Park St C3	
Pheasant St B2	
Pitchcroft	
Racecourse A1	
Police Station 🛈 . . B2	
Portland St C2	
Post Office 🅟	
. . . . A1/A2/B2	
Quay St B2	
Queen St B2	
Rainbow Hill A3	
Recreation Ground . A2	
Reindeer Court. . . . B2	
Rogers Hill A3	
Royal Porcelain	
Works 🏛. C2	
Sabrina Rd A1	
St Dunstan's Cr . . . C3	

St John's C1	
St Martin's Gate . . . B3	
St Paul's St. B3	
St Wulstans Cr C3	
Sansome Walk A2	
Severn St C2	
Shaw St B2	
Shire Hall A2	
Shrub Hill ≠ B3	
Shrub Hill	
Retail Park B3	
Shrub Hill Rd B3	
Slingpool Walk C1	
South Quay B2	
Southfield St. A2	
Sports Ground . A2/C1	
Stanley Rd B3	
Swan, The 🎭 A1	
Swimming Pool A2	
Tallow Hill B3	
Tennis Walk A2	
The Avenue C1	
The Butts B2	
The Cross B2	
The Shambles B2	
The Tything. A2	
Tolladine Rd B3	
Tybridge St B1	
Vincent Rd B3	
Vue 🎦. C2	
Washington St A3	
Woolhope Rd C3	
Worcester Bridge . . B2	
Worcester Library &	
History Centre . . . B3	
Worcester Royal	
Grammar School . A2	
Wylds La. C3	

Teignmouth Devon 15 A6
Tellisford Som'set 57 E7
Temple Cornw'l 9 A5
Temple Wilts 49 C8
Temple Cloud Bath/NE Som'set 56 E4
Temple Cowley Oxon 67 B7
Temple Grafton Warwick 76 B5
Temple Guiting Glos 71 B7
Templecombe Som'set 38 B4
Templeton Devon 34 D2
Templeton Bridge Devon 34 D2
Terhill Som'set 46 E3
Terras Cornw'l 8 E1
Tetbury Glos 64 D2
Tetbury Upton Glos 64 C2
Tetcott Devon 18 A3
Tevorrick Cornw'l 8 A1
Tewkesbury Glos 70 A3
Thatcham W Berks 61 C7
The Banks Wilts 58 A5
The Barton Wilts 59 A6
The Batch Som'set 48 A2
The Batch S Gloucs 57 B5
The Bourne Worcs 76 A2
The Butts Som'set 49 B7
The Camp Glos 70 F4
The Cleaver Heref'd 68 B4
The Common Oxon 72 B4
The Common Wilts 52 E1
The Common Wilts 64 E5
The Eaves Glos 62 A4
The Fence Glos 62 A2
The Flat Glos 69 D9
The Folly Som'set 48 A3
The Folly W Berks 61 C6
The Fox Wilts 65 E7
The Frenches Hants 41 B9
The Gibb Wilts 57 A8
The Graig Monmouths 68 F4
The Green Glos 71 B5
The Green Hants 52 F2
The Green S Gloucs 57 B5
The Green Warwick 77 A7
The Green Wilts 50 E2
The Green Wilts 50 E4
The Grove Worcs 75 D7
The Ham Wilts 50 A2
The Hill Worcs 75 E6
The Holt Hants 61 D8
The Holt W Berks 60 B3
The Hoo Glos 77 E6
The Hook Worcs 75 D6
The Kendals Dorset 49 F8
The Knapp S Gloucs 63 D5
The Leigh Glos 70 B3
The Linleys Wilts 58 C2
The Marsh Wilts 65 F6
The Moors Heref'd 68 A4
The Mount Dorset 24 A4
The Mount Hants 61 D5
The Mythe Glos 75 F7
The North Monmouths 62 A2
The Oval Bath/NE Som'set 57 D6
The Park Glos 70 B4
The Park Glos 70 C4
The Park N Som'set 55 A8
The Pill Monmouths 62 E1
The Pitts Wilts 40 A4
The Point Devon 22 D1
The Pound Glos 69 A8
The Purlieu Glos 63 A5
The Quarry Glos 63 C6
The Ramplings Worcs 75 F7
The Reddings Glos 70 C4
The Rhydd Heref'd 68 A3
The Ridge Wilts 58 C2
The Rocks S Gloucs 63 F7
The Roundabout S Gloucs 62 E4
The Row Oxon 73 E7
The Scarr Glos 69 B8
The Shoe Wilts 57 B8
The Slade W Berks 61 C7
The Spa Wilts 58 D3
The Stocks Wilts 58 D3
The Strand Wilts 58 E3
The Thorn Heref'd 68 C5
The Tynings Glos 70 D4
The Verne Dorset 24 D2
The Wrangle Bath/NE Som'set 56 E2
Theale Som'set 48 B1
Theobald's Green Wilts 58 C5
Thicket Mead Bath/NE Som'set 57 E5
Thickwood Wilts 57 B8
Thorley I/Wight 29 C7
Thorley Street I/Wight 29 C7
Thornbury Devon 31 E8
Thornbury Heref'd 74 A2
Thornbury S Gloucs 62 D4
Thornbury Park S Gloucs 62 D4
Thorncross I/Wight 29 D8
Thorndon Cross Devon 19 B7
Thorne Coffin Som'set 37 C8
Thorne St. Margaret Som'set 35 B6
Thornecombe Dorset 37 F5
Thornend Wilts 58 A4
Thorney Som'set 37 B6
Thorney Hill Hants 28 A4
Thornfalcon Som'set 36 B3
Thornford Dorset 38 D2
Thorngrove Som'set 47 E7
Thornhill Wilts 59 A6
Thornhill Head Devon 31 C8
Thornicombe Dorset 39 F7
Thorns Beach Hants 29 A8
Thorverton Devon 34 F3
Three Ashes Som'set 49 B5
Three Burrows Cornw'l 4 A2
Three Hammers Cornw'l 18 C1
Three Horse Shoes Devon 21 A8
Three Legged Cross Dorset 40 E4
Threemilestones Cornw'l 4 B3
Threewaters Cornw'l 8 B3
Throckmorton Worcs 76 C2
Throop Dorset 26 B3
Throwleigh Devon 20 B3
Thrupe Som'set 48 B4
Thrupp Glos 64 B2
Thrupp Oxon 66 C2
Thrupp Oxon 73 D8
Thrushelton Devon 19 C5
Thruxton Hants 52 B2
Thruxton Heref'd 68 A2
Thurdon Cornw'l 31 D5
Thurlbear Som'set 36 B3
Thurlestone Devon 12 D4
Thurloxton Som'set 46 E5
Tibberton Glos 69 C9
Tibberton Worcs 75 A8
Tichborne Hants 53 E8
Tickenham N Som'set 55 A9
Tickmorend Glos 64 C1
Tidcombe Wilts 61 E2
Tiddington Warwick 77 A7
Tideford Cornw'l 10 D2
Tideford Cross Cornw'l 10 C2
Tidenham Glos 62 C3
Tidmington Warwick 77 E8
Tidnor Heref'd 74 E1
Tidpit Hants 40 C4
Tidworth Wilts 52 B1
Tigley Devon 14 C3
Tilland Cornw'l 10 C2
Tillers Green Glos 69 A7
Tilsdown Glos 63 C7
Tilshead Wilts 51 B5
Tiltups End Glos 64 C1
Timbercombe Som'set 46 E4
Timberscombe Som'set 45 C6
Timsbury Bath/NE Som'set 57 E5
Tincleton Dorset 26 B2
Tinhay Devon 18 C4
Tinkers Hill Hants 52 B4
Tintagel Cornw'l 17 C6
Tintern Parva Monmouths 62 B2
Tintinhull Som'set 37 E8
Tiptoe Hants 28 A5
Tipton Cross Devon 22 B3
Tipton St. John Devon 22 B3
Tirley Glos 70 B2
Tisbury Wilts 50 F3
Titchberry Devon 30 A4
Titcomb W Berks 60 C4
Tithill Som'set 46 F3
Titson Cornw'l 30 F4
Tiverton Devon 34 D4
Tivington Som'set 45 B5
Tockenham Wilts 58 A5
Tockenham Wick Wilts 65 F5
Tockington S Gloucs 62 E4
Todber Dorset 39 B5
Toddington Glos 71 A6
Todenham Glos 77 E7
Tog Hill S Gloucs 57 B6
Tolborough Cornw'l 17 E8
Toldish Cornw'l 8 D1
Tolgus Mount Cornw'l 4 B1
Tolladine Worcs 75 A7
Tolland Som'set 46 E2
Tollard Farnham Dorset 40 C2
Tollard Royal Wilts 40 C1
Toller Fratrum Dorset 25 A6
Toller Porcorum Dorset 25 A6
Toller Whelme Dorset 37 F8
Tollerford Dorset 25 A6
Tolpuddle Dorset 26 B2
Tone Som'set 35 B7
Tone Green Som'set 35 B8
Tonedale Som'set 35 B7
Toot Baldon Oxon 67 B8
Toothill Swindon 65 F7
Topsham Devon 22 C1
Torbay Torbay 15 C6
Torbryan Devon 14 B4
Torcross Devon 13 D7
Torfrey Cornw'l 9 E5
Tormarton S Gloucs 57 A7
Torpoint Cornw'l 10 D4
Torquay Torbay 15 C6
Torr Devon 11 C8
Torr Devon 11 E7
Torre Som'set 45 C7
Torre Torbay 15 B6
Tortworth S Gloucs 63 D6
Tosberry Devon 31 B5
Totford Hants 53 D8
Totgarrick Cornw'l 8 E1
Totland I/Wight 29 C6
Totnell Dorset 38 E2
Totnes Devon 14 C4
Tottens Wilts 41 A7
Touches Som'set 36 E4
Toulton Som'set 46 E3
Towan Cornw'l 16 F2
Towan Cross Cornw'l 6 F5
Towednack Cornw'l 3 C5
Towerhead N Som'set 55 E8
Town Street Glos 70 B2
Townlake Devon 19 E5
Town's End Dorset 26 A4
Town's End Dorset 27 D6
Town's End Dorset 38 E1
Towns End Hants 61 E8
Towns End Som'set 38 C4
Towns End Som'set 46 C2
Town's End Som'set 49 B5
Townsend Bath/NE Som'set 56 E3
Townsend Oxon 66 E4
Townsend Som'set 36 D5
Townsend Som'set 47 E7
Townsend Som'set 48 A2
Townsend S Gloucs 62 F3
Townsend Wilts 58 E4
Townshend Cornw'l 3 D7
Townwell S Gloucs 63 D5
Traboe Cornw'l 4 F2
Tracebridge Som'set 35 B6
Tram Inn Heref'd 68 A3
Trapshill W Berks 60 D4
Travelmond Cornw'l 9 C7
Tre-Essey Heref'd 68 C4
Tre-gagle Monmouths 68 F4
Treaddow Heref'd 68 C4
Treamble Cornw'l 7 D6
Treator Cornw'l 16 E3
Trebahwartha Cornw'l 4 E3
Trebarber Cornw'l 7 C8
Trebartha Cornw'l 18 E2
Trebarvah Cornw'l 3 E6
Trebarvah Cornw'l 4 D2
Trebarwith Cornw'l 17 C6
Trebeath Cornw'l 18 C2
Trebehor Cornw'l 2 F3
Trebetherick Cornw'l 16 E3
Treble's Holford Som'set 46 E2
Treborough Som'set 45 D7
Trebudannon Cornw'l 7 C8
Trebullett Cornw'l 18 E3
Treburley Cornw'l 18 E3
Treburrick Cornw'l 7 A8
Trebyan Cornw'l 8 C4
Trecrogo Cornw'l 18 D3
Tredarrup Cornw'l 17 B8
Tredaule Cornw'l 18 D1
Tredavoe Cornw'l 2 E5
Tredington Glos 70 B4
Tredington Warwick 77 D8
Tredinnick Cornw'l 2 D4
Tredinnick Cornw'l 9 B6
Tredinnick Cornw'l 9 D7
Tredrizzick Cornw'l 16 E4
Tredworth Glos 70 D2
Treen Cornw'l 2 C4
Treen Cornw'l 2 F3
Treesmill Cornw'l 8 D4
Treffany Hill Cornw'l 9 D7
Trefynwy = Monmouth Monmouths 68 E4
Tregada Cornw'l 18 D3
Tregadillet Cornw'l 18 D2
Tregajorran Cornw'l 4 B1
Tregare Monmouths 68 E2
Tregarland Cornw'l 9 D8
Tregarne Cornw'l 4 F3
Tregaswith Cornw'l 7 C8
Tregatta Cornw'l 17 C6
Tregavarras Cornw'l 5 B7
Tregear Cornw'l 7 E8
Tregeare Cornw'l 18 C1
Tregellist Cornw'l 16 E5
Tregenna Cornw'l 17 F6
Tregeseal Cornw'l 2 D3
Tregonce Cornw'l 16 F3
Tregonetha Cornw'l 8 C2
Tregonhawke Cornw'l 10 E4
Tregonna Cornw'l 8 A1
Tregony Cornw'l 5 B6
Tregoodwell Cornw'l 17 D7
Tregorrick Cornw'l 8 E3
Tregoss Cornw'l 8 C2
Tregowris Cornw'l 4 F3
Tregrehan Mills Cornw'l 8 E3
Tregullon Cornw'l 8 C4
Tregunna Cornw'l 16 F4
Tregunnon Cornw'l 18 D1
Tregurrian Cornw'l 7 B8
Trehan Cornw'l 10 D4
Trehemborne Cornw'l 7 A8
Treheveras Cornw'l 7 F7
Trehill V/Glam 54 B1
Trehunist Cornw'l 10 C2
Trekeivesteps Cornw'l 9 B7
Trekelland Cornw'l 18 D3
Trekelland Cornw'l 18 E2
Trekenner Cornw'l 18 E3
Treknow Cornw'l 17 C6
Trelan Cornw'l 5 G2
Trelash Cornw'l 17 B8
Trelassick Cornw'l 7 E8
Treleigh Cornw'l 4 B2
Treligga Cornw'l 17 D6
Trelights Cornw'l 16 E4
Trelill Cornw'l 17 E5
Trelinnoe Cornw'l 18 D3
Trelion Cornw'l 8 E1
Trelissick Cornw'l 4 C4
Trellech Monmouths 62 A2
Trelleck Cross Monmouths 62 B2
Trelleck Grange Monmouths 62 B1
Trelonk Cornw'l 5 B5
Trelowia Cornw'l 10 D1
Trelowth Cornw'l 8 E2
Trelowthas Cornw'l 7 F8
Treluggan Cornw'l 5 C5
Tremail Cornw'l 17 C8
Tremaine Cornw'l 18 A1
Tremar Cornw'l 9 B8
Trematon Cornw'l 10 D3
Trembraze Cornw'l 9 B8
Tremollett Cornw'l 18 E2
Tremore Cornw'l 8 C3
Tremorfa Card 54 A4
Trenale Cornw'l 17 C6
Trenance Cornw'l 7 C7
Trenance Cornw'l 8 A1
Trenant Cornw'l 9 B7
Trenarren Cornw'l 8 F3
Trenarrett Cornw'l 18 D1
Trenault Cornw'l 18 D2
Trencreek Cornw'l 7 C7
Trendeal Cornw'l 7 E8
Trendrean Cornw'l 7 D7
Treneague Cornw'l 8 A2
Trenear Cornw'l 4 D1
Treneglos Cornw'l 17 C9
Trenewan Cornw'l 9 E6
Trengune Cornw'l 17 B8
Trenhorne Cornw'l 18 E2
Treninnick Cornw'l 7 C7
Trenode Cornw'l 9 D8
Trenoweth Cornw'l 4 D3
Trent Dorset 38 C1
Trentishoe Devon 43 B7
Trenwheal Cornw'l 3 D8
Trequite Cornw'l 17 E5
Trerank Moor Cornw'l 8 D2
Trerose Cornw'l 4 E3
Trerulefoot Cornw'l 10 D2
Tresawle Cornw'l 5 A5
Tresawsen Cornw'l 7 F6
Trescowe Cornw'l 3 D7
Tresean Cornw'l 7 D6
Tresevern Croft Cornw'l 4 C2
Tresham S Gloucs 63 D7
Tresillian Cornw'l 5 A5
Treskillard Cornw'l 4 C1
Treskinnick Cross Cornw'l 17 A9
Tresmeer Cornw'l 18 C1
Tresowes Green Cornw'l 3 E7
Tresoweshill Cornw'l 3 E7
Tresparrett Cornw'l 17 B7
Tresparrett Posts Cornw'l 17 B7
Trespeane Cornw'l 18 D1
Tressinney Cornw'l 17 D7
Treswithian Cornw'l 3 B8
Treswithian Downs Cornw'l 3 B8
Trethevy Cornw'l 17 C6
Trethewey Cornw'l 2 F3
Trethosa Cornw'l 8 E1
Trethowel Cornw'l 8 E3
Trethurgy Cornw'l 8 D3
Tretire Heref'd 68 C4
Trevadlock Cornw'l 18 E2
Trevalga Cornw'l 17 C6
Trevance Cornw'l 8 A1
Trevanger Cornw'l 16 E4
Trevanson Cornw'l 8 A2
Trevarrack Cornw'l 3 D5
Trevarren Cornw'l 8 C1
Trevarrian Cornw'l 7 B8
Trevarrick Cornw'l 5 B7
Trevarth Cornw'l 4 B2
Treveal Cornw'l 7 D6
Treveighan Cornw'l 17 E6
Trevellas Cornw'l 7 E5
Trevemper Cornw'l 7 D7
Treverbyn Cornw'l 8 D3
Treverbyn Cornw'l 9 B7
Treverva Cornw'l 4 D3
Trevescan Cornw'l 2 F3
Trevethan Cornw'l 4 B2
Trevia Cornw'l 17 D6
Trevigro Cornw'l 10 A2
Trevilla Cornw'l 4 C4
Trevillian Cornw'l 17 B8
Trevilson Cornw'l 7 D7
Treviscoe Cornw'l 8 D1
Treviscoe Barton Cornw'l 8 D1
Trevithal Cornw'l 2 E5
Trevivian Cornw'l 17 C8
Trevoll Cornw'l 7 D7
Trevone Cornw'l 16 E2
Trevowah Cornw'l 7 D6
Trew Cornw'l 3 E8
Trewalder Cornw'l 17 D6
Trewarlett Cornw'l 18 D3
Trewarmett Cornw'l 17 C6
Trewarne Heref'd 68 D4
Trewassa Cornw'l 17 C7
Treween Cornw'l 18 D1
Trewellard Cornw'l 2 D3
Trewen Cornw'l 18 D2
Trewen Heref'd 68 D4
Trewennack Cornw'l 4 E1
Trewetha Cornw'l 16 D5
Trewethern Cornw'l 16 E5
Trewidland Cornw'l 9 D8
Trewint Cornw'l 10 C1
Trewint Cornw'l 17 A8
Trewint Cornw'l 18 D1
Trewithian Cornw'l 5 C5
Trewoodloe Cornw'l 10 A2
Trewoofe Cornw'l 2 E4
Trewoon Cornw'l 8 E2
Treworga Cornw'l 5 B5
Treworlas Cornw'l 5 C5
Treworthal Cornw'l 5 C5
Treyarnon Cornw'l 16 F2
Trickett's Cross Dorset 40 F4
Tricombe Devon 23 A6
Trill Devon 23 A7
Trimstone Devon 42 C4
Trinity Devon 34 E4
Triscombe Som'set 46 D3
Trispen Cornw'l 7 E7
Troan Cornw'l 7 D8
Trolway Heref'd 68 C3
Troon Cornw'l 3 C9
Troswell Cornw'l 18 B2
Trow Devon 23 C5
Trow Green Glos 69 F5
Trowbridge Card 54 A4
Trowbridge Wilts 58 E1
Trowle Common Wilts 58 E1
Trudoxhill Som'set 49 C7
True Streek Devon 14 C4
Trull Som'set 36 B2
Trumpet Heref'd 74 E3
Truro Cornw'l 4 B4
Truscott Cornw'l 18 C3
Trusham Devon 21 D7
Truthwall Cornw'l 3 D6
Trythogga Cornw'l 2 D5
Tubney Oxon 67 C5
Tuckenhay Devon 14 D4
Tuckermarsh Devon 10 B4
Tuckingmill Cornw'l 18 B1
Tuckingmill Cornw'l 3 B9
Tuckingmill Wilts 50 F3
Tuckton Bournem'th 28 B2
Tudorville Heref'd 69 C5
Tuffley Glos 70 D2
Tufton Hants 53 B6
Tumpy Green Glos 63 B6
Tunley Bath/NE Som'set 57 E5
Tunnel Hill Worcs 75 D6
Turfdown Cornw'l 8 B4
Turfmoor Devon 36 F3
Turkdean Glos 71 D8
Turleigh Wilts 57 D8
Turlin Moor Poole 27 B6
Turmer Hants 41 E5
Turnchapel Plym'th 11 E5
Turner's Green W Berks 61 C7
Turners Puddle Dorset 26 B3
Turner's Tump Glos 69 D6
Turnworth Dorset 39 E6
Tutnalls Glos 62 B4
Tutshill Glos 62 C2
Tutts Clump W Berks 61 B8
Tutwell Cornw'l 18 E4
Twelveheads Cornw'l 4 B3
Twerton Bath/NE Som'set 57 D6
Twigworth Glos 70 C2
Twinhoe Bath/NE Som'set 57 E6
Twitchen Devon 44 E2
Two Bridges Devon 13 F2
Two Burrows Cornw'l 7 F5
Two Mile Oak Cross Devon 14 B4
Twyford Dorset 39 C7
Twyn-y-Sheriff Monmouths 68 F2
Twyn-yr-odyn V/Glam 54 B2
Twyning Glos 75 E7
Twyning Green Glos 75 E8
Tyneham Dorset 26 D4
Tyning Bath/NE Som'set 57 E5
Tyntesfield N Som'set 56 B2
Tythecott Devon 31 C8
Tytherington Som'set 49 B7
Tytherington S Gloucs 63 E5
Tytherington Wilts 50 C3
Tytherleigh Devon 36 F4
Tywardreath Cornw'l 8 E4
Tywardreath Highway Cornw'l 8 D4

U

Ubley Bath/NE Som'set 56 E2
Uckinghall Worcs 75 E7
Uckington Glos 70 B4
Udley N Som'set 56 D1
Uffcott Wilts 59 A7
Uffculme Devon 35 D6
Uffington Oxon 66 E3
Ugborough Devon 14 D1
Ugford Wilts 51 E6
Uley Glos 63 C7
Ullcombe Devon 36 E2
Ullenwood Glos 70 D4
Ullingswick Heref'd 74 C1
Ulwell Dorset 27 D7
Umberleigh Devon 32 B5
Underdown Devon 20 B4
Underwood Plym'th 11 D6
Up Cerne Dorset 38 F3
Up Exe Devon 34 F3
Up Exe Devon 34 F3
Up Hatherley Glos 70 C4
Up Mudford Som'set 38 C1
Up Somborne Hants 52 E4
Up Sydling Dorset 38 F2
Upavon Wilts 59 F8
Upcott Devon 32 E4
Upcott Som'set 26 B1
Upcott Som'set 34 A3
Uphall Dorset 37 F9
Upham Devon 34 E2
Uphempston Devon 14 C4
Uphill N Som'set 55 E6
Uplands Glos 64 A2
Upleadon Glos 69 B9
Uploders Dorset 24 A5
Uplowman Devon 35 C5
Uplyms Devon 23 B8
Upottery Devon 36 E2
Upper Basildon W Berks 61 A8
Upper Brailes Warwick 77 E9
Upper Broadheath Worcs 75 A6
Upper Buckenhill Heref'd 69 A5
Upper Bucklebury W Berks 61 C7
Upper Burgate Hants 41 C5
Upper Canada N Som'set 55 E7
Upper Canterton Hants 41 D8
Upper Cheddon Som'set 46 F4
Upper Chicksgrove Wilts 50 F4
Upper Chute Wilts 61 E2
Upper Clatford Hants 52 C4
Upper Coberley Glos 71 D5
Upper Colwall Heref'd 75 D5
Upper Egleton Heref'd 74 C2
Upper End Glos 71 E8
Upper Enham Hants 52 A4
Upper Fivehead Som'set 36 B4
Upper Framilode Glos 69 E8
Upper Godney Som'set 48 C1
Upper Green Monmouths 68 D1
Upper Green W Berks 60 D4
Upper Grove Common Heref'd 68 B5
Upper Ham Worcs 75 C7
Upper Ham Worcs 75 E7
Upper Heyford Oxon 73 B8
Upper Hill S Gloucs 63 C5
Upper Howsell Worcs 75 C5
Upper Inglesham Swindon 65 C9
Upper Kilcott Glos 63 E7
Upper Lambourn W Berks 66 F3
Upper Langford N Som'set 56 E1
Upper Ley Glos 69 D8
Upper Littleton N Som'set 56 D3
Upper Lydbrook Glos 69 D6
Upper Milton Oxon 72 D4
Upper Milton Som'set 48 B2
Upper Minety Wilts 64 D5
Upper Moor Worcs 76 C2
Upper Morton S Gloucs 63 D5
Upper Oddington Glos 72 B3
Upper Pennington Hants 29 A6
Upper Quinton Warwick 77 C6
Upper Ratley Hants 41 B9
Upper Seagry Wilts 64 F3
Upper Siddington Glos 65 C5
Upper Slackstead Hants 52 F4
Upper Slaughter Glos 72 C2
Upper Soudley Glos 69 E7
Upper Stanton Drew Bath/NE Som'set 56 D4
Upper Street Hants 41 C5
Upper Strensham Worcs 75 E8
Upper Studley Wilts 58 E1
Upper Swell Glos 72 B2
Upper Town Heref'd 74 C1
Upper Town N Som'set 56 C2
Upper Town Wilts 58 A4
Upper Upham Wilts 60 A1
Upper Vobster Som'set 49 B6
Upper Waterhay Wilts 65 D6
Upper Welland Worcs 75 D5
Upper Weston Bath/NE Som'set 57 C6
Upper Wick Glos 63 C6
Upper Wick Worcs 75 B6
Upper Wilcove Cornw'l 10 D4
Upper Wolvercote Oxon 73 E8
Upper Woodford Wilts 51 D7
Upper Woolhampton W Berks 61 C8
Upper Wootton Hants 61 F8
Upper Wraxhall S Gloucs 57 B7
Upper Wyche Worcs 75 D5
Uppincott Devon 34 F2
Uppington Dorset 40 E3
Upthorpe Glos 63 B7
Upton Cornw'l 30 F4
Upton Cornw'l 9 A8
Upton Devon 13 D5
Upton Devon 35 F6
Upton Dorset 26 D1
Upton Dorset 27 B6
Upton Hants 60 E4
Upton Oxon 67 E7
Upton Oxon 72 E3
Upton Som'set 45 F6
Upton Som'set 47 F9
Upton Warwick 76 A5
Upton Wilts 50 E2
Upton Bishop Heref'd 69 B7
Upton Cheney S Gloucs 57 C5
Upton Crews Heref'd 69 B6
Upton Cross Cornw'l 9 A8
Upton Hellions Devon 34 E1
Upton Lovell Wilts 50 C3
Upton Noble Som'set 49 D6
Upton Pyne Devon 21 A8
Upton St. Leonards Glos 70 E3
Upton Scudamore Wilts 50 B2
Upton Snodsbury Worcs 76 B1
Upton upon Severn Worcs 75 D7
Upwey Dorset 25 C8
Urchfont Wilts 59 E5
Uton Devon 21 A6

V

Valley Truckle Cornw'l 17 D6
Vellanoweth Cornw'l 3 D6
Vellow Som'set 46 D1
Velly Devon 31 B5
Venn Devon 14 F3
Venn Devon 31 B6
Venn Green Devon 31 D7
Venn Ottery Devon 22 B3
Venny Tedburn Devon 21 A6
Venterdon Cornw'l 18 F4
Venton Devon 11 D7
Venton Devon 20 B3
Ventongimps Mill Cornw'l 7 E6
Vernham Dean Hants 60 E3
Vernham Row Hants 60 E3
Vernham Street Hants 60 E4
Vertington Som'set 49 F6
Verwood Dorset 40 E4
Veryan Cornw'l 5 C6
Veryan Green Cornw'l 5 B6
Victoria Cornw'l 8 C2
Victoria Park Dorset 25 C8
Viney Hill Glos 63 A5
Vinny Green S Gloucs 57 A5
Virginstow Devon 18 B4
Viscar Cornw'l 4 D2
Vobster Som'set 49 B6
Vole Som'set 47 A7

W

Wadborough Worcs 75 C8
Waddeton Devon 15 D5
Waddicombe Devon 44 F4
Waddon Devon 21 E7
Waddon Dorset 25 C7
Wadebridge Cornw'l 8 A2
Wadeford Som'set 36 D4
Wadswick Wilts 58 C1
Wadwick Hants 53 A5
Wagg Som'set 47 F8
Waggs Plot Devon 36 F4
Wainhouse Corner Cornw'l 17 A8
Wakeham Devon 14 F1
Walcombe Som'set 48 B3
Walcot Swindon 65 F8
Walcot Warwick 77 A5
Walditch Dorset 24 B4
Wales Som'set 38 A1
Walford Heref'd 69 C5
Walham Glos 70 C4
Walhampton Hants 29 A6
Walkford Dorset 28 B4
Walkhampton Devon 11 B6
Wall Cornw'l 3 C8
Wall Mead Bath/NE Som'set 57 E5
Waller's Green Heref'd 74 E3
Wallingford Oxon 67 E8
Wallisdown Poole 27 B8
Wallow Green Glos 63 C8
Wallston V/Glam 54 B2
Wallsworth Glos 70 C2
Walpole Som'set 47 C6
Walrow Som'set 47 B6
Walson Monmouths 68 C2
Walton Som'set 48 D1
Walton Warwick 77 B8
Walton Cardiff Glos 70 A4
Walton Elm Dorset 39 C5
Walton-in-Gordano N Som'set 55 B8
Walton Park N Som'set 55 B8
Walton St. Mary N Som'set 55 B8
Wambrook Som'set 36 E3
Wanborough Swindon 65 F9
Wanderwell Dorset 24 B4
Wanson Cornw'l 30 F3
Wanstrow Som'set 49 C6
Wanswell Glos 63 B5
Wantage Oxon 67 E5
Wapley S Gloucs 57 A6
Warborough Oxon 67 D8
Warbstow Cornw'l 17 B9
Warbstow Cross Cornw'l 17 B9
Warden Hill Glos 70 C4
Ware Devon 23 B8
Wareham Dorset 27 C5
Warfleet Devon 15 E5
Warkleigh Devon 33 B5
Warleggan Cornw'l 9 B6
Warleigh Bath/NE Som'set 57 D7
Warminster Wilts 50 C2
Warminster Common Wilts 50 C2
Warmley S Gloucs 57 B5
Warmley Hill S Gloucs 57 B5
Warmwell Dorset 26 C2
Warndon Worcs 75 A7
Wash Common W Berks 61 D6
Washaway Cornw'l 8 B3
Washbourne Devon 14 E3
Washbrook Som'set 47 A8